# Collaborative Business Process Engineering and Global Organizations:
## Frameworks for Service Integration

Bhuvan Unhelkar
*University of Western Sydney, Australia*

Abbass Ghanbary
*University of Western Sydney, Australia*

Houman Younessi
*Rensselaer at Hartford, USA*

**BUSINESS SCIENCE REFERENCE**

Hershey · New York

| | |
|---|---|
| Director of Editorial Content: | Kristin Klinger |
| Senior Managing Editor: | Jamie Snavely |
| Assistant Managing Editor: | Michael Brehm |
| Publishing Assistant: | Sean Woznicki |
| Typesetter: | Chris Hrobak |
| Cover Design: | Lisa Tosheff |
| Printed at: | Yurchak Printing Inc. |

Published in the United States of America by
Business Science Reference (an imprint of IGI Global)
701 E. Chocolate Avenue
Hershey PA 17033
Tel: 717-533-8845
Fax: 717-533-8661
E-mail: cust@igi-global.com
Web site: http://www.igi-global.com/reference

Library of Congress Cataloging-in-Publication Data

Unhelkar, Bhuvan.
 Collaborative business process engineering and global organizations :
frameworks for service integration / by Bhuvan Unhelkar, Abbass Ghanbary, and
Houman Younessi.
  p. cm.
 Includes bibliographical references and index.
 Summary: "This book is about achieving organizational synergy in an era of
business which is rapidly moving towards electronic collaboration, providing
clear definition of the next phase of this collaborative evolution of the
Internet"--Provided by publisher.
 ISBN 978-1-60566-689-1 (hardcover) -- ISBN 978-1-60566-690-7 (ebook)  1.
Strategic alliances (Business) 2.  Information technology.  I. Ghanbary,
Abbass, 1965- II. Younessi, Houman. III. Title.

 HD69.S8U54 2010
 658'.044--dc22

2009007770
British Cataloguing in Publication Data
A Cataloguing in Publication record for this book is available from the British Library.

All work contributed to this book is new, previously-unpublished material. The views expressed in this book are those of the authors, but not necessarily of the publisher.

**Gaurav and Vaibhav**
        —*Bhuvan Unhelkar*

**Naghmeh and Avessta**
        —*Abbass Ghanbary*

**Sheyda and Daniel**
        —*Houman Younessi*

# Table of Contents

# Foreword

This book, *Collaborative Business Process Engineering and Global Organizations: Frameworks for Service Integration,* provides a model for collaborative business that not only has a well researched foundation but has also been deployed and tested by the authors in practice.

In the last 10 years, the Internet and Web, supported by several advances in information and communication technology (ICT), has transformed irrevocably the way we work, the way we collaborate with individuals and partner organizations and the way we communicate with each other. As a result there is dramatic change in business landscape. The Web enables businesses to extend and expand their operational boundariesand technological boundaries, as well as helps to achieve better synergy among the triad of a business – people, process and technology – both internal and external to an enterprise.

The Web is no longer just a one-way communication and information dissemination medium, that many businesses have exploited quite effectively. Web is now also global platform for fielding applications, for interaction, coordination and collaboration, and for socializing. Advances in the Web, which are now traced into stages as Web 1.0, Web 2.0 and Web 3.0, are heralding a new era, a paradigm shift, in business – which is popularly known as Business 2.0, Collaboration 2.0, CRM 2.0, BI 2.0, and Innovation 2.0.

In response to call for chapters for the *Handbook of Research on Web 2.0, 3.0 and X.0: Technologies, Business, and Social Applications* (IGI Global, 2009) that I am currently editing, I have had contributions both from researchers and practitioners on a wide range topics, from business-IT/Web strategies, and Web-enabled business processes, to novel applications of Web in areas such as cross-organizational collaboration, synergizing an enterprise, and the environment. This is just one evidence that alerts (and warns) everyone of us that the Web is no longer a mere tool for communication; it is a global platform as well as a business mechanism that supports a number of different business activities, processes and functions going *beyond* the traditional, often predefined, business-to-consumer (B2C) and business-to-business (B2B) transactions.

A large number of senior executives believe now businesses - small and large, local and global - need to seriously consider and innovatively and effectively employ ICT and Web as strategic business tools to sustain and excel in the highly competitive world we live in now. Though the opportunities for exploiting these new strategic business tools are many and varied, one area that is gaining greater interest is one-to many and many-to-many dynamic, real-time business-to-business coordination and collaboration. The challenges of conducting and realizing full potential of many-to-many collaborative businesses are, however, huge, and you need to indentify, understand, and address those challenges effectively, and embark on a new journey in this not well-known trail. This book is a helpful, timely resource to help you and show you directions when you are at a cross-road in this endeavor.

Businesses no longer operate in isolation – they need to collaborate with other businesses in the same as well other industry sectors; they need to transition into what we might call collaborative businesses. Though already there are some businesses that falls under this category of collaborative businesses, many of them have met with problems and barriers in the conception of, or transition to, their new collaborative business model, and their journey has not been smooth, either.

The authors of this book - Bhuvan Unhelkar, Abbass Ghanbary and Houman Younessi – who have multidisciplinary expertise and complementary skills and real-world experience have come together to present through this book a robust research-based approach to transitioning traditional businesses to collaborative businesses. This book points you right directions and appropriate methodologies for transitioning into collaborative businesses, and encourages you to consider the various significant aspects of collaborative business processes and strategies.

Beginning with a discussion on foundations of collaborative business and an overview of technologies that support business collaboration, the authors take you through several components and constituents of collaborative business - architectures, organizational structures and quality assurance, to name a few, all encapsulated in what the authors call "Collaborative Business Process Engineering (CBPE). They also discuss often neglected but important socio-cultural aspects and change management that are keys to success of such collaborations. They put together several practical aspects of CBPE in a Collaborative Web Based System (CWBS), and demonstrated applications of CWBS through two case studies.

You the readers – whether you are a business executive, a business/IT consultant, a developer of business process engineering tools, a researcher, an academic, or someone interested in collaborative business – will surely find this book worth reading and an invaluable resource in your practical work. I wish this book my very best.

*San Murugesan*
*Professor of Information Systems*
*Multimedia University, Malaysia*
*san1@internode.net*

\* \* \*

**San Murugesan** *is a professor at Multimedia University, Malaysia; an Adjunct Professor in the School of Computing and Mathematics at the University of Western Sydney, Australia; and an independent business, IT, and education consultant. Dr. Murugesan's expertise and interests include green computing, cloud computing, Web 2.0 and 3.0, mobile computing, Web engineering, information retrieval, e-business, innovation, IT project management, and offshoring. In 2006, the Council of the Australian Computer Society elected Dr. Murugesan to the grade of Fellow of the Australian Computer Society (ACS), an honor that is awarded to those who have made a distinguished contribution to the field of information and communications technology. Dr. Murugesan is a distinguished visitor of the IEEE Computer Society and a sought-after speaker. He is the editor of the forthcoming new "Handbook of Research on Web 2.0, 3.0 and X.0: Technologies, Business, and Social Applications" (IGI Global, 2009). He was General Chair of the 5th International Conference on Web Engineering, and he has served as cochair and organizer of other international workshops and conferences. He serves as Associate Editor of the "Journal of Web Engineering", "International Journal of E-Business Research", and "International Journal of Health Information Systems and Informatics." Dr. Murugesan served in various senior positions at Southern Cross University and the University of Western Sydney, both in Australia, and the Indian Space Research Organization, Bangalore, India. He also served as Senior Research Fellow of the US National Research Council at the NASA Ames Research Center. He can be reached at san1@internode.net.*

# Preface

This book is about achieving organizational synergy in an era of business which is rapidly moving towards electronic collaboration. Times are gone when businesses had well defined boundaries and where they only competed against each other. Modern-day businesses are highly complex, with fuzzy boundaries and where collaboration is as significant as competition, if not more. The core driver of this collaborative business era is electronic and mobile communication. In this book we discuss technologies of collaboration, their challenges and risks, and also how they offer opportunities within and amongst collaborative businesses. Such discussion is based on research and practical experiences of the authors in enabling collaborative business environments within the information and communication technology (ICT) domain. The model of collaborative business presented in this book aims to bring together the business processes of multiple organizations in order to deliver unified service to a customer while transcending time, location, and technological boundaries. Thus, this book synergizes multiple organizations and their business processes to provide a unified view of collaborative business from a customer's viewpoint. The impact of such collaboration on people (developer, user and customer), organizational structure and behavior, process of globalization, socio-cultural and change management are also investigated. The Internet has evolved through the increasingly complex areas of handling information, transaction, operation and collaboration. Acollaboration is initiated when two known organizations (a.k.a. business-to-business [B2B]) start transacting in the market. These collaborations expand and thrive using the communications technologies and systems that are based on services oriented architecture (SOA). The collaborative issues discussed in this book are of tremendous significance when they are purely electronic and are undertaken in a dynamic manner through an "open market" interaction on the Internet. These collaborations involve even further challenges when organizations in need of collaboration are not known to each other but are only interacting through electronic transactions–leading to the concept of "dynamic" collaboration where physical proximity and personal knowledge of each other play lesser and lesser role in completing collaborative transactions.

The authors strongly believe that this book has significant new material to offer relative this new order in global collaborative business environment. Although the topic of collaboration has a rich literature base, such base is primarily aimed at discussing collaboration across two or more businesses that are known to each other and have financial, legal, social and even more often than not geographical commonality and proximity. This book provides clear definition of the next phase of this collaborative evolution of the Internet. The authors hope that the readers find this book a valuable and practical book in order to increase their knowledge and understanding of collaborative business.

## Scope

The scope of this book is to discover the full potential and functionality of a service based approach (using the technologies of Web services/SOA) in order to provide a framework that will enable collaboration amongst multiple organizations. Furthermore, these collaborations are meant to be dynamic–that is, organizations get together to collaborate electronically for a specific purpose or business goal and, after that goal is consummated, they disperse. These organizations may not be necessarily known to each other. Furthermore, their geographical location would be of little interest in consuming transactions, and they would have diverse technical environments.

Later in the book, we propose the *collaborative business process engineering (CBPE)* model of business collaboration which incorporates an understanding of business processes that enable these multiple organizations to collaborate with each other electronically. Through the CBPE model discussed in this book, businesses can collaborate by discovering each other for the products and services that they offer across the Internet and consume each others' offerings using Web services. This book can thus be described as a practical output of a detailed investigation into how Web services (WS) influence the business processes of a cluster or group of organizations. There is a need for the study of such processes that appear unified to the customer (end-user) but are in fact in the background, comprising numerous organizations, their individual business processes and their diverse underlying technologies. Finally, this book also discusses the socio-cultural aspects of adoption of collaborative business as we believe that with the application of the aforementioned emerging technologies in businesses, the social aspects of the ensuing collaborations will become important – mainly because these social impacts are likely to be unique from previous understandings of social interactions in business.

## Justification

The justification for this book is that it draws the attention of business to the possibilities afforded them by engaging in the new collaborative business environment that is growing due to electronic and mobile technologies. This book encourages business strategies that enable multiple organizations to get together rapidly and independent of their locations through Web portals and execute electronic business transactions. These Web portals enable all involved parties to interact with each other rapidly and globally. Thus, the justification for this work is as follows:

- Preparing the organization for the new collaborative environment in the business world.
- Preparing the organization to use ICT as a collaborative business strategy as against a competitive environment.
- Preparing the organization to change and upgrade their organizational infrastructure that would facilitate dynamic collaboration.
- Preparing the organization to have a forward-looking strategic vision that makes them ready for the collaborative business environment.
- Preparing the organization to up skill their people, and upgrade their processes, infrastructure and technology so as to enable electronic business collaboration.
- Preparing the organization to realize the important challenges and risks in adopting emerging collaboration technologies.

There is no doubt that the future success of an organization is based upon the way it adapts the new technologies in its business undertaking–including new hardware, software and telecommunication technologies that enable it to remain competitive in the market. The success of the organizations also depends upon the way they use their resources, work within the constraints and collaborate with each other. Business collaboration provides organizations with better opportunities to provide customer relationship management (CRM), supply chain management (SCM) and enterprise resource planning (ERP) systems. These are some of the significant discussions in this book and that justify the publication of this work.

# READERS

This book is aimed at the followed audiences:

a.  Strategic decision-makers in industry who are involved in the process of improving their business operations and services through adoption of technology through or for the purpose of collaboration. This book will provide the decision-makers in business with a robust approach to collaboration that will encompass business as well as technological considerations. The strategies outlined in this book will equip business decision-makers to play a *proactive* role in adopting communications technologies in their business processes. Furthermore, discussions in this book on socio-cultural aspects of communications technologies including customer demographics, usability, change management, security and privacy concerns, project management as well as user training should be of immense interest to these audiences from industry as also the action points towards the end of the chapters, and the case study chapters towards the end.

b.  Academics involved in teaching courses/subjects that relate to "business strategies", "collaborative business", "mobile technologies for business" and so on, will find this book spot-on. Each chapter is organized with key points, introduction, detailed discussions and action points. The action points, apart from being of value to practitioners, can also be used for discussions and interactions within the classroom environment. These action points can be developed into corresponding exercises that can be worked out by students to consolidate their grasp of the chapter/topic. Thus, this book has an appeal even for classroom teaching for final year students in information and communication technologies. Subjects (units) taught include: business strategies, mobile information systems, advance topics in e-business, IT project management, and business process reengineering, to name but a few.

c.  Researchers and higher degree students that are involved in understanding, delving deeper and finding new knowledge within the area of collaborative businesses and mobile technologies. Higher degree students including masters and PhD students, as well as academic researchers and teachers, will find the "research base" of this book quite attractive. Most chapters have a research base and is based on a significant literature review encompassing a number of books, articles and websites cited as well as intensive research (both quantitative and qualitative) conducted by the authors.

# CONTENTS

We have based this book on extensive research conducted by the authors over more than three years, informed by a detailed qualitative study using a number of cases dealing with collaboration across multiple organizations. Furthermore, we have brought into play the well-known pedagogy of "student-centered learning" to facilitate the use of this book for higher degree courses as well as for its use in industry. The book contains twelve chapters, each neatly laid out to make it convenient for the readers to select the topics discussed. Furthermore, the book contains a detailed preface, discussing the reasoning for the book including the need for collaboration; detailed references, and bibliography at the end; a comprehensive index; a section describing the meanings of acronyms and keywords; and an exhaustive case study. As far as individual chapters are concerned, each chapter has the following structure:

- Chapter key points; introduction; main discussion of the chapter; action points; end notes and references.

How to use the book (Chapter Summaries)

| Chapter | Description |
|---|---|
| Chapter 1 | Fundamentals of Collaborative Business |
| Chapter 2 | Emerging Technologies for Business Collaboration |
| Chapter 3 | Global Collaborative Business |
| Chapter 4 | Collaborative Business Process Engineering (CBPE) Model |
| Chapter 5 | Advanced Technologies and Architecture in the Proposed Collaborative Businesses |
| Chapter 6 | Collaborative Web Based System (CWBS) |
| Chapter 7 | Organizational Structure and Technology Adaptation |
| Chapter 8 | Quality Assurance of the CWBS |
| Chapter 9 | Socio-Cultural Factors and Collaboration |
| Chapter 10 | Change Management in Collaboration |
| Chapter 11 | Case Study 1: A Security Service Organization (Medium-sized Organization) |
| Chapter 12 | Case Study 2: An Energy Provider Organization (Large Organization) |

# WORKSHOP

The "practical" aspects of collaboration and the extension of this collaboration across multiple organizations are discussed in this book have also been presented in seminars and conferences. As a result, we now have sufficient material included here to form the basis of a one day workshop. The following is a generic outline of such a one day seminar that can be optionally extended to a two-day workshop for a more comprehensive hands-on discussion on collaborations in business. For the academic community, each chapter in this book can correspond potentially to a 3-hour lecture topic, with Chapters I, II and III used earlier in the semester to establish the Collaborative Business Process Engineering (CBPE) models introduced in Chapter IV.

| Mapping of the Chapters in this Book to a ONE Day Workshop | | | | |
|---|---|---|---|---|
| Day | Session | Presentation & Discussion Workshop Topic | Relevant | Comments |
| 1 | 8:30 – 10:00 | Business Collaborations: Advantages and Challenges | Ch I | • Static versus dynamic collaboration.<br>• Outlining the value to global collaborations. |
| 1 | 10:30 – 12:00 | Collaboration and Technologies; Proposed Model for Collaboration (*CBPE*) | Ch II,III & IV | • E-collaboration through open market/portal.<br>• Technologies supporting collaboration.<br>• Global issues of collaboration.<br>• Proposed model of collaboration. |
| 1 | 1:30 – 2:30 | Technology Acceptance & Organizational Structure | Ch VI & VII | • Implementation of the proposed model.<br>• Organizational issues while adapting new technologies.<br>• Change to organizational structure as a result of collaboration. |
| 1 | 2:30 – 3:30 | Quality Assurance, Socio-Cultural and Change Management | Ch VIII, IX & X | • Testing and quality assurance.<br>• Mistrust and social perspectives.<br>• Change management due to collaboration. |
| 1 | 3:30 – 5:00 | Case studies | Ch XI & XII | • Practical appreciation of *CBPE* by working out a case study |

## LANGUAGE

The authors firmly believe in gender-neutral language. *Person* is therefore used wherever possible. However, in order to maintain the simplicity of reading *he* has been used freely, interspersed with *she*. Terms like *user* and *manager* represent roles and not people. Therefore, these terms don't tie down real people who may transit through many roles in a lifetime, or even in a job. Furthermore, individuals often play more than one role at a given time – like *consultant, academic* and *analyst*. As a result, the semantics behind the theory and examples may change depending on the role one is playing, and should be kept in mind as one peruses this book. *We* throughout the text primarily refer to the reader and the authors. Occasionally, *we* refer to the general IT community of which the authors and most readers are members. *We* also refer to the teams in which the authors have worked.

## COMMENTS AND CRITICISM

Comments about and criticisms of this work are welcome. The authors will be thankful to you, the esteemed readers, for your comments. These comments and criticisms expected from our readers will surely add to the overall knowledge available on the subject. We offer our *a priori* gratitude to all readers and critics.

*Bhuvan Unhelkar*
*Abbass Ghanbary*
*Houman Younessi*
(Feb, 2009. Sydney, Australia; Hartford, USA)

# Acknowledgment

The authors are grateful to a number of parties for their support and encouragement during the drafting of this book. Numerous students and fellow researchers at University of Western Sydney, University of Technology, Sydney, as well as at Rensselaer Polytechnic Institute need special mention in this work. Furthermore, members of various discussion forums including those at the Australian Computer Society, Computer Society of India and Mobile Internet Research and Applications Group (MIRAG) have regularly provided comments and feedback, and have enabled the survey on collaboration across the globe. Our thanks to all these wonderful people. As always, we are grateful to our families for enabling us to write this book and we remain grateful to them for their encouragements and support:

BU – Asha, Sonki and Keshav Raja; and extended family, Chinar & Girish Mamdapur
AG - Naghmeh and Avessta
HY - Sheyda and Daniel

Robyn Lawson
M. Ranjbar
Naghmeh Khandan
Akshai Aggarwal
Vivek Handa

Vijay Khandelwal
Amit Lingarchani
Javed Matin
San Murugesan
Ekata Mehul

Sargam Parmar
Amit Pradhan
Prabhat Pradhan
Prashant Risbud
Prince Soundararajan
Pinku Talati
Amit Tiwary
Asha Unhelkar
Padmanaabh Desai
Mindy Wu
Mamta Padole

Ekata Shah
Jignesh Vyas
Jigisha Gala
Shivprakash Agrawal
Mukesh Bhargav
Vipul Kalamkar
Mehul Shah
Mandar Mehta
Saurin Mehta
Bharti Trivedi

# Chapter 1
# Fundamentals of Collaborative Business

*The significant problems we face cannot be solved at the same level of thinking we were at when we created them.*

Albert Einstein (1879–1955)

## CHAPTER KEY POINTS

- Argues for the significant need to understand and approach for collaboration amongst businesses in the technologically connected 21$^{st}$ century
- Discusses the competitive advantage when a business embarks on the collaborative approach
- Introduces the concept of collaborative business processes that are carried out electronically across multiple organizations that may be spread globally
- Discusses how business has utilized and continues to use the web technology by incrementally increasing its value in business as well as handling its complexity
- Discusses the current collaborative approach between businesses and proposes a new electronic collaborative model for multiple businesses spread globally.
- Discusses the challenges to business arising out of electronic collaboration.

DOI: 10.4018/978-1-60566-689-1.ch001

## BUSINESS IN THE 21ST CENTURY

The modern business age is about astute collaboration. This is so because the nature of competition amongst businesses has changed significantly. The core change has resulted from the advances of electronic communications. The ability of businesses to execute their business processes independent of geographical or technological boundaries has brought about an utterly different type of business eco-system. The new business model mandates the business to look around, observe its associated businesses, establish alliances with them and provide unified solutions to its customers in a way that encapsulated the underlying 'mix' of complexities and combinations of services and products desired by the customer. Thus, in a way, competition has transcended itself and businesses have started associating with each other at a different level, with changed scope and global standards. The discussion on collaboration in this book is to understand the way in which it is affecting businesses and what is required of the businesses in order to handle collaboration without giving up competition completely. Collaboration allows you to work with your business partners and, at the same time, compete in the market for customer's attention and share of their business. With the advances in information and communications technologies, the business community is encouraged to consider many different and innovative business models that bring together a judicious combination of collaboration and competition. These emerging innovative business models take a number of different forms that result in globalized businesses, mergers and alliances across countries, differentiation of products and services, electronic business-to-business relationships, revised economic models with value added focus, changes to productivity processes, customer demands and fulfillment, legal rules and regulations that apply often vary depending on the market and so on. Electronic collaboration (e-collaboration), powered by web-enabled applications and electronic technologies, is thus rapidly expanding into the day to day workings of many organizations - linking individuals and systems towards achieving better information sharing, real-time interactive communication and seamless collaboration. For example, a group of individuals with access to electronically enabled collaborative systems can instantly form a virtual team on a complex project, or be part of a virtual organization or a virtual community with common interests but scant physical access. Electronic collaboration can also become technically very complex, with its virtual net encompassing various organizations, allowing for real-time information exchange to pass through a dynamically formed cluster of organizations supporting and achieving a mutually complimentary business objective – leading to what we are calling here as collaborative commerce.

The significant impact of the need for collaboration on businesses brings about substantial changes to the way in which business operates. Earlier, during the reengineering revolution, Hammer and Champy (1993) presented a process-based model for businesses that required the businesses to undergo substantive and revolutionary changes. Later, Bill Gates (1999) introduced the concept of a digital nervous system (DNS) as the basis of the business communication network to facilitate the transformation or reengineering of business processes into new digital business processes. Most business enterprises focus on a few essential elements such as customers, suppliers, products and services, costs, employees, and skills. Each of these areas contains a collection of business data. Through human intelligence, data is interpreted and transformed into meaningful information to assist people at all levels to make decisions. However, if such interpretation and transformation are performed or supported through the use of information technology in a significant way, then the organization is said to have a digital nervous system (DNS). Gates describes a digital nervous system as, "the digital processes that closely link every aspect of a company's thoughts and actions." One can extend the concept of the DNS beyond a single business and to multiple businesses that collaborate with each other electronically. Such engineering of collaborative business requires a strategic approach to the business philosophy, business processes and business organization that is different from that of a separate, stand-alone activity and moving towards a suite of ongoing and dynamically changing processes that brings together many businesses and their activities together.

Gates (1999) further suggests organizations should consider three imperative concepts as a part of their re-thinking or re-engineering effort:

- Firstly, organizations should review their current business processes periodically;
- Secondly, they should try to have the least number of people involved in decision-making of each business process; and
- Thirdly, they should consolidate procedures and activities to decrease failure rates.

Collaborative organizations need to reflect on these aforementioned organizational imperatives in the context of the need to electronically collaborate with each other. Thus, there will often be a need to model business processes of the organization itself, as well as those of the business partners in the collaboration. During this effort, it is not unusual to find that there are similar or even identical processes across multiple collaborating and globally spread organizations. Modeling and studying these business process models lead to improvement in efficiency in offering products and services to customer as it is now possible to provide many different products and services of different organizations under a single portal that the customer is accessing. Study of the organizational structures of collaborations also open up opportunity to reduce duplication of jobs, inappropriate allocation of human resources, and ambiguous global management responsibilities as the organization becomes a collaborative global organization. Although creating a new business process or reengineering an existing one is a complex and sophisticated project in a globally collaborating business organization, there is a need to define, model, test and validate global processes that can be adopted within and amongst the organizations.

Apart from understanding collaboration from the vendor's viewpoint, there is also a need to understand collaboration from a customer's viewpoint. For example, the customer is interested in a comprehensive one-stop solution; the customer in modern electronic business environment approaches an airline not only for the air ticket, but to also seek associated travel services such as hotels, cars, insurance and credit facilities. Another increasingly popular example is of a modern-day electronic customer who is about to enter a hospital as a patient, but is exploring the opportunities for medical-tourism (Lingarchani, 2008). The need for a complete, customizable, assorted and yet transparent solution from a customer's viewpoint requires the business that is the primary contact of the customer to deal with many other interrelated businesses that provide goods and services in order to arrive at the desired final package for the customer. For example, in the aforementioned example of a customer that comes electronically to an airline to buy a ticket to travel would need multiple other facilities of hotels and cars that cannot be satisfied directly by the airline. The airline, then, has to necessarily collaborate with other businesses (such as hotels and car rental companies) in order to provide the solution desired by the customer. This need for businesses to collaborate in the electronic age is further complicated by the fact that the customer may not be an individual but, rather, a large organization (such as a conference organizer) that is seeking a large volume of business in a short span of time. The ability to provide for this demand would require the airline to collaborate with not only natural collaborators like hotels and car rental companies but also other *airlines*. Thus, the need to collaborate in the electronic age is not only between different types of businesses but businesses of the same type that were earlier always aiming to compete. This need for collaboration in an electronic age and all the associated challenges and advantages of such collaboration are many fold and ever increasing. We discuss them further in the subsequent pages of this chapter and the rest of this book.

## BUSINESS ARGUMENTS FOR GLOBAL COLLABORATIONS

Businesses are increasingly interested in collaboration with each other. The market dynamics and the demands from the customers have made this collaboration imperative. However, the business owners and decision makers are keen to collaborate with other businesses and also globalize only if it helps them grow their own business. Therefore, businesses need to consider the competitive advantages of their foray in global collaboration. Lan and Unhelkar (2005) have discussed in detail numerous related and supporting globalization factors that influence the ability of businesses to collaborate with each other. These factors include information systems planning, information systems organization alignment, information systems effectiveness, productivity measurement, business reengineering, competitive advantage, information quality, office automation, identification of global business opportunities, systems reliability, availability, and transferability.

Collaboration amongst businesses can take different shapes and formats. For example, there are possibilities of executing some collaboration on a long term basis through mergers and acquisitions. There are also possibilities of joint partnerships, sourcing agreements and so on. Businesses have been keen to grow by forming alliances with external parties and organizations. Such alliances enable a business to differentiate its products and services. An allied business can potentially provide products and services to customers that are unique, value efficient, and reasonably priced. Electronic collaboration, as discussed here, takes this concept of business alliance further and builds on top of the technologies of communications. Electronic business itself can be understood as a business that uses Internet tools in overall or partial operations of the organization leading to substantial virtual processes, sourcing and supply strategies.

Economic value added focus – refers to the increasing financial pressure on organizations to achieve high process performance as they affect or are affected by sourcing and supply, and increasing focus on economic value added.

Work in managerial economics (Younessi, 2009, HRMB2) has shown us that technological change is one of the major factors that effect revenue. This influence is often through impact on the efficiency by which we generate supply. Technological change may have primary or secondary impacts on the supply side of the equation. The primary impact is largely due to increased production capability for the same unit of input afforded us through improved production efficiency. The secondary effect may be described as the impact of technology on means other than that of production; e.g. improved communication, more accurate invoicing etc.

*Ceteris paribus*, a shift in technology to the "right", that is a shift towards use of more highly sophisticated technology, will shift the relevant supply isoquant (say the capital/labor isoquant) to the right (see Figure 1) and would positively impact revenue.

Electronic collaboration amongst businesses has the potential to provide cost control, reduced cycle time, increasing flexibility and improved profits.

*Figure 1. Shift towards highly sophisticated technology*

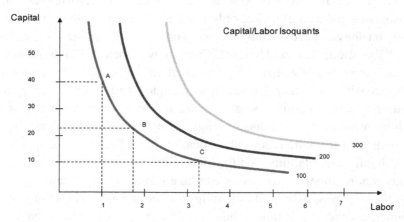

Order fulfillment and customer demand management here refers to fundamental changes in distribution, and the need to change the methods used in customer order fulfillment and customer demand management. Globalization of markets here refers to the need to adopt standard processes for producing, selling and distributing products and services. Systems reliability, availability, and transferability of information systems should be ensured in terms of the nature of use by various types of users through a variety of platforms or environments. This refers to the capability of incorporating diverse error handling strategies to react to any possible and unforeseeable situations in information systems. Moreover, the availability and transferability of information systems are considered as important to overall systems reliability in the global organization. Due to the multinational business units in the global organization, each business unit may need to access information in different time periods. Maintenance strategy needs to cope with this multinational characteristic to eliminate the consequences of the system's downtime. Global information systems operating on the Internet are expected to operate in a 24 x 7 manner. Components and modules of global information systems should also be designed flexibly enough to transfer and adapt from one business unit to another without requiring undue technical modifications.

An understanding of the factors that affect the competitive advantage of business due to global collaborations can be based on Porter's (1990) discussions. Porter has suggested that the following attributes determine the environment for business: the inputs to production, the availability of resources, the requirement of necessary skills, the business strategy, and the structure of the organization. These four determinants of the competitive advantage are extended and discussed here. (see Figure 2)

*Figure 2. Factors in competitive advantage of global organizations*

Figure 2 depicts the factors in providing Competitive Advantage in the Global Organization (based on Porter, 1990). Production is the fundamental input to competition. Significant advantage arises from the high quality inputs such as product knowledge, diverse acquisition of technology and infrastructure and variety of human and capital resources. Demand conditions; advantages arise from the characteristic of global market and products. In a global market customers demand products from anywhere in the world. Redesigning products or services is essential to fulfill the global conditions and satisfy the global customer requirements. Thus, products can be manufactured anywhere on the globe where conditions are optimum and distributed to the nearest or furthest markets. Related and supporting industries; advantages in increasing productivity arise from the availability of global resources (specialized suppliers and related industries). Through the global supplier channel, organizations are able to find required supporting materials and services at reduced costs. The presence of global resources also works better with a global production strategy. That is, selected global suppliers provide the required materials or services directly to the closest global production sites. This result in the reduction of time required for transportation and thus shortens the production cycle.

Firm strategy, structure, and rivalry diverse and multicultural conditions in the global business environment present advantages to enterprises in organizing, structuring, and managing the business strategy and structures to survive the global rivalry.

In attaining global competitive advantage, organizations require competence in areas such as organizational structure, skills, and resources. These competences are crucial to attaining competitive advantage but perhaps even more important is making sure that the competitive advantage is always through adding value to the customer. Ford Motor Company is a good example to illustrate how such changes have taken place. In order to reach the global competitive advantage Ford transformed its organizational structure through five stages of change in its competence. In the first stage, competence of overseas business units was based on products, designs and methods provided by the home country (the headquarters). In stage 2, competence of the overseas business unit was based on its own production with the designs and methods provided by the home country. When the overseas business unit had the capability of production and designing products locally, then it had reached the third stage. In the forth and fifth stages, the capability of production and design were based regionally and globally respectively. In accordance with the above stages, competence to change became the driver for the organization towards globalization, while customer requirements became the trigger of transformation from stage to stage. Furthermore, to maintain a global competitive edge, the organization needs to ensure that changes in organizational structure and its business strategy have met with customer satisfaction within the framework of global transformation process.

Information is a direct product of processes that capture knowledge about the persons, places, things and events discovered while conducting business transactions. In a global organization, sources of information are enormous. Information is produced by virtually everyone from any level in the organization. As a result, enterprises often face situations such as missing or inaccurate information. This would cause business processes to fail and would increase costs as information will need to be reproduced or rediscovered. Hence, organizations must apply quality principles to effectively manage information. However, managing and controlling information and its quality seem to be a complex and challenging task.

## Effect of Information Systems

Global information systems facilitate global business operations by bringing together technical elements of software applications and enabling them to 'talk' with each other. There are, however, wide ranging issues to be dealt with when introducing a global information system. Apart from the software environment, application configuration and security issues, there are also changes to job specifications, skills requirements, management, and organizational structures that need to be considered by business. Anticipated changes related to the new systems should be documented and the business plan should be drawn up to reflect those changes.

As per Laudon & Laudon (2002), an information systems plan refers to: "A roadmap indicating the direction of systems development: the rationale, the current situation, the management strategy, the implementation plan, and the budget." These aspects of an information systems plan need to be reflected in the effort of an organization to implement effective global information system. In considering global information systems, it is imperative for the information system function to align itself with the business processes, strategies and goals of the organization. Information systems are developed based on the requirements, behaviors and activities of all business parties who have intercommunicated with the organization's core business functions and objectives. These parties include suppliers, customers, government agencies, and all the collaborating businesses. The goals and strategic vision of these business entities must be incorporated in the development of information systems. In addition, the alignment of information systems with business functions in a global organization must also take into account the organizational type or structure.

Configuring and implementing an effective global information system requires understanding of the goal of the organization when using such a system for collaborative purposes. Furthermore, collaborative business processes need to be modeled and the people involved in the use of the information systems need to be taken in confidence. These people include senior managers, operational staff, salespeople, customers, suppliers, and many other general employees. All these users should be invited to participate in the modeling of processes, configuration of the application, training and deployment.

Global information systems that facilitate collaboration have a direct impact on the models of collaborative business processes. Organizations have to understand and recognize that business processes in the collaborative global context are significantly different from the traditional or existing ones. In order to design the appropriate information systems to facilitate business operations in the global environment, organizations should rethink and redesign their business processes to align with the global business strategic vision. This is in accordance with Hammer and Stanton (1995) "official definition" of reengineering which is, "the fundamental rethinking and radical redesign of business processes to achieve dramatic improvements in performance". Four key words (fundamental, radical, dramatic, and processes) contained in the definition are identified to further explore their significance in the globalization perspective. Fundamental; in preparing for business process reengineering, organizations must ask themselves questions in relation to the current and future business operations and strategic vision. These questions can be as simple as "what are the current business processes?", "what are the new business processes that would emerge after the global transition?", and "what are the activities involved in the processes (both current and future)?" and so forth. By asking these questions, organizations are forced to map an overall picture of ways they are expecting to conduct their business in a collaborative manner. Radical; refers to the design of collaborative business processes from the very beginning and not just tweaking the existing business processes by making modifications or improvements. Instead, by reengineering business processes for collaboration, the old processes are removed and the new ones are created to cope with the global nature of collaboration. Dramatic;

refers to the depth of changes to the existing business processes. Dramatic improvement differs from marginal improvement, as the former requires giving up the old ones and replacing them with something totally new, while the latter requires only fine-tuning of the existing processes. Processes; are the objects of the reengineering concept. A business process refers to a collection of activities that together carry out operations that achieve business routines and satisfy customer requirements. According to Virdell (2003), a business process can be defined as a set of interrelated tasks linked to an activity that spans functional boundaries. Besides activities and tasks, business processes also have starting points, ending points and deliverables, and these business processes are repeatable. In a global business environment, many business processes are implemented through collaborative teams across borders. Hence, the view of trans-border business processes is crucial to success in the business reengineering process for global organizations.

The technologies that facilitate electronic collaboration amongst many businesses also influence the internal workings of those organizations. For example, the organization's blueprints as identified by Laudon & Laudon (2002) that deal with coordination, management and maintenance also undergo changes when reconfigured for electronic collaboration. The organization, and its various levels and functions are linked through the work that is being performed across the organization. Computing and information technologies that support these activities need to be identified and made available for all business units in planning for globalization. Furthermore, group collaborations including, particularly, in outsourced projects require collaborations amongst multiple members of virtual teams (Unhelkar, 2008, smart sourcing report). Electronic collaboration technologies enable scheduling individuals and groups – the technologies that facilitate this activity include electronic calendars, groupware, and intranet. Communicating with individuals and groups – the tasks include initiating, receiving, and managing data in the format of voice, image, digital, and text. The supporting technologies may consist of e-mail, voice mail, digital answering systems, groupware, and intranets. Managing data on individuals and groups – this activity mainly focuses on the management of data and information of employees, customers, vendors, suppliers, or even competitors. The enabling technologies include database systems and spreadsheet applications. Managing projects – it refers to the management of collaborative work and projects in both local and global environments. The technologies that can be applied to this activity may include groupware, teamware, and project management applications.

# ELECTRONIC TECHNOLOGY AS BASIS FOR COLLABORATION

Web Services (WS) technologies and their extensions to Mobile Technologies (MT) provide a basis for electronic collaborative businesses. While collaboration in the business world is influenced by technology, since the business world itself is a part of the overall socio-cultural fabric, it is also worth considering the impact of these emerging WS technologies on the society in general. As mentioned earlier, these emerging technologies cause the restructure of the organization and its existing business processes. The changes to the organization and the introduction of new processes enable the business to collaborate with other businesses and thereby grow globally. This growth is invariable based on finding greater number of customers (see Ginige, (2002) for a detailed discussion). The overall impact of mobility has been summarized by Unhelkar (2005a), who states that mobility has had a significant impact on the quality of life for individuals and the society in which they live. This impact of emerging technologies on society revolves around the way communication, through mobile devices, has changed the way people relate to each other, their corresponding ethics (in their private and working lives) and how security and privacy concerns have changed due to these technologies. However, while location-aware mobile connectivity has dramatically increased the ability of individuals to communicate, it has also produced challenges in terms of privacy and new social protocols. The effect of globalization now needs to be further considered in the context of a global-mobile society.

There have been many studies in understanding Business-to-Business collaboration, such as those conducted by Grewal, Comer and Mehta (2001) and Barnes-Vieyra and Claycomb, (2001). These studies indicate that B2B e-commerce use has proved more difficult than expected. The business as well as Information Technology (IT) communities are looking for answers on how to proceed with B2B collaboration. The significance of B2B e-commerce makes it imperative to research it for three reasons (Grewal, Comer, and Mehta, 2001):

1. B2B collaboration is becoming a viable alternative to traditional markets;
2. The commercial potential of B2B collaboration is enormous; and
3. Not enough is known about the factors that influence the nature of organizational participation in B2B collaboration.

B2B integration (or Business Integration) is a secured coordination amongst two or more known businesses and their information systems. This B2B integration has dramatically transformed the way business is conducted between specific business partners, suppliers, customers and buyers. The Internet has made B2B e-commerce more accessible at a lower cost than older communication methods (Sharma, 2002).

B2B facilitate e-commerce by helping to avoid value migration (that is, capture of growth in revenue, profits, and market value by competing firms) attributable to declining market prices (disinflation), rising competitive intensity, advanced technology (enabling increased communication flows), and reverse marketing strategies, hence ecommerce is more customer-focused rather than product-focused.

B2B e-commerce is defined by Barnes-Vieyra and Claycomb (2001), as a supply chain innovation that generates cross-firm process integration. The use of the World Wide Web has secured the trading of goods, information, and services before, during, and after the sale. The ideas presented in this book extend the aforementioned concept of the Business-to-Business (B2B) collaborations and apply them to multiple organizations in a dynamic manner. Furthermore, collaborating organizations may not even be known to each other and yet get together electronically to satisfy a particular business demand.

Thus, this book attempts to model collaborative services that can be offered and consumed by organizations that may be unknown to each other electronically. This ability to offer services by publishing them on the Internet, and then locating and consuming them, results from the ability of WS to "transcend" technological boundaries and environments, as discussed later in this book. Web Services technology enables applications from different organizations to communicate with each other regardless of the specific platform requirements. This book is an attempt to extract the full potential of this opportunity offered by Web Services technology. A service is a component that can be invoked by a requester dynamically; furthermore, the technical platform of Service-oriented Architecture (SOA) describes how the service could be invoked and how the services attributes are implemented.

Most studies until now only have concentrated on the business processes "internal" to the organization. This book investigates the cross-organizational processes within multiple organizations when these organizations are not necessarily known to each other, in order to provide the required services/products by customer.

As a part of the development of the model for successful *Collaborative Business Process Engineering (CBPE)*, many important issues and challenges have been identified and studied. Based on the three-dimensional process framework developed by Unhelkar (2005a, 2007), these issues and challenges in *CBPE* could be broadly categorized into technical, methodological and social challenges. These three types of challenges are now explained in the context of *CBPE*.

*Technically*, the challenge is to investigate the simplicity of implementation of Web Services and their corresponding security and performance issues. These technical issues, revolving around SOA, further expand into identifying the availability and management of the various channels of transaction capabilities between the collaborating organizations. *Methodologically*, the challenge is to identify, model, evaluate and investigate the impact of collaborative business processes on the structure and dynamics of the collaborating organizations. *Socially*, collaborations lead to challenges in terms of privacy, trust, and legal as well as cross-cultural issues, between organizations that may be lying across vast geographical boundaries.

This book also addresses the impact of collaboration on social system (people *"trust"*; reward *"why collaborate?"*; and authority structure *"who is in charge of the collaboration?"*) as well as technical system (processes *"before and after engineering"*; tasks *"security, convenience and availability of the channels"*; and technology *"Web Services"* and *"Mobile Technology"*).

The discussions in this book is thus a unique attempt to examine and model processes for a cluster or group of organizations and how these processes can be engineered to incorporate emerging technologies in them. Logically, this discussion delves into the advantages and limitations of the aforementioned emerging technologies, and uses those advantages and limitations in creating a base for engineering business processes of multiple organizations.

## ELECTRONIC BUSINESS PROCESSES

A business process is a set of coordinated tasks and activities that provides significant guidance in achieving a specific organizational objective. According to Virdell (2003), a business process can be defined as a set of interrelated tasks linked to an activity that spans functional boundaries. Besides activities and tasks, business processes also have starting points, ending points and deliverables, and these are repeatable. Furthermore, business processes are usually closely supported by software applications. The rapid advent of the Internet allows these software applications, and the many organizational processes that are built around these software applications, to communicate easily with each other. The resultant transactions cross geographical and time boundaries with relative ease. Subsequently, current business processes can span multiple organization boundaries transcending across many different countries and operating under varying socio-political and legal climates. The sheer potential of these Internet-based business processes is such that there is a pressing need to study them carefully and in detail. These business processes that transcend geo-political boundaries, particularly when these business processes employ Internet-based connectivity, are changing the business landscape to include hitherto unknown possibilities. The potential of Internet-based business processes, their effect on organizations and customers, and the challenges faced by the business world resulting from these processes comprise a vast field requiring formal research and study.

This book discusses and models the business processes that enable the organization to transcend its boundaries – geographic and technological – resulting in collaborative business processes of multiple organizations. Furthermore, this book also delves deeper into the possibilities offered *beyond* simple (or static) connectivity between two business applications, and reaches into the areas of dynamic collaborative business processes. Finally, this book also encompasses all the dimensions of technology, methodology and sociology (as discussed by Unhelkar, 2005a, 2007), and the corresponding points-of-view of these dimensions in the context of understanding and modeling these business processes. Such modeling, it is envisaged, will eventually result in a truly collaborative and dynamic global market. The ability of organizations to electronically get together, perform a certain goal, and then disperse, is a *new* reality of collaborative business. This new reality rests heavily on Internet-based software applications that support the business processes of these collaborating organizations. This book lays down the path for such dynamic Internet-based collaborations between myriad businesses.

## BUSINESS USE OF THE WEB

The use of the Internet's communication capabilities by businesses is shown in Figure 3. The triangle in the figure represents increasingly complex yet fruitful use of these technological capabilities by business. This figure maps the technological evolution of the Internet and its usage by business (based on S'duk & Unhelkar, 2005).

As seen in Figure 3, Internet technology has evolved through the four layers of the triangle – namely, informative, transactive, operative and collaborative layers. Each layer of the triangle builds upon the lower layers. The ability of a business to thoroughly implement the preceding layers has a positive effect on the success of the subsequent layers.

These layers correspond roughly to the four distinct eras of business utilizing the Web. As each layer moves closer to the top of the triangle, it becomes *smaller* to depict the reduced usage of the Web by business, more *complex* to depict the technical requirements to facilitate this usage, and last, but not least, more *risky* and *expensive* to implement than the previous layers. Once a business has successfully traversed each layer and positioned itself at the top of the triangle then it has maximized its usage of the Web as today's technology permits by achieving the strategic business goals.

*Figure 3. Model of the Internet's evolution (based on S'duk and Unhelkar, 2005)*

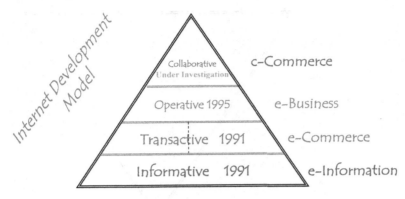

The tip of the triangle depicted in Figure 3 represents the collaborative business (c-business) era. That collaborative era is a natural evolution of the business which initially starts with the e-information (informative) era. Figure 4 shows the required effort needed by the organisation to reach the successful level in each individual era of the Internet development model.

As demonstrated in Figure 4, the success of the e-collaboration era is the most difficult task and needs concentrated effort by the organizations. The organizations need to make sure that they have identified the importance of the collaboration for the survival, how they manage to distribute the knowledge, identify the associated cost factors, develop and test the collaborative software products, identify the post transfer issues and evaluate their organization as well as the organizations responses. In the e-business era, the organizations need encouragement, adapt high affiliated costs and employ people who are capable of handling the transformation of the business. In the e-commerce era, the organizations need to identify the right electronic markets for their product, change existing policies, develop new purchase process, investigate the possibility for international market and use the right e-commerce software. The lowest tip of the triangle which is the e-information era needs least amount of effort since the organizations just need to make sure that they post the right information and that such posting of information does not violate the privacy and security of the recipients.

The benefits of these efforts are demonstrated in Figure 5, wherein the possible opportunities of each individual era of the Internet usage model for the organizations is shown. This triangle is similar to the triangle shown in Figure 4 wherein the greater is the effort of the organization, the greater are the opportunities for the organizations in each individual era.

As shown in Figure 5, the e-collaborative era provide more opportunities for organizations to advance their services, provide their customer with better CRM,

*Figure 4. Needed efforts for the success of the Internet development model*

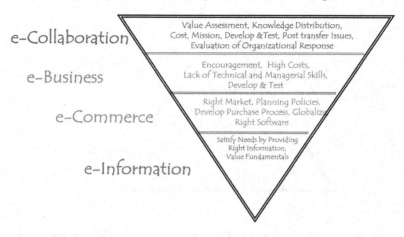

*Figure 5. Possible opportunities from the Internet evolution*

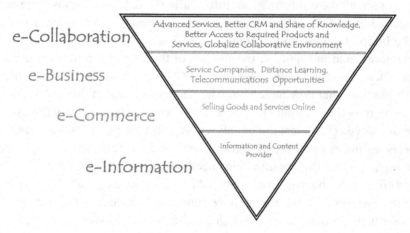

share knowledge, provide better access to the required products and services and provide better opportunity to globalize collaborative environment. E-business provides more opportunity for service companies, distance learning and creates more telecommunications opportunities. E-commerce only provides opportunity to sell goods and products while e-information create the least opportunity for the organizations since they can only provide information about the content of their company in regards to the products and services they manage to offer. These Internet usages are further discussed here with the aim of understanding their impact on Internet-based collaborative businesses.

## The Informative Stage of Internet Usage

The informative aspect of the Web can be considered as the first or the most basic use of the Internet. This was the first utilization of the Internet and its use was initiated after the Massachusetts Institute of Technology (MIT) published the first newspaper (*The Tech*) online. Initially, this usage of the Internet meant scanning of the company's brochures and putting them up on the Web. Therefore, this informative use of the Internet was also called "brochure ware". Even today, this informative aspect of the Internet usage is the most used aspect of the Internet and it includes providing online newspapers and business advertisements. Collaborative business model requires that the information provided in this stage is gleaned from various sources and service providers. For example, today's collaborative newspapers provide information to the electronic reader that is sourced from international agencies, financial markets, weather bureaus and sports channels. These sources of information need not be owned by the newspaper that is presenting this information to the user.

## The Transactive and Operative Stages of Internet Usage

The informative layer of the Internet usage is followed by e-commerce (transactive era). This transactive layer encompasses two-way interactions between business and the users, for example, free services such as free web-pages and chat rooms, which were offered for community building. Online sales have grown rapidly for such products as books, music and computers. These sales transactions form the transactive aspect of the Web. Ordinary business is not capable of satisfying the sales of the goods and services online as demanded by the customers. As a result, the mechanism of electronic transactions between two organizations is required. While the transactive aspect of the use of the Internet deals with *external* parties (that are outside of the business), the operative aspect *also* includes the *internal* processes of the business being conducted electronically. Thus, it is when all aspects of the business including the *operative* aspect of the business is moved on to the internet that one can say it is e-Business. In other words, we use the term "e-business" is used when the Internet technology is used not only to collaborate with customer, supplier and business partners but also more to internal business processes or the Web. As a result, e-business demonstrates the utilization of the Internet's communication capabilities to handle *all* aspects of business, including information, transaction and operations, both externally and internally.

An e-business is an enterprise with the capability to exchange values (goods, services, money, and knowledge) digitally via computer networks (Hackbarth and Kettinger, 2000). An e-business is also a business that uses distributed information technology, knowledge management, and trust mechanisms to transform key business processes and relationships with customers, suppliers, employees, business partners, regulatory parties, and communities (Craig and Jutla, 2001). As per Abu-Musa (2004), the concept of e-business is not only rapidly changing the way that companies buy, sell, and deal with customers, but also changing the relationships with its employees.

Thus, the concept of e-business deals with the carrying out of business activities that lead to an exchange of value, where the parties interact electronically, using network or telecommunications technologies (Jones, Wilikens, Morris and Masera, 2000).

The competitive environments of electronic business (e-business), with frequent and rapid changes to their digitally enabled supply, production, and logistics and distribution networks, are increasingly dependent on electronic interconnections that are innovative in their functionality (Lai, 2006).

E-businesses result in organizations sharing their data and information both inside and outside the business boundary. This sharing is achieved by unlocking data in the back-end computer systems and opening them up in a secured manner to conduct electronic transactions.

While e-business means conducting business online using paperless methods, it needs a multi-disciplinary approach to a business process (Lawson and Alcock, 2003). Thus, one of the most important issues, as far as e-business is concerned, is the ability to bring together information technology, business processes and secured communications across organizational boundaries, resulting in an efficient business. Such a business increases its chances to globalize easily (Lan and Unhelkar, 2005).

As seen in Figure 3, e-business evolution has taken more time than the earlier adoption of e-information and e-commerce. This is so because the diffusion of new technology can take decades, and involves more than simply reproducing and distributing the technology. This longer time duration for diffusion of technology in this layer is understandable the behavioral change required for this increasingly complex layer has been greater. The potentials (e.g. collaboration) emerging from this latter technology are much more sophisticated and disruptive than introduction of previous forms of technology that was merely a labor (energy) replacement mechanism. Indeed, making full use of these new technologies relies on the IT skills of staff within organizations (Roseberg, 1976 cited in Forester, 1985). Therefore, as the IT skill set within organizations improves, so does the ability of people to use the Internet for internal business processes as well as external ones. Chapter 4, later in this book, deals in detail with the social aspect of collaboration.

The external and internal business processes are in many ways based on the Online Transaction Processing (OLTP) of the earlier era of software applications. In OLTP applications, a class of program facilitates and manages transaction-oriented applications, typically for data entry and retrieval transactions in a number of industries. The online transaction-processing increasingly requires support for transactions that run on different computer platforms in a network.

Improvements in transaction processing by business applications have provided immense benefits to businesses – enabling them to collaborate rapidly and effectively. Through OLTP, doors are opened up for organizations to expand their reach to a much broader market, improve communication, enable efficient business practices and increase the overall value to the customer (based on Lawson et al., 2001).

Increasing business dynamics, changing customer preferences, and disruptive technological shifts create the need for two kinds of flexibility that inter-enterprise information systems must address: the ability of inter-enterprise linkages to support changes in offering characteristics while offering flexibility, and the ability to alter linkages to partner with different players such as partnering flexibility (Sanjay, Malhotra and ElSawy, 2005).

Flexibility is also an effective means by which an e-business can hedge against uncertainty in a swiftly changing environment. Systems, applications, and business processes – in short, the entire environment supporting e-business – must seamlessly adapt to changes without costly and time-consuming infrastructure overhauls. Decision-makers therefore have a growing need for knowledge about e-business flexibility. However, flexibility remains largely an abstraction in the e-business domain (Shi and Daniels, 2003).

## The Collaborative Stage of Internet Usage and Business Intelligence

The rapid development of web and ICT technologies has caused e-collaboration to evolve from its original role as a substitution for traditional face-to-face collaboration into a genuine creator of novel associations between businesses and customers. Moreover, the development of e-collaboration technologies is changing the nature of group collaboration, its functionality and its productivity. Thus, the use of electronic technologies adds a new and interesting dimension to what is commonly understood as collaboration. E-collaboration and collaborative systems not only bring geographically dispersed teams but also create a synergy between them that lets them function as a unified group – albeit only for the sake of satisfying the specific needs of a customer. Such c-business (that is, a collaborative business in the collaborative era) is initiated when a significant number of electronically collaborating applications start transacting in the market. Collaborations are widely acknowledged as a means to share and leverage knowledge within a context forged by the organization's history, culture, and its external environment (Fahey et al., 2001). Collaboration, by its very nature, is *democratic*. Such business does not always control what its customers do. As per Siegel (1999), good collaborative businesses take the bold steps of facilitating collaboration between their customers. Such collaboration between customers can lead to interesting discussions and subsequent results, such as the specifications for a car. Another example is the discussion about the quality of a book (the latter having been tried out by amazon.com).

Electronic collaboration or e-collaboration is defined as collaboration among individuals engaged in a common task using electronic technologies (Kock et al., 2001). The rapid development of Internet-based communication has caused e-collaboration to evolve from its original role as a substitution for traditional face-to-face collaboration into a genuine creator of novel associations between businesses and customers (Unhelkar, 2003).

The integration of e-collaboration and virtual technologies increases the effectiveness and speed of interactions between organizations, thereby enhancing strategic decision-making and genuine operational agility (Barekat, 2001).. These collaborations are well supported by technologies that are built on top of the Internet. For example, there are web-based chat tools, web-based asynchronous conferencing tools, e-mail, Internet-based list servers, collaborative writing tools, and group decision-making tools, as discussed by Kock et al. (2001) that operate on the Internet.

Collaborative commerce or c-commerce is seen to focus on developing collaborative relationships and providing new revenue opportunities by enabling organizations and network of organizations to sell their services and products more efficiently and at lower costs (Fairchild & Peterson, 2003). The presence of c-commerce indicates a network of firms with similar collaborative natures with established collaborative business platform and strategies (Fairchild & Peterson, 2003).

Driven by external forces and the need to streamline information exchange and work coordination, private and public sector organizations are increasingly being compelled to adopt a more collaborative approach. For instance, the increased threat from global terrorism has seen greater collaboration and cooperation between intelligence and law enforcement agencies to track terrorists on a global scale. In United States of America alone, there are 13 intelligence agencies and more than 50 organizations that run their own ant-terrorist units. This inter-agency collaboration is being expanded to include travel reservation agencies to enable screening of passenger databases to identify terrorist suspects (Morris, 2002). According to Fairchild and Peterson (2003), financial service institutions are spearheading the collaborative commerce ventures, bundling IT-enabled transactions and interactions amongst suppliers, customers and partners into a global business-to-business trading communities.

Modern-day business collaborations use inter- and intra-organizational processes efficiently and effectively. This efficiency of communication has percolated in all arenas of organizational activities, including customer relationships, resource planning, and, in the context of this discussion, collaboration. Given the cost of communication and their importance in order fulfilment process, organizations want to collaborate so as to sustain them in the globally competitive and challenging world of electronic business. Furthermore, with this invigorated growth of e-business era moving to e-collaborative era, software vendors and consultants have been promising businesses the utopian Internet-based systems that would provide them with the capability to respond in real-time to changing product demand and supply and offer easy integration functionality with backend information systems. Although a number of Internet-based collaborative systems are available for adoption, enterprises do not guarantee to implement the systems in conjunction with their existing information systems. Additional work to bring a synergy between disparate IT systems and the business processes is required in undertaking collaborative business transformations.

## The Desired Evolution in the Collaborative Layer (Wisdom)

The discussion here is focused on the tip of the triangle of Figure 3, namely the collaborative business layer. The reason for further and detailed discussion of the collaborative business layer is because collaborative business environment based on Internet technology is considered as major stage of the Web evolution for businesses: "Collaborative-Business". Based on Curtis, Kellner, and Over (1992), a process model is an abstract definition of an actual or proposed process. The collaborative process model here is also, to a certain extent, an abstraction of the actual process that a collaborative group of organizations can undertake. Consequently, in Figure 3, the tip of the triangle represents this current, abstract, current stage of the Internet usage by business. This book applies the abstraction in the tip of the triangle in Figure 3 in practice by evaluating, modeling and implementing the business processes of multiple organizations in a collaborative manner. The term *Collaborative Business Process Engineering (CBPE)* is considered most appropriate to explain the resultant dynamic collaboration between multiple organizations through the business processes that transcend the individual boundaries.

The collaborative process model in this book is expected to result in a new collaborative business environment that provides opportunities for organizations and people within to interact with each other in what can be considered a genuinely "free market" environment. The collaborative business process discussed especially here deals with situations in which the organizations may not be known to each other beforehand. The dynamic and "open market" nature of what is being proposed is new, and it requires the rigors of process engineering. The engineered process could become a part or an extension of an existing business process or it can be a fully re-engineered process.

Collaborations are the key results of being able to communicate electronically. Electronic or e-collaborations, powered by web-enabled applications and electronic technologies, are not merely popular within an organization but are also a creative cause for and rapid facilitators of a group of organizations. Linking individuals and systems towards achieving better information sharing, real-time interactive communication and seemingly seamless collaboration is the goal of any business that wants to capitalize on the Internet revolution. Electronic communication mechanisms provide instant capabilities to form groups, link organizations and create "virtual" teams as well as business clusters at a global level. The end result is a global village that is built on the capabilities of the Internet. However, collaborations are not the first achievement of the Internet world. The Internet usage has started from some basic informative concepts through to commerce and collaborations. When a group of businesses collaborate with each other electronically, it results in the usage of the Internet that can be labeled electronic collaborative usage. Collaborative usage is widespread amongst businesses that are still coming to grips with the needs of standards in setting up and promoting their businesses, as well as improving their comfort levels in terms of security and privacy. Collaborative processes enable relationships between a network of organizations to identify each other through the provided products and services electronically, thereby making them cheaper to sell or buy as well as enabling the businesses to reach a wide range of market. Despite its understandable slowness in catching up, it is this collaborative nature of the Internet usage that is bound to provide maximum advantages to businesses both in terms of globalization and in managing their own internal processes effectively.

These newly engineered processes, resulting from *CBPE*, enable an organization to become part of a global collaborative environment. The modeling of these collaborative business processes, however, needs a detailed understanding of the architecture and design of a process itself: therefore, this book can benefit immensely by understanding the corresponding software-modeling processes. For example, Graham, Henderson-Sellers and Younessi, (1997) discuss various software development methods through their *OPEN* (Object-Oriented Process, Environment and Notation) – wherein they discuss and provide strong support for process-modeling. Unhelkar (2003) has also discussed elements of process architecture.

The discussions of the aforementioned authors, especially the use of lifecycles and patterns, processes to capture requirements, configuration and enactment of processes – all of this has relevance to the *CBPE* model discussed in this book. This relevance of process-modeling, discussed in the software literature to the *CBPE* model can be seen in Figure 6. The activities, deliverables and roles, as presented in Figure 6, have their origins in software processes such as OPEN.

Figure 6 demonstrates that the collaborative business process has brought together organizations in a collaborative environment using relevant technologies. As has been

*Figure 6. Collaborative business process environment*

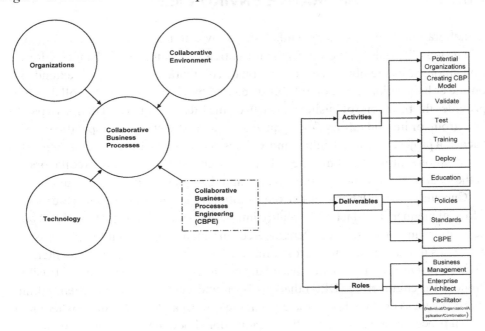

noted by Vij and Patel, (2006), current information retrieval systems provide only a list of ranked documents with a very brief summary against user-supplied keywords. However, the proposed *CBPE* improves the search engine's information retrieval results by increasing the compactness of clusters based on the processes discussed here. In order to achieve this efficiency, *CBPE* restructures the infrastructure, refines the activities, deliverables and roles, and links these elements to the existing environment. The *CBPE* presented in Figure 6 is also made up of these elements of activities, deliverables, and roles. These elements therefore comprise:

- *Activities:* Potential organizations, creating the *CBPE* model, validation of the model, testing of the model, training of users, deploying the system and educating the end-users.
- *Deliverables:* Policies and standards involved in the management of the proposed collaborative system.
- *Roles:* Business management, Enterprise Architecture (EA) and the facilitator.

The evolution of the technology is clearly demonstrated in this section by stating how the Internet technology has evolved from not only being informative to also becoming effective in providing a collaborative environment.

## CURRENT COLLABORATIVE ENVIRONMENT

Collaboration, as discussed by Yildiz, Marjanovic and Godart (2006) is an activity of a group of people that results in the formation of a team that exchanges information amongst its members. This definition of collaboration can also be extended to online collaboration. For example, as discussed by Unhelkar (2003), collaboration provides the backbone of business growth on the Internet when collaborative parties as a group of individuals and/or organizations come together for a specific purpose such as a project or a task. Linking individuals and systems towards achieving better information sharing, real-time interactive communication and seamless collaboration is the goal of any business that wants to capitalize on the Internet revolution.

Currently, this collaboration between multiple organizations does not take place in a formal manner. This lack of formality implies that the existing technical and business environment has not been "engineered" in a manner that would encompass new processes that are conducted across multiple business organizations. The literature review presented here indicates that all the business-process modeling and Business Process Re-engineering (BPR) that has been undertaken so far has been within a single business entity. This is true even in the case of a global business wherein the global processes are still within the organizational boundary. When these business processes are indeed extended beyond the boundaries of an organization, they are invariably extended to another "known" and dedicated business partner. These business processes have resulted in what is described as Business-to-Business (B2B) processes. However, throughout the usage of the Internet, the question of modeling integrated but dynamic business processes that transcend multiple organizational boundaries is still an open question.

### Alternative Collaboration Models

An alternative collaboration with regard to multiple organizations is possible when a gateway is positioned to facilitate the interactions amongst organizations, as illustrated in Figure 6 This demonstrated gateway in Figure 6 is the only existing channel of collaboration between the two organizations (ordinary B2B model). The model presented in Figure 6 clearly demonstrates the shortcomings of this form of collaboration, since the organizations are not in direct contact with each other.

The Gateway (an individual organization) can collaborate with many other organizations. For example, your bank (Gateway) can pay different bills to different service providers (electricity, water, phone service) through their BPay addresses. Figure 7 is an illustration of the existing environment of collaboration.

This book is focused on cross-organizational processes. The new engineered processes must be able to facilitate collaboration and negotiation with organiza-

*Figure 7. Potential opportunities for a "gateway" based approach to collaboration*

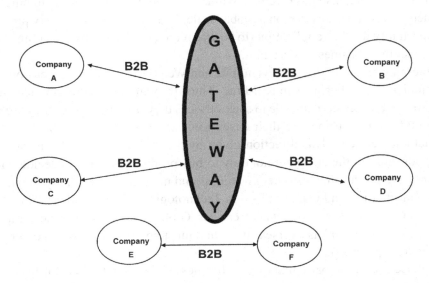

tions that are getting together electronically. These organizations may be physically unknown to one another, may be in remote geographic locations and may have different technical environments. Goethals and Vandenbulcke (2006) explain that Web Services may be used for integrating systems for unknown parties. In creating this type of integrations, the infrastructure used should be built in such a way that it could easily adapt to new requirements.

Fong (2005) further argues that the limited empirical evidence of successful e-collaboration is attributed not only to the short history of e-collaboration and software, but also to the challenges associated in business with this revolutionary way of operating and sharing information.

The challenges of e-collaboration are mainly classified where individual organizations use varying technologies and data standards that give rise to islands of networks that now need to be integrated and coordinated. Web Services can overcome this problem of interoperation. This is so because WS enable applications to talk with each other through protocols such as the Extensible Markup Language (XML). Such XML-based interaction is relatively new and different from the B2B interactions between two dedicated applications. WS are understood as independent application components that take the Web to a new stage of business interactions in which software applications can transmit and receive the required data, irrespective of their existing platform under operation.

Customers are better informed with information at their fingertips over the Internet. The Internet also has offered a window of opportunity for users to purchase products and receive services on a global scale. Web Services technology provides an opportunity for Web applications to be discovered by other software components to conduct their business transaction.

Emerging technologies such as mobile and Web Services allow the customer to communicate with business in real-time. Thus, through these emerging technologies, not only are customers able to seek services they need now – but they are also able to inform the business of their exact needs and upcoming expectations of the product and services. This direction given by the customer to the business gives the opportunity to the customer not only to buy products but also to decide on the way they are produced. Customer awareness and maturity significantly impact the use of Information and Communication Technologies (ICT) in order to direct the business to globalize its product and services. Globalization matures the company, since the organization has overseas trade and must become sensitive to other (foreign) market potentials.

The success of global collaborative businesses depends heavily on the sociocultural nuances of participating organizations. Organizations are encouraged to embrace diversity and turn the multicultural characteristics into strategic advantages. The multicultural characteristic will provide organizations with a certain level of competitive edge in the global business environment. Countries, and societies within countries, need to be understood so we can provide collaborative products/services to them.

Traditional e-collaboration plays a strategic role in business direction, and the proposed new business process (*CBPE*) has emerged from the traditional e-collaboration, by examining beyond the boundaries of the internal processes of the organization. E-collaboration, facilitated by Internet technology, is more than mere substitution of traditional collaboration. The *CBPE* also changes the organizational infrastructure, resulting in a flatter reporting hierarchy, while people at similar levels in collaborating organizations continue to interact with each other. Thus, human interaction is a significant factor in collaborative business. The technical infrastructure facilitates rapid emergence of e-collaboration. However, technical issues such as storage and system architecture also need to be addressed for the success of a collaborative business.

## Business-to-Business (B2B) Collaboration

The B2B integration architecture on the receiving website is responsible for the complete processing of B2B events. The underlying software system not only has to provide the connectivity, but also the back-end system storage, process and security management. An active sub-component of this architecture, the B2B engine, is responsible for the communication aspects of B2B events with the various trading partners (Bussler, 2002). This B2B engine implements the various aforementioned functionalities required by the customer and makes it available to the overall B2B integration architecture.

The current collaborative environment has been researched, discussed and implemented across myriad businesses, globally. This current environment for business collaboration is able to satisfy customer needs once the website and the business that is represented by the website are "known" to the customer. Furthermore, the response is able to satisfy the customer demand only to its capacity and ability. For example, this same collaborative environment is unable to assist the customer if the customer has much greater demand than the ability of a particular business can satisfy. The travel scenario described above is not able to provide a solution that requires a complex request, such as two airlines, three hotels and four car companies, to get together to satisfy the travel needs of a large client (such as, say, a touring party or a school excursion). The customer has to physically search and book with different businesses (service providers) in order to satisfy his or her travel needs. There is no provision, within the current business models, to easily enable the customer to create a major tour package *without* the customer searching, booking and submitting *multiple* applications. Therefore, this current approach to business collaboration can be classified as *static collaboration*. Such static collaboration is mundane, routinely occurring between millions of businesses, not warranting much argument.

## PROPOSING A NEW MODEL OF BUSINESS COLLABORATION

The current collaborations, that take place daily, occur between two or more organizations that are known to each other. Such electronic collaborations imply that the business applications belonging to the organizations are in prior electronic contract with each other and that such collaborations have been "set up" prior to the occurrence of business transactions. Figure 8 shows such an existing collaborative environment in a travel agency example.

Figure 8 depicts a current Business-to-Business (B2B) collaborative environment, using a travel industry example. Herein, a customer has multiple needs in order to undertake travel: the need to book and purchase an airline ticket, to book a hotel room, to hire a car and to purchase travel insurance. These needs of the customer are submitted through an "application" that contains his or her specific requirements. The customer enters the desired destinations, desired date and time of the departure, desired date and time of return and required services (the airline ticket, car, hotel room and hired car). This application, made up of these various parameters, is then

*Figure 8. Current model of collaboration (Travel agency example)*

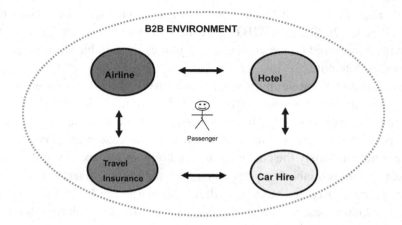

submitted to one of the businesses. Once the application is received by the specific website of a business, it can register the details, make the bookings and provide the customer with a schedule. Furthermore, this website also provides the customer with an invoice and, possibly, an easy electronic way of making the payments.

Figure 9 demonstrates how the collaborative environment could be improved to receive the full potential of collaborations where multiple organizations are involved in partnerships. These organizations are not necessarily known to each other.

Figure 9 shows how this particular investigation aims to redress the shortcoming of the B2B scenario depicted in Figure 8. In Figure 9, the proposal is for a new collaborative environment that is based on the model created in this work as: *Collaborative Business Process Engineering (CBPE)* model. Figure 9 demonstrates, simply, that by interoperation amongst multiple organizations, the customer is able to present requirements for multiple airlines, hotels and other required services or products through *one* simple application. Thus, for example, if a customer needs to purchase tickets, insurance policies and book hotel rooms and cars for 150 people, the customer submits only one single application to the proposed collaborative system. This collaborative system is capable of accessing multiple airlines, insurance companies, hotels and car rental agencies. The underlying *CBPE* system model would automatically access various other organizations and collaborate with them in order to satisfy the needs of the customer. For example, if one organization is unable to provide for the needs of 150 people in a touring party, the underlying *CBPE* system model will access more than one hotel and car company to satisfy these needs of the customer. These multiple organizations from specific industries need not necessarily be known to the customer, or to each other. And yet the customer is able to book multiple numbers of tickets, travel insurances, hotel rooms and hired

*Figure 9. Proposed model of collaboration (Travel agency example)*

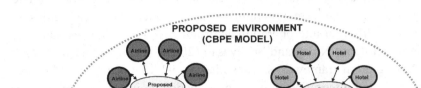
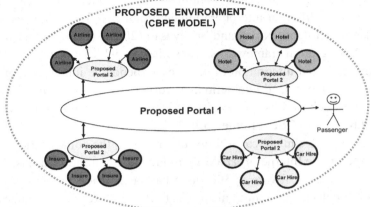

cars from multiple different organizations by submitting just one single application. The scenario presented in Figure 9 is classified as *dynamic collaboration.*

Note how the scenario depicted in Figure 9, and described above is different from the well-known B2B scenario. The differences in the B2B scenario of Figure 8 and the proposed collaborative scenario of Figure 9, can be listed as follows:

1.  The B2B businesses set up a relationship beforehand, whereas in a true collaborative *(CBPE)* -based scenario, the collaborations between the businesses may not be set beforehand.
2.  The B2B businesses "know" each other, and are therefore more secure in their transactions; the *CBPE*-based businesses may not be known to each other, leading to higher security risks.
3.  The *CBPE*-based collaborative businesses are dynamic – in the sense that they get together on a portal to achieve a particular business objective, but then can disperse after the business objective has been satisfied; the B2B businesses remain in continuous contact with each other.
4.  The collaborations between multiple businesses create business challenges; the issues of trust and legal enforcement become very important in terms of these collaborations in *CBPE*, compared with B2B collaborations.
5.  There appears to be a dearth of in-depth modeling of these collaborative business processes, compared with the B2B processes.

This book addresses these differences and produces answers to the challenges emanating from these differences. As is noted later, the collaborative business process scenario encompassing multiple organizations does not appear to have been addressed previously in the formal literature. However, there are a few studies that try to evaluate the different interoperation environments for businesses. One such study, by Hogg, Chilcott, Nolan and Srinivasan (2004), highlights the various issues in B2B integration frameworks. These issues, which need to be addressed, include process-based integration of services, dependable integration of services, and support of standardized interactions, security, and privacy. The current work, reported in this book, addresses these issues in the context of collaborative business processes through the *CBPE* framework.

The underlying technical capabilities that result in the collaboration envisaged here are based on the Internet's capability to facilitate communications. This communication between software applications has been made possible through the technologies for electronic communications. Earlier, before the open Internet-based communications, these technologies included Microsoft's DCOM (Distributed Component Object Model) and the Object Management Group's (OMG's) CORBA (Common Object Request Broker Architecture).

However, Internet-based collaborations that are now being made possible between multiple businesses are dependent on the technologies of Web Services (WS) and Mobile Technologies (MT). Therefore, this work studies these technologies and investigates their impact on transitioning to successful *CBPE*. Some earlier studies in these emerging technologies of WS and MT have already been reported by Ghanbary and Unhelkar (2007a), Ghanbary and Unhelkar (2007b) and Ghanbary (2006b). These publications have identified and described the concept of *Collaborative Business Process Engineering (CBPE)* as distinct from the traditional Business Process Re-engineering (BPR). This book presents the full analysis of these aforementioned publications, together with the testing and evaluation of the *CBPE* model and case studies that demonstrate how the model is applied in practice. The major parts of this CBPE model can be said to be based on the study of the following questions:

- What is the nature of interoperation in the existing practice (model) of collaboration?
- What is the impact of interoperability emanating from Web Services on organizations that collaborate electronically? (Here we address the dynamic aspect of collaborations wherein organizations can enter and exit the collaboration at will.)
- What are the characteristics and the mechanisms to model collaborative business processes that transcend organizational boundaries (also technical boundaries) as against business processes within a single organization?

- What are the factors influencing collaborative business processes (such as trust, security, confidence level and availability of channels)?
- What are the benefits of the constructed model of collaboration (*CBPE* Model) in terms of its efficiency as well as its practicality?
- What are the impacts of mobile technology on the *CBPE* model?
- How do organizations adapt the new technologies (such as mobile and Web Services technologies)?
- What are the methodological and social consequences of the proposed environment of the collaboration?

The above questions are inter-related, leading from one question to the next. The dependencies of these questions and their answers are an important factor in the creation of the *CBPE* model.

## CHALLENGES IN ELECTRONIC COLLABORATION

Most organizations traditionally face challenges in "managing the human side of introducing new technologies" (Fahey et al, 2001), human issues can be major. This is supported by a recent survey of UK public sector executives and senior management showing that 50% of public sector agencies were able to share data with other government agencies, but only 11% were able to share information with private sector partners (Morris, 2002).

For e-collaboration efforts to succeed in achieving the desired objectives, employees need to modify their current work practices and mindsets. Not only the willingness to share knowledge is required, Fahey et al (2001) emphasize on the importance of issues concerned with developing and enriching human relationships with individual customers which call for "touch" and "trust" between both parties.

Certain industries have begun to realize the benefits of collaboration and information sharing. For instance, data are commonly shared and cross-checked to ensure the legitimacy of claims within insurance industry. However, there are organizations within the insurance sector that face the difficulty of sorting through data related to various ways of storing ages, different interpretations and formats related to same piece of information and also handling different languages. In other sectors, such as for instance the automotive sector, Ford, General Motors and Daimler Chrysler have created supplier portals and attempted to transform automotive supply chains using e-commerce. However, it was found that 40% of the product CAD (computer aided design) files from suppliers did not comply with the stringent quality standards which caused a setback in their e-commerce venture (Morris, 2002).

Data-sharing can be significantly improved provided it is presented in a neutral format, independent of any platform or system. Else, it can be costly to convert large chunks of disparate information into a standardized format that can be used by multiple organizations. For instance, the costs of a project that links fingerprint databases held US FBI and US Immigration and Naturalization Service are estimated to be at £143 million (Morris, 2002).

Other issues that can adversely impact collaborative relationships include collaborating organizations of different sizes, having different company cultures, or non-complementary core competencies (Morris, 2002). This indicates that collaborative commerce is not to be thought as "one size fits all", organizations must take into account their internal structures and environment, the considerable barriers such as costs of establishing data-sharing systems, and the compatibility of their chosen collaborative partners.

## ACTION POINTS

1.  Enforce a business strategy to adopt collaboration in the internal and external division of your organization.
2.  Evaluate the impact of the Internet development model on your organization.
3.  Evaluate the opportunities created by each era of the Internet development model for your organization.
4.  List your organization's business process and evaluate how theses business processes can collaborate with other organization's business processes.
5.  Identify the challenges associated with the collaboration in your organization.

## REFERENCES

Abu-Musa, A. A. (2004). Auditing e-business: New challenges for external auditors. The Journal of the American Academy of Business , 4(1/2), 28–41.

Arunatileka, D., & Unhelkar, B. (2003). *Mobile technologies, providing new possibilities in customer relationship management*. Paper presented at the 5th International Information Technology Conference, Colombo, Sri Lanka.

Barekat, M. (2001). The real time-enterprise [r]evolution. Manufacturing Engineering , 80(4), 153–156. doi:10.1049/me:20010404

Barnes-Vieyra, P., and C. Claycomb (2001). Business-to-business e-commerce: Models and managerial decisions. Business Horizons , 44, 13–20. doi:10.1016/S0007-6813(01)80030-6

Bussler, C. (2002). Data management issues in electronic commerce: The role of B2B engines in B2B integration architectures. SIGMOD Record , 31(1), 67-72. doi:10.1145/507338.507351

Cabrera, L. F., & Kurt, C. (2005). *Web services architecture and its specifications: Essential for understanding WS.* Redmond, WA: Microsoft Press Corporation.

Chen, M., A. N. K. Chen, and B. B. M. Shao (2003). The implications and impacts of Web services to electronic commerce and research practices. Journal of Electronic Commerce Research , 4(4), 128–139.

Craig, J., & Jutla, D. (2001). *E-business readiness: A customer-focused framework.* Boston, MA: Addison-Wesley.

Curtis, B., M. I. Kellner, and J. Over (1992). Process modelling. Communications of the ACM , 35(9), 75–90. doi:10.1145/130994.130998

Fahey, L., Srivastava, R., Sharon, J. S., & Smith, D. E. (2001). Linking e-business and operating processes: The role of knowledge management. *IBM Systems Journal Knowledge Management, 40*(4).

Fairchild, A. M., & Peterson, R. R. (2003). Business-to-business value drivers and ebusiness infrastructures in financial services: Collaborative commerce across global markets and networks. In *Proceedings of the 36th Hawaii International Conference on System Sciences* (pp. 239-248).

Fong, W. L. M. (Ed.). (2005). *E-collaborations and virtual organizations.* Hershey, PA: IRM Press.

Forester, T. (1985). *The information technology. Revolution.* Oxford, UK: Blackwell.

Gates, B. (1999). *Business @ the speed of thought: Using a digital nervous system.* Australia: Viking.

Ghanbary, A. (2006a). Evaluation of mobile technologies in the context of their application, limitation & transformation. In B. Unhelkar (Ed.), *Handbook of research in mobile business*. Hershey, PA: Information Science Reference.

Ghanbary, A. (2006b). Collaborative business process engineering across multiple organisations. In *Proceedings of the ACIS Conference, ACIS 2006*, Adelaide, Australia.

Ghanbary, A., & Arunatileka, D. (2006). Enhancing customer relationship management through mobile personnel knowledge management (MPKM). In *Proceedings of the IBIMA International Conference*, Bonn, Germany.

Ghanbary, A., & Unhelkar, B. (2007a). Collaborative business process engineering (CBPE) across multiple organisations in a cluster. In *Proceedings of the IRMA Conference,* Vancouver, Canada.

Ghanbary, A., & Unhelkar, B. (2007b). Technical & logical issues arising from collaboration across multiple organisations. In *Proceedings of the IRMA Conferenc, IRMA 2007*, Vancouver, Canada.

Ginige, A. (2002). New paradigm for developing evolutionary software to support business. In E. K. Chang (Ed.), *Handbook of software engineering & knowledge engineering* (Vol. 2). World Scientific.

Goethals, F., & Vandenbulcke, J. (2006). Using Web services in business-to-business integration. In M. Fong (Ed.), *E-Collaborations and Virtual Organizations*. Hershey, PA: IRM Press.

Graham, I., Henderson-Sellers, B., & Younessi, H. (1997). *The open process specification*. New York: ACM Press.

Grewal, R., M. Comer, and R. Mehta (2001). An investigation into the antecedents of organizational participation in business-to-business electronic markets. Journal of Marketing , 65(3), 17–33. doi:10.1509/jmkg.65.3.17.18331

Hackbarth, G., and W. J. Kettinger (2000). Building an e-business strategy. Information Systems Journal , 17(3), 78–93.

Hammer, M., & Champy, J. (1993). *Reengineering the corporation, a manifesto for business revolution*. UK: Nicholas Brealey Publishing.

Hammer, M., & Champy, J. (2001). *Reengineering the corporation, a manifesto for business revolution.* UK: Nicholas Brealey Publishing.

Hammer, M., & Stanton, S. A. (1995). *The reengineering revolution*. Cambridge, MA: Harvard Business School.

Hogg, K., Chilcott, P., Nolan, M., & Srinivasan, B. (2004). An evaluation of Web services in the design of B2B application. In *Proceedings of the 27ᵗʰ Australasian Conference on Computer Science, Australian Computer Society, Inc. 26 ACS '04.*

Jones, S., M. Wilikens, P. Morris, and M. Masera (2000). A conceptual framework for understanding the needs and concerns of different stakeholders. Communications of the ACM , 43(12), 81–87. doi:10.1145/355112.355128

Kock, N., R. Davison, R. Wazlawick, and R. Ocker (2001). E-collaboration: A look at past research and future challenges. Journal of Systems and Information Technology , 5(1), 1–9.

Lai, J. Y. (2006). Assessment of employees' perceptions of service quality and satisfaction with e-business. In *Proceedings of the 2006 ACM SIGMIS CPR conference on computer personnel research: Forty-four years of computer personnel research: achievements, challenges and the future*, Claremont, California (pp. 236-243).

Lan, Y., & Unhelkar, B. (2005). *Global enterprise transition: Managing the process*. Hershey, PA: Idea Group Publishing.

Laudon, C., & Laudon, J. (2002). *Business information systems: A problem solving approach*. Fort Worth, TX: Dryden Press.

Lawson, R., and C. Alcock (2003). Factors affecting adoption of electronic commerce technologies by SMEs: An Australian study. Journal of Small Business and Enterprise Development , 10(3), 265–276. doi:10.1108/14626000310489727

Lingarchani, A. (2008). Extending collaborative business model with mobility and its implementation in the medical tourism industry. In. B. Unhelkar (Ed.), *Handbook of research in mobile business: Technical, methodological and social perspectives, second edition*. Hershey, PA: Information Science Reference.

Morris, A. (2002). The challenge of collaborative commerce. IEE Review , 48(6), 33–37. doi:10.1049/ir:20020604

Porter, M. E. (1990). *The competitive advantage of nations*. New York: The Free Press.

Sanjay, G., A. Malhotra, and O. A. ElSawy (2005). Coordinating for flexibility in e-business supply chains. Journal of Management Information Systems , 21(3), 7–46.

S'Duk, R. & Unhelkar, B. (2005). Web services extending BPR to industrial process reengineering. In *Proceedings of the Information Resource Management Association, International Conference*, San Diego, California.

Sharma, A. (2002). Trends in Internet-based business-to-business marketing. Industrial Marketing Management , 31(2), 77–84. doi:10.1016/S0019-8501(01)00185-7

Shi, D., and R. L. Daniels (2003). A survey of manufacturing flexibility: Implications for e-business flexibility. IBM Systems Journal , 42(3).

Siegel, D. (1999). *Futurize your enterprise: Business strategy in the age of the e-customer.* Hoboken, NJ: John Wiley and Sons. Retrieved October 10, 2006, from http://www.futurizenow.com

Unhelkar, B. (2003). *Process quality assurance for UML-based projects.* Upper Saddle River, NJ: Pearson Education, Inc.

Unhelkar, B. (2003). Understanding collaborations and clusters in the e-business world. In *Proceedings of the We-B Conference*, Perth, Australia.

Unhelkar, B. (2004). Globalization with mobility. Proceedings of the ADCOM, 2004, 12.

Unhelkar, B. (2005a). An initial three dimensional framework for mobile enterprise transitions. Cutter IT Journal, 18(8).

Unhelkar, B. (2005b). Transitioning to a mobile enterprise: A three-dimensional framework. Cutter IT Journal , 18(8), 5–11.

Unhelkar, B. (2005c). *Practical object oriented analysis.* Australia: Thomson Social Science Press.

Unhelkar, B. (2007). Beyond business integration–management challenges in collaborative business processes. *ICFAI Journal.*

Unhelkar, B., & Deshpande, Y. (2004). Evolving from Web engineering to Web services: A comparative study in the context of business utilization of the Internet. In Proceedings of the ADCOM, 2004, 12.

Venkatesh, V., M. Morris, G. Davis, and F. Davis (2003). User acceptance of information technology: Towards a unified view. MIS Quarterly , 27(3), 425–478.

Vij, S., & Patel, V. (2006). Clustering, profiling, ranking & summarization of retrieved information. In *Proceedings of the Seventh International Conference on Operations and Quantitative Management, by AIMS International and Indian Institute of Management,* Jaipur, India.

Virdell, M. (2003). *Business process and workflow in the Web services world.* Retrieved from http://www-128.ibm.com/developerworks/webservices/library/ws-work.html

# Chapter 2
# Emerging Technologies for Business Collaboration

*We don't know one-millionth of one percent about anything.*

Thomas Alva Edison (1847–1931)

## CHAPTER KEY POINTS

- Describes what comprises emerging technologies of today.
- Discusses the manner in which the emerging technologies facilitate business collaboration.
- Discusses the role of Web Services (WS) technology in dynamic business collaboration.
- Discusses the use of Mobile technology in dynamic business collaboration.
- Discusses the use of Enterprise Application Integration (EAI) in dynamic collaboration.
- Discuss the use of Web 2.0 and Service Oriented Architecture (SOA) in dynamic collaboration.

DOI: 10.4018/978-1-60566-689-1.ch002

## APPRECIATING EMERGING TECHNOLOGIES

This chapter describes the fundamentals of technologies such as Web Services (WS) and mobile technologies that provide the basis for modem-day business collaboration. These technologies, introduced here, are further discussed and evaluated later in Chapter 5 from the point of view of demonstrating their application to the *CBPE* environment. With the use of WS and mobile technologies, clients and users of organizations can access their applications from anywhere and at any time regardless of their physical location and platform. Appreciation of the capabilities of WS opens up many opportunities for businesses to interact with each other electronically. This chapter starts by identifying the important issues already extant in current ways in which businesses collaborate with each other. These issues and their understanding provide a good starting point for businesses to consider basing their strategies on collaborative services. While electronic collaboration has been investigated in the past, there has not been an ample focus on the dynamic aspect of such collaborations that result from the rapidly evolving communications technologies. This dynamic aspect of collaboration, based on Internet-based communications, is also explored in this chapter. The opportunities for many different groups or categories of organizations to collaborate – such as business, government and community sector organizations is also considered here. Formal analysis of collaboration, their business processes, their organizational structures and the support technologies and applications can provide many benefits including:

- Ability to leverage strengths and expertise of various organizations that may not be in physical proximity and, instead, spread globally
- Access to information, knowledge and even material and other production resources that would lower costs through their sharing and smart sourcing
- Improved service coordination across multiple organizations with better pathways or referral systems for customers
- One-stop-shop for customers looking for multiple services over the Internet
- Holistic and efficient approach to meeting client needs with wide range of services, enhanced quality and consistent responsiveness.
- Organizational knowledge and improved service system capability that includes greater innovation, flexibility to respond to emerging client needs and changing operations and operational environments
- Increased capacity to successfully submit tenders or expressions of interest to agencies through collaboration amongst partners.

The way to leverage these aforementioned advantages of ICT (such as the Internet and mobile technologies) for businesses and also on people's lives is to undertake a carefully construed transformation of the businesses to collaborative businesses. For example, at the beginning of the Internet age, with the aid of its communications capabilities, businesses were radically transformed into what was then known as "e-business". This kind of transformation of business also changed the social fabric of the environment in which the business operated. Consider the numerous opportunities that have opened up for many services in health, travel and government sectors as a result of the communication abilities of electronic businesses. Information that used to take days, if not weeks, is now available to the users at their fingertips. Knowledge, that was the exclusive privilege of a few, is now being freely shared across the globe. There is no doubt that many of these technological services and products, that were first considered by people as luxuries, are now a daily necessity. Today, there is a need to take an even greater plunge and move from e-business to collaborative business. The information and communications technologies (ICT) that can make this many-to-many relationships between businesses collaboration possible are already available and they need to be formally utilized and incorporated in collaborative businesses. Formal collaborative business would make use of ICT to come up with innovative ways of providing services that are otherwise not possible with simple electronic transactions.

Collaborative business, as discussed here, has come a long way. In the past, collaboration was possible only through physical communication based on geographical proximity and connectivity. In that era, businesses (particularly retailers) were hesitant to share information with other businesses. However, today, through technologies such as Web Services (WS), there are tremendous opportunities for businesses to share information and provide services to their customers by collaborating with each other globally and in a timely manner. Furthermore, even at individual level, customers are able to collaborate through simplified, standardized solutions based on common architectures and data models. Rising customer expectations have a direct connection to the advancement of technology. Customers tend to rely on technology and, at times, have very high expectations even when the technology itself may not have sufficient capability to provide the results. The need to model processes and use technology to satisfy those processes can help in satisfying the growing and dynamically changing needs of modern-day technologically savvy customers. Only collaborative businesses whose processes are built around communications technologies are capable of handling the real-time needs of the customers. The luxuries of customization and modification within a proprietary infrastructure will have to be discarded by business (based on Horvath, 2001) as they move into the brave new world of collaboration.

The advent of the Internet and computer-mediated communication has intensified the nature of collaboration between businesses. The Internet enables business applications to communicate and interact with each other in a real-time manner.

The resultant electronic collaborations (e-collaborations) are also broadly defined as collaboration among individuals engaged in a common task using electronic technologies (Kock and Nosek, 2005). These electronic collaboration across multiple organizations that share products and services in an electronically open and free market are based on the application of Web Services technologies. Goethals and Vandenbulcke (2006) support this by mentioning that Web Services could be used for integrating system for collaboration even amongst unknown parties.

Murugeson and Deshpande (2001) discuss the various models of electronic business that need to be extended for collaboration. Organizations wanting to move towards collaborative business must plan and manage change (cultural, technological, internal and external) and understand the key risks in their attempts to collaborate. Technologically, it is important that the development cycle is iterative and incremental (Maharmeh and Unhelkar, 2008) and that the technological element of the collaboration project is delivered in a short time (an iteration lasting maximum of three months). "Build quickly and move to the learning stage, then build the next stage and fix the previous ones based on what has been learned" (Philipson, 2001).

Managing the change resulting from collaborative business is an important part of the business strategy. These changes, discussed in detail in Chapter 10 later in this book, include changes in business and market strategies, organizational restructure and management strategies. There is a need for the decision makers, the senior managers to support these inevitable changes. Managing the transformation to a collaborative business by having a reliable and calculated plan is the crucial factor for success. The transition must remain persistent, alongside the detailed knowledge of the development of the individual clusters.

Mobile Technologies along with WS could be considered as the emerging technologies of today that are rapidly becoming established technologies for business applications. The major areas of a business that need attention when they consider these emerging technologies to undertake collaborative business are (Ghanbary, 2006):

- Software applications that would facilitate business processes to collaborate across multiple organizations.
- Methods to transit from already e-transformed businesses into collaborative may be m-enabled. Collaborative business process engineering is an important part of this research.

Information and Communications Technologies (ICT) that are used by business applications primarily comprise Web Services (WS) and mobile technology (MT). These technologies are of immense value in the new collaborative environment that transcends multiple organizational boundaries and enables dynamic cross-organizational business processes. Therefore, this chapter concentrates on the Web Services technologies, Business-to-Business (B2B) interactions and collaborations, and the influence of mobility on business collaboration. These technological and business issues are studied here from current as well as future collaborative environment's viewpoint. This discussion is thus made up of describing the technologies, identifying their potential and their limitations, and subsequently using these technologies to create the CBPE model, discussed later in the book. Thus, here we examine the available technologies in a scholarly manner in order to specifically achieve the following:

- Define the technologies of WS and how they facilitate service-based applications.
- Define the concept of collaboration in a B2B environment.
- Define the limitations of the current collaborative environment.
- Define the challenges and risks in proposing the new collaborative environment.
- Define the fundamental technologies that facilitate the proposed model of *Collaborative Business Process Engineering (CBPE)*.
- Define the implication of mobile technologies in business collaboration.

Emerging technologies include (but may not be restricted to) Web Services (WS), Web 2.0 (as the upcoming and continuously improving versions of the Internet), grid computing, mobile technologies, nanotechnologies, genomics, robotics, artificial intelligence and sensors. These emerging technologies not only provide enormous opportunities for enhancing the quality of life (Eng, 2005) but also have phenomenal impacts on businesses as we are discovering here

For example, the enhanced ability of businesses to communicate with each other has led to global business opportunities and global customer relationships that are not possible without the help of these technologies. Similarly, mobile technologies, including mobile applications, devices, networks and content management systems have become catalysts for changes to customer relations, creation of customer groups, inventory management processes and also deep organizational structure changes within the business.

Businesses accomplish their goals by moving beyond automating their existing processes and reaching a wider customer base, business partners and regulatory bodies such as governments by engaging most efficiently with them through the Internet and mobile technologies (Alag, 2006). Mobile technologies have also resulted in a high degree of personalization for the users (Unhelkar, 2008). This personalization capability of MT has dramatically shifted customer expectation towards the new era of management called mobile Customer Relationship Management (M-CRM).

As stated by Hsu, Burner and Kulviwat (2005), personalization provides significant advantages to business in terms of enhanced customer services directed towards the needs of an individual. Today, mobile technologies facilitate this personalization much better than any other technology. This is so because mobile technologies are inherently personal due to the need for an individual to carry a mobile gadget – which then provides his or her patterns in terms of shopping, movements and choices. The ability of users to access their applications from anywhere and at any time leads to location- and time-independent dimension to the usage of mobility by businesses, as this phenomenon did not exist in the traditional land-based Internet (Arunatileka, 2007). Therefore, this chapter discusses mobile technologies for a collaborative environment, leading to what is called Mobile Web Services (MWS).

## EMERGING TECHNOLOGIES AND COLLABORATION

The following sections provide detailed discussion of the aforementioned technologies that facilitates the *CBPE* model. The concepts of SOA (Zimmerman et al., 2005), Business Process Choreography (Leymann et al., 2002) ESB (Keen et al., 2004) and Web Services technologies (Booth et al., 2004) form part of the technologies supporting the model of *CBPE* – as depicted in Figure 1.

These technologies enable the *CBPE* model to extract the full potential for business collaborations. These technologies include Web Services, Enterprise Application Integration (EAI), Service-oriented Architecture, Enterprise Service Bus, Mobile and Web 2.0.

The left-hand-side box on the bottom presents the advantages of the technological facilitation while the right-hand-side box presents the challenges, such as channels of collaboration, trust and control. The following sections describe the aforementioned technologies and their influence on the proposed collaborative model.

### Web Services and Collaboration

A Web Service (WS) is a software application or a system that can be accessed over a network by Extensible Markup Language/Simple Object Application Protocol (XML/SOAP) messaging. A Web service is defined by Preist (2004) as a computational entity that is accessible over the Internet (using Web service standards and protocols). The term *'Web service'* means to provide a service over the Internet, with the agreed standards (http://www.Ambysoft.com).

The W3C (World Wide Web Consortium) has defined that Web Services provide a standard means of interoperating between different software applications, running on a variety of platforms and/or frameworks. Web Services provide a conceptual

*Figure 1. Technologies Facilitating and Supporting CBPE*

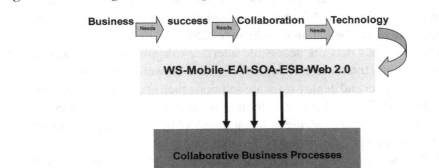

model and a context for understanding Web Services and the relationships between the components of this model. Web Services architecture is interoperability architecture: it identifies those global elements of the global Web Services network that are required in order to ensure interoperability between Web Services (Booth et al., 2004).

A Web Service (WS) is a delivery mechanism that can serve many different consumers on many different platforms at the same time. Web Services technology act as an enabler to connect incompatible stand-alone systems to integrate a complex distributed system in a way that was not possible with previous technologies (Stacey and Unhelkar, 2004).

Web Services enable Web applications to "talk" with each other independent of their technical environments which could be defined as open standard (XML, and SOAP) -based Web applications that interact with other Web applications for the purpose of exchanging data. Initially used for the exchange of data on large private enterprise networks, Web Services are evolving to include transactions over the public Internet by providing generic coordination mechanisms that can be extended for specific protocols (Curbera, 2003). The collaborative coordination of business processes through WS includes the execution of short-running transactions within an organization (similar to traditional distributed transactions) and long-running transactions across organizations. Web Services incorporate standards using open protocols that enable processes made up of service calls and data transmission. The availability of these services over the Internet allows the consuming programs to request a service running on another server (a Web Service) and use that program's response in a website, WAP service, or other application (S'duk and Unhelkar,

2004). These WS enabled calls transcend organizational firewalls, resulting in an opportunity for a cluster or group of organizations to simultaneously transition to web-based entities (Unhelkar and Deshpande, 2004).

Web Services as a network accessible interface to application functionality are built using standard Internet technologies (Snell and Tidwell, 2002), while as a novel approach to engineer and deploy software solutions such as cooperative information systems (Tilley et al., 2002). Another definition states that they are any services that are available over the Internet, use a standardized XML messaging system, and are not tied to any one operating system (Cerami, 2002).

XML Web Services are the fundamental building blocks that provide exchange of information over different computing standards on the Internet. XML uses open standards to communicate and collaborate amongst applications. Thus we see that WS tend to offer opportunities that are way beyond the commonly discussed business integration - that merely deals with document exchanges. Web Services hold the promise of considerable gains for many organizations by giving them the opportunity to develop techniques to effectively integrate disparate applications by leveraging computer technology (Kirda et al., 2001). The above statement emphasizes that not only can integrated systems provide better business value by sharing data, communicating results and improving overall functionality, but the ability to integrate systems also opens up doors to synergies between systems of disparate organizations.

One of the challenges of the collaboration occurs when the involved organizations have to make the investment necessary for replacing redundant or older systems as well as building a dynamic platform that incorporates multiple standards (Fong, 2006). The challenge is further increased when, in unstructured e-collaboration (without prior contract), creating or exchanging of non-standard documents takes place.

The ability to promote as well as locate services, however, is provided through Universal Data Dictionary Integration (UDDI). UDDI is a platform-independent, XML-based registry, allowing businesses worldwide to list themselves on the Internet. Enterprise UDDI Services is a key element of Web Services infrastructure that provides a standards-based solution for discovery, sharing, and reuse of Web Services, helping to maximize the productivity of developers and IT professionals. The purpose of UDDI is to allow users to discover available Web Services and interact with them dynamically. The process can be divided into three phases: searching (discovery), binding, and executing.

The UDDI specifications provide a mechanism to register and locate WS. It defines an electronic business registry in which businesses can describe their business and register their WS as well as discover and integrate with other businesses that offer Web Services (Roy and Ramanujan, 2001). However, as per Goethals and Vandenbulcke (2006), UDDI may not be the best means for realizing Web Services discovery, since the current UDDI directories are accessible to almost anyone. In fact, UDDI will allow companies to publish information about the Web Services they offer in a Universal Business Registry (UBR) that will be accessible by anyone. There is a need to store information in the UDDI registries after properly indexing them. Private UDDI or WSIL (Web Services Inspection Language) can also help in improving the use of directories for posting usable services. .

The business-to-business dedicated interactions, resulting in the current B2B collaborative environment, can be considered as a *static* collaboration. Static collaboration is collaboration that always follows the same pattern – for example, the sending and receiving of the same type of invoices and same kind of queries between two known organizations. However, with UDDI, organizations need not restrict themselves to two known parties – many different organizations post the services they want to offer on the UDDI, and other organizations can search and find these services and *consume* them. As per Pollock (2002), there will be a need for integration projects within the organization and these projects will not be just technical but also logical. Following are our observations based on the understanding of the technologies of Web Services:

- Internet access will be a default for every program or piece of software to be written
- Generic browsers for accessing the Internet will not be necessary as programs will access the Internet directly through their own generic mechanisms
- Solution providers need to write code that is service-based and that is able to talk with other code, over the Internet.
- XML is the current lowest Common Denominator for these communications mechanisms between various pieces of code.
- WS Provide integration within and amongst Enterprise Applications thereby facilitating Global collaborative business.
- WS provide environment (technical) independence, beyond DCOM and CORBA.
- WS enables existing legacy assets of an organization to be made available on the Web.
- WS enables application-to-application businesses.
- Technology enables Globalization, called Enabling Technologies.
- WS-based on the Internet, provide maximum globalization opportunity.
- Interaction and implications of the Web Services in Web 2.0 technology.
- Extensible Markup Language (XML) provides the support for the development of the Web 2.0 applications. Web 2.0 builds on the existing Web server architecture, but relies much more heavily on the back-end software of Web Services technology.

## Mobile Technology and Collaboration

Since Mobile Technologies (MT) form the basis for collaboration and have a great impact on business integration, the following section discusses the implications of mobile technology in collaboration. As Toffler (1980) predicted, people's dependence on technology has increased to a level at which technology affects every aspect of human life. Mobile technology, which is an integration of communication and computer technology, has created very high expectations in humans' behavior. These human expectations from mobility also influence businesses strategies, business development and, in the context of this discussion, business collaboration. Therefore, it is only appropriate that the literature on mobile technology and mobile business is reviewed here.

When mobility is also involved in these transitions, then as discussed by Brans (2003), there is also a need to consider portable devices, networks, application gateways and supporting enterprise applications in order to bring about a smooth transition of the business. The particular need to consider mobility in transitioning to collaborative business is felt because of the immense growth in mobile devices that have easily surpassed the number of desktop computers in use. The number of WAP-enabled devices has also surpassed the numbers of PC-enabled Internet users. Pashtan (2005) mentions over 100 million wireless Internet users in 2003, a number which has now more than doubled. The growth of mobile users has been experienced everywhere. A similar investigation by Gohring (2005), found that 53 per cent of phones being used by 4,000 surveyed mobile users around the globe are data-enabled. Armed with such data-capable phones, those customers are increasingly using online services, such as Internet or mobile e-mail access and collaborative businesses need to consider these users and their access mechanisms when they undertake transformations.

Mobile Technologies, which are a convergence of communication, computer and Internet technologies with mobility, are a relatively new but rapidly growing area. The access and connection to the Internet and the functionality of WS or MWS have also become very simple and ubiquitous. These facilities have opened up opportunities for organizations to revolutionize their business processes. Undoubtedly, improvements in communications technology have impacted not only the business domain but also the socio-cultural domain. The reason that the service model is so attractive in mobile collaborative business is its ability to incorporate standards and open protocols for calling services and transmitting data (Unhelkar and S'duk, 2004). WS make software functionality available over the Internet so that programs can request a service running on another server (a Web Service) and use that program's response in a website, Wireless Application Protocol (WAP) services, or other applications. Possibilities are endless.

## Mobile Technology

Unhelkar (2005) characterizes mobility as a significant factor impacting the quality of life of individuals and the society in which they live. Correct application of mobile technologies into business processes provides an opportunity to business enterprises likely to gain advantages such as increased profits, satisfied customers and greater customer loyalty. These customer-related advantages will accrue only when the organization investigates its customer behavior in the context of the mobile environment.

The application of mobile technologies can be classified into two different categories: on-line and off-line services. The applications of on-line services are the executed applications when the mobile devices are connected to the mobile Internet.

The applications of online wireless mobile Internet depends on **mode** (of the user; such as whether the user is walking while using the service, or whether being driven around – such as in an ambulance), **place** (remote area which may not be easily accessible to the wireless transmissions, or city metropolitan area that may have a high density of users), **goal** (aim of the connection such as in an emergency or for leisure), **immediacy** (instant action and reaction to demand) and **load** (how occupied the Internet-provider is at the time of the connection). The congestion of the network clearly depends on the usage, which varies at different times of the day. As expected, during business hours the network load on the Internet service-provider is heavy.

The major on-line mobile applications provide information, check e-mails, enable payments, mobile banking, mobile shopping, mobile education, general government bulletins, messaging and enable leisure activities. Mobile applications also facilitate services such as Location-Based Services (LBS), Global Positioning Services (GPS) and Car Navigation System (CNS).

Off-line mobile applications are also an important consideration for business. The major off-line services offered by related network-providers include personalized diaries, games, ordinary communications, built-in memory, expert systems, remote supervision and connectivity to local devices through Bluetooth and infrared. These can be extra features on particular mobile devices. Note that although these applications need not be necessarily off-line, their ability to operate for some duration without wireless connectivity enables them to add value to the user's activities.

The aforementioned on-line and off-line application of mobile technology helps us understand how this technology can be used in order to enhance collaboration. For example, Chapter 14 of this book identifies a simple application using GPS that enables an organization to locate the nearest tradesperson to the site by the aid of GPS in mobile technology.

Thus, increasingly, we notice that the consumer's demands and corporate objectives to satisfy those demands can be different in the m-enabled world. These usages in m-enabled society are classified in three categories of *interaction* (voice, email chat, digital postcards, etc.), *trading and business* (banking, shopping, auctions, advertising, ticketing, etc.) and *mobile-provided services* (news, entertainment, driving directions and many more).

Mobile technology provides organizations with a platform that enables them to access their customers in different ways. For example, with mobile technologies, customers can be reached independent of their specific locations; or, alternatively, customers can be reached and provided support and services in the *context* of their location. The Internet has also provided opportunities for service-providers such as Paypal, an online payment-processing company founded in 1999 (https://www.paypal.com/), to offer more cost-effective payment related services that are similar to banking services to its customers. The Paypal service, introduced in 2000, has become the most used payment system for clearing auction transactions on eBay (Schneider, 2004), competing directly with the traditional banks. Thus the experience of the customer and business in dealing with each other is changing with the advancement of technology resulting in opportunities to generate more revenue in many areas, such as banking, shopping, travel and health.

While the location-aware mobile connectivity has dramatically increased the ability of individuals to communicate, it has also produced challenges in terms of privacy and new social protocols. The effects of globalization now need to be further considered in the context of a global-mobile society and this requires us to investigate WS and mobility together.

WS have promised to expand and enrich the existing distributed computing arena with their ability to connect disparate systems and allow communication between them from anywhere and on any platform (Stacey and Unhelkar, 2004).

This promise of Web Services to revolutionize the way in which companies interact with each other and also how they come together or discover each other to form business alliances also needs to be studied together with mobility.

A specific form of WS, using mobile technology, is described next. This new technology is that of Mobile Web Services (MWS). MWS has the capabilities of text, voice and videoconferencing using wireless devices, as well as the ability to connect to the World Wide Web.

## Mobile Web Services

The application of Mobile Technologies and mobile services provide a robust basis for the expansion of the customer base of the organization. This is so because mobile and Web Services technologies together (Mobile Web Services) create opportunities for multiple organizations to interact in one application. The Web Services initiative effectively adds computational objects to the static information of yesterday's Web, and therefore offers distributed services capability over a network (Davies et al., 2004). Web Services have the potential to create new paradigms for both the delivery of software capabilities and the models by which networked enterprises will trade.

The collaborating organizations that have m-enabled WS technology make it possible for sale-/service-providers to benefit all people involved in the process. A mobile application that is using WS to transmit its data is classified as MWS. Mobile users interact with the system by mobile terminal browsers (software components in mobile phones). GPS-enabled terminals can provide location data and so allow the retrieval of information which is pertinent to their location (Puustjarvi, 2006).

According to the Australian Computer Society's (ACS, Sept 08, 2005) report on MWS, with Web Services, phones now have the potential to actually consume useful web-based services. First of all, turning one's phone into a SOAP (Simple Object Access Protocol) client might have some performance costs related to slow data speeds and processing both HTTP commands and XML. Secondly, most phones do not come with Web Services support built in. Finally, the user can hide the Web Services complexity and leverage existing technologies to make use of their widespread availability. This would require a gateway to sit in between the phone and the Web Service to handle the passing and conversion of messages (http://www.acs.openlab.net.au/).

Microsoft service-providers define MWS as an initiative to create Web Services standards that will enable new business opportunities in the personal computer and mobile space and deliver integrated services across fixed (wired) and wireless networks. Mobile Web Services use existing industry standard Extensible Markup Language (XML)-based Web Services architecture to expose mobile network services to the broadest audience of developers (http://www.microsoft.com/).

The functionality of MWS is examined in the light of how MWS could enhance the current process, enhancing its functionality to talk to the Peoplesoft system directly via the Web, eliminating the second data entry at Head Office which is happening in the current process.

The Next Generation Enterprises (NGEs) rely on automation, mobility, real-time business activity monitoring, agility, and self-service over widely distributed operations to conduct business. Mobility is one of the most invigorating features, having an enormous impact on how communication is evolving into the future (Umar, 2005).

## Enterprise Application Integration (EAI) and Collaboration

Enterprise Architecture (EA) builds on business knowledge and allows business specialists to apply their respective knowledge to determine the most effective technology and process solutions for the business (Finkelstein, 2006).

Enterprise Application Integration (EAI) is also a relevant approach to integrating core business processes and data-processing in the organization. EAI automates the integration process with less effort. EAI is a business computing term for plans, methods, and tools aimed at modernising, consolidating, and coordinating the overall computer functionality in an enterprise (Lee, Siau and Hong, 2003).

EA helps integrate different enterprise systems, such as Supply Chain Management (SCM), Selling Chain Management, CRM, Enterprise Resource Planning (ERP), procurement, human resource, payroll and Knowledge Management (KM). EAI plays an important role in integrating these applications and, thereby, enables efficient functioning of the enterprise. Using mobile devices as part of the enterprise model can help real-time information access amongst systems on production planning and control, inbound and outbound logistics, material flows, monitoring functions, and performance measurements (Rolstadas and Andersen, 2000). Information and Communication Technology (ICT) architectures have not paid enough attention to integration of the services in the past.

Enterprise Application Integration ensures when existing applications are linked together electronically. This is done in order to provide a single integrated response to a user request. Enterprise Application Integration (EAI) automates and extends data integration processes. Data integration involves storing the data of an application that can be manipulated in ways that other applications can easily access. This integration is as simple as using a standard relational database for data storage, or perhaps implementing mechanisms to extract the data into a known format such as Extensible Markup Language (XML) or a comma-separated text file that other applications can consume (Gorton and Liu 2004).

Such electronic exchange enables firms to have information systems (IS) that encourage unhindered flow of information. As mentioned before, the paradigm that addresses this need of firms is popularly known as Enterprise Application Integration (Erasal et al., 2003). EAI involves developing and devising ways to efficiently reuse what already exists, while adding new application and data (Jinyoul, Siau and Hong, 2003).

EAI provides the means to integrate strategic business solutions within and across the parts of organizational information system infrastructures. The increased deployment of enterprise application alongside legacy systems means that companies are being compelled to adopt Information System (IS) infrastructures that connect applications, data and information together (Sharif et al., 2004).

EAI is a pertinent approach to integrating core business processes and data-processing in an organization (Reiersgaard et al., 2005). EAI maps the business processes, rather than technology-driven processes, by providing the linkage to applications at the business level.

The map of the internal business processes of an organization provides an opportunity for these business processes to collaborate with the business processes of other "collaborating" organizations. The mapping of these business processes enables *CBPE* to place the organization within the right industry categorization, so that the services that are provided are easily recognizable.

## Service Oriented Architecture (SOA) and Collaboration

Web Services (WS) technologies, built around the Extensible Markup Language (XML), provide many opportunities for integrating enterprise applications. However, XML/Simple Object Access Protocol (SOAP), together with Web Services Definition Language (WSDL) and Universal Description Discovery and Integration (UDDI) form a comprehensive suite of WS technologies that have the potential of providing capabilities for integrating processes across multiple organizations.

The WS technology adopted by Web 2.0 opens up doors to collaborative Enterprise Architecture Integration (EAI) and Service-oriented Architecture (SOA), resulting in Business Integration (BI). WS can be used in order to align and integrate business processes of organizations (internal and external processes) to satisfy the needs of Enterprise Architecture (EA).

Thus far, the concept of Business Integration (BI) has mainly focused on integrating the business processes internal to an organization. However, this book provides definitions to identify how organizations can extend this integration with these business processes belonging to "other" enterprises.

The concept of "Web 2.0" began with a conference brainstorming session between O'Reilly and MediaLive International. According to O'Reilly (2005), Web 2.0 is a business revolution in the computer industry caused by the move to the Internet as platform, and an attempt to understand the rules for success on that new platform.

Web 2.0 allows the network itself to become a platform for delivering services and allowing users to access applications entirely through a browser (O'Reilly, 2003). Web 2.0 technology is WS-enabled (second generation of Web), contributing to easy collaboration and integration of applications on a network-based system.

According to Murugesan (2007), Web 2.0 is a collection of technologies, business strategies and social trends, more dynamic and interactive than its predecessor Web 1.0 technology. Web 2.0 facilitates flexible Web design, creative reuse and updates. Web 2.0 facilitates collaborative content creation and modification, as well as enabling the creation of the new applications by reusing and combining different applications on the Web or by combining data and information from different sources.

The flexibility of the Web 2.0 technology supports collaboration of business processes and even social trends – which are all based on the use and reuse of the services. Use and reuse of services across the entire enterprise is one of the significant aims of SOA – which is achieved through the use of SOA for Enterprise Architecture (EA). Therefore, Web 2.0 technology is an instrument for the organization to develop EA and SOA.

Service Oriented Architecture (SOA) is an architecture that makes the services of a system interact and perform a task supporting a request. SOA is classified as part of Enterprise Architecture. As such SOA can be viewed as a "sub-architecture" of an Enterprise Architecture. SOA predates the advent of Web Services. Technologies such as Common Object Request Broker (CORBA) and Distributed Component Object Model (DCOM) afforded the opportunity to create SOA. However, Web Services is an ideal technology for developing sophisticated architecture (Barry, 2003).

SOA is a collection of services capable of interacting in three ways, commonly referred to as "publish, find and bind" (Harrison and Taylor, 2005). A service must be able to make its interface available to other services (publish), other services must be capable of discovering the interface (find), and finally, services must be able to connect to one another to exchange messages (bind). The loose coupling of an SOA is achieved firstly through the separation of data exchange from the software agents involved in the exchange, and secondly through the discrete nature of the service.

SOA also describes how the service could be invoked and how the service attributes are implemented. The concepts of SOA and The Open Group Architecture Framework, TOGAF (website) relate to each other when Technology Architecture is invoked by different requesters. TOGAF contains two reference models that can be used in this way: a platform-centric Technical Reference Model that focuses on the services and structure of the underlying platform necessary to support the use and reuse of applications, and an Integrated Information Infrastructure Reference Model that focuses on the applications space, and addresses the need for interoperability and for enabling secure flow of information where and when it is needed (Harding, 2005).

## The Role of SOA in CBPE

Web Services integration enables a dynamic e-business model that fosters collaboration with heterogeneous business services and opens the doors for new business opportunities (Chung, 2005). A SOA is an application framework that takes everyday business applications and breaks them down into individual business functions and processes, called services. Figure 2 explains how SOA impacts on the requirements of *CBPE*.

Figure 2 shows the importance of SOA in developing the applications of **CBPE**. The technology and the architectural aspects of this integration based on collaboration have also been demonstrated. The requirements of **CBPE**, as far as the multiple organizations are concerned, are the required technology, required methodology, social threats, how to implement the integration, how to architect the integration and investigate the structural changes to the organization after the integration.

Web Services technology enables applications in separate technical environment to talk with each other, leading to opportunities to collaborate electronically across the globe. On the other hand, SOA is a platform, a backbone, on which the actual services can rest. Therefore, SOA is a strategic development of technology within an organization to enable it to deal with the rest of the world.

*Figure 2. The Role of SOA in CBPE*

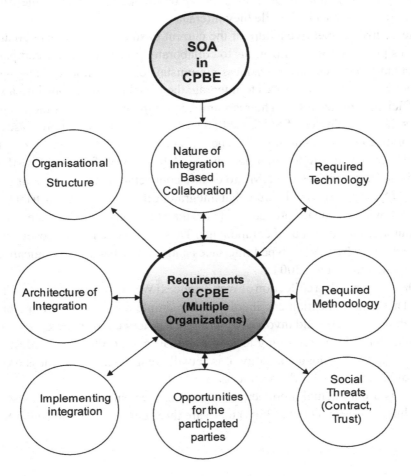

Web Services are self-contained, modular, Internet-based applications, offered by different providers that have standard interfaces to enable efficient integration and implementation of complex business applications (Marjanovic, 2006). Composite Web Services enable flexible, on-demand integration of individual services offered by different providers to meet a specific business objective. This integration is made possible by the fact that Web Services are platform–neutral, so as long as they comply with the common standard they can be integrated into a more complex structure.

SOA gives an opportunity to architect new processes enabling multi organizational collaboration. SOA, especially Web Services, are emerging as middleware to implement cross-organizational processes (Yildiz, Marjanovic and Godart, 2006). The very recent advances in this domain such as WS-Coordination, WS-Agreement and WS-Policy are the actual agreements among involved Web Services. These technologies aim to specify the protocols supported by collaborating services, such as the order in which individual services can be invoked or how the relevant message should be exchanged while they interact.

The highly competitive nature of the current business environment creates tremendous pressure for organizations to collaborate. It is essential for companies to understand rapidly changing business circumstances. The rapidly changing environment encourages enterprises to integrate their business functions into a system that efficiently utilizes ICT. The recommended implementation of the integration utilizes the technologies of SOA, EAI and TOGAF to integration processes in the collaborative environment of the business processes of multiple organizations.

Web Services technology implements SOA by means of standard XML-based initiatives. Web Services use XML to enable connection between various applications. SOA is a system architecture that integrates different systems distributed over a network with a standard procedure. Thus, the SOA considers the system as made up of autonomous distributed components. These components are loosely coupled with each other by strictly-typed interfaces and standardized communication protocols (Nakamura et al., 2004).

SOA is essentially a collection of Web Services (WS) that communicate with each other. This communication can involve either simple data passing from a browser to a Web server or it could involve two or more services coordinating some activity (Dorenhoefer, 2005). According to Knorr and Gurman, (2007) the hardest part of constructing SOA is not technology; it is actually redrawing the business processes that provide the basis for the architecture.

SOA is a contractual architecture to offer and consume software as services. According to Gustavo et al., (2004) there are three entities that make up a SOA:

1.  Service-providers: The owner of the services. They define descriptions of their services and publish them in the service registry.
2.  Service Requesters: They use a "find" operation to locate services of interest. They are also known as service consumers.
3.  Service Registry: Returns the description of each relevant service.

According to Jammes et al. (2005), the basic interaction patterns of a device-level SOA can be described according to five levels of functionality. These functionalities are described here briefly from the point of view of utilizing them in *CBPE*.

*   *Addressing:* This is the foundation for device networking. The Internet Protocol (IP) based networking is supported by the IP protocols and IPv6. According to Philip Argy (2007), the National President of the Australian Computer Society (ACS), IPv6 will create a network that is vastly larger the current Internet, extending the current IP addresses. The created network will also be more secure, easier to implement, and enable a ubiquitous nanotech-nology-connected world with vastly increased potential for innovation. In *CBPE*, each organization registered is allocated to a specific portal through an IP address. The individual IP address enables the services to be reused while searching for an individual product and service. IPv6 provides support for the *CBPE* model by creating a larger network and the IPv6 potential for innovation.
*   *Discovery:* Once the addressing of networking is established, devices need to discover each other. A discovery protocol enables a device to advertise its services on the network. A search request is sent out for all devices and then the devices that match the request send a corresponding reply. In *CBPE*, the UDDI stores the services and products offered. The *CBPE* system has the capability of discovering the products and services irrespective of the used platforms.
*   *Description:* The device metadata may include information like manufac-turer name, version and serial number. Each service exposed by a device defines the command message or actions, as well as the associated message formats. In *CBPE*, the system has the capability of registering such a descrip-tion through recommended suites of attributes that specify the products or services being discovered.
*   *Control:* To invoke an action on a device service, a controlling service sends a control message to the network endpoint for that service. In *CBPE,* the system has a portal manager controlling the transaction. The manager could be an electronic artificial intelligence device or a person.

- *Eventing:* In addition, devices may communicate through asynchronous eventing, usually implemented by "publish–subscribe" mechanism. Through eventing, a service exposes events corresponding to internal state changes, to which controlling devices can subscribe in order to receive event notifications whenever the corresponding internal state change occurs. In *CBPE,* the proposed UDDI has the capability of registering the event for future transactions. Furthermore, changes to the state of a service have the capability of broadcasting that state-change to all other subscribing services.

The current SOA is widely used to offer Web Services on wired networks. However, no significant investigation has been carried out in the field of mobile services that would provide availability and dynamic discovery service for mobile users. According to Brantner, Helmer, Kanne and Moerkotte (2006), while the software industry has moved towards service-oriented architectures (SOA) in the last few years, this has mostly been undertaken for non-mobile enterprise systems. Nowadays, mobile devices are ubiquitous and they need to be considered in the context of SOA.

However, they are characterized by limited resources such as processing power, memory, display screen and connection bandwidth (Sanchez-Nielsen et al., 2006). SOA is a flexible and extensible architecture for designing and realizing industry solutions and applications. Therefore, SOA needs to consider both mobile and non-mobile services and applications. SOA also needs to align IT strategy with business strategy. The application of SOA in *CBPE* is discussed in section 4.5.1 of this chapter.

## Influence of Web 2.0 and SOA on the CBPE Model

Web Services and their importance in Web 2.0 technology continue to be investigated in the context of their use in collaborative business. At the same time, there is a need to consider the importance of the Mobile technologies – which provide rich areas of application to collaborative environment amongst organizations that are not necessarily known to each other. The chapter also describes how organizations have moved from paper-based to electronic business (e-business), mobile business (m-business) and how they could transform to collaborative business (c-business).

SOA breaks down the software systems into sets and sub-sets of services. These services from building blocks can use new applications that have a very high level of integration and reuse. Web 2.0 is characterized by action-at-a-distance interactions and ad-hoc integration. Web 2.0 treats data as the most important component of the organization, specifically while developing the new software systems. The

SOA concept evolves from earlier component-based software frameworks, while Web 2.0 promotes Web experiences that encourage users to participate in sharing information and enriching services (Lin, 2006).

According to Hazra (2007), SOA governance provides transparency in the usage of services enabling consumers to search for, discover and locate desired services and obtain consistent services (response) from any specific service-provider.

The idea of writing the code once and then using it everywhere in SOA results in less code, lower cost and increased standardization. SOA bonds independent services and resources, whilst Web 2.0 applications follow a platform that helps users create and share content with a broad audience, resulting in online collaborative platforms.

Web 2.0 and SOA enable creation of multiple applications that benefit many organizations. SOA and Web 2.0 define the network as a platform across all connected devices. Based on Philipson (2007), the SOA and Web 2.0 create ecosystems for communicating, connecting, collaborating and creatively expressing ideas and information in revolutionary new ways.

Web 2.0 is considered as a platform for building systems that are tied together by a set of protocols, open standards and agreements for cooperation. SOA is considered the philosophy of encapsulating application logic in services with a uniformly defined interface and making these publicly available via a discovery mechanism. The SOA and Web 2.0 technologies are developed on the notion of reusing and composing existing resources supporting the collaboration and coupling of remote resources. Both Web 2.0 and SOA applications enable the loose coupling of distant resources and structural change (Schorth and Janner, 2007).

Web 2.0 and SOA also have divergent elements. First of all, many Web 2.0 applications incorporate a social aspect, such as facilitating human interaction. Web 2.0 applications deal with human-readable content (such as text and pictures). In contrast, conventional SOA merely aims at interconnecting dispersed business functionality and facilitating seamless machine–machine collaboration. Secondly, Web 2.0 is clearly about presentation and user interface integration, whereas SOA deployments are more abstract and less visible to its users (Schorth and Janner, 2007).

SOA, as a software design principle, is able to streamline and harmonize the *CBPE* model and is able to set up a cross-organizational collaboration. Web 2.0 incorporates the technical concepts of SOA to provide the techniques and design principles facilitating the *CBPE* to locate and consume the desired and available services and products online. Integration of the Web users into application design via all relevant channels (such as mobile channels) on the basis of various platforms (by the aid of Web Services) allows the discovering, mashing and tagging of diverse resources.

## ACTION POINTS

1. Identify the impact of the emerging technologies on your organization and evaluate these impacts on the collaborative nature of the organizational business processes.
2. Investigate the impact of web services technology on your organization's system infrastructure and identify how this technology enables you introduce a new streamlines of business activities.
3. Investigate the impact of mobile and mobile web services on your organization's infrastructure and state how mobility changes your business environment since you can perform the organization's activities disregard of location and time.
4. Enforce Enterprise Application Integration and evaluate the impact of this technology on the business processes of your organization.
5. Describe the Service Oriented Architecture (SOA) and explain why SOA is doable rather than purchasable.
6. Identify how Web 2.0 and Service Oriented Architecture facilitate the collaboration of your organization.

## REFERENCES

Argy, P. (2007, September). Time to move on IPv6 opportunity. *Australian PC Authority.*

Arunatileka, D. (2007). *Mobile transformation of business processes to enhance competitive delivery of service in organisations.* Unpublished doctoral dissertation, University of Western Sydney.

Australian Computer Society. (2005, September 8). *Business process basics, ACS learn.* Retrieved October 11, 2005, from www.acs.openlab.net.au/content.php?article.35

Barry, D. K. (2003). *Web services and service-oriented architecture. The savvy manager's guide.* San Francisco: Morgan Kaufmann Publishers.

Booth, D., Haas, H., McCabe, F., Newcomer, E., Champion, M., Ferris, C., & Orchard, D. (2004). *Web services architecture* (W3C Working Group Note). Retrieved October 2, 2007, from http://www.w3.org/TR/ws-arch/#introduction

Brans, P. (2003). *Mobilize your enterprise*. Upper Saddle River, NJ: Pearson Education.

Brantner, M., Helmer, S., Kanne, C. C., & Moerkotte, G. (2006). Ontologies for location-based services. In B. Unhelkar (Ed.), *Handbook of research in mobile business*. Hershey, PA: Idea Group Reference.

Cabrera, L. F., & Kurt, C. (2005). *Web services architecture and its specifications: Essential for understanding WS*. Redmond, CA: Microsoft Press Corporation.

Cerami, E. (2002). *Web services essentials*. Sebastopol, CA: O'Reilly and Associates.

Chung, J. Y. (2005). An industry view on service-oriented architecture and Web services. In *Proceedings of the 2005 IEEE International Workshop on Service-Oriented System Engineering (SOSE'05)*. IEEE.

Curbera, F., R. Khalaf, N. Mukhi, S. Tai, and S. Weerawarana (2003). The next step in Web services. Communications of the ACM , 46(10). doi:10.1145/944217.944234

Davies, N. J., D. Fensel, and M. Richardson (2004). The future of Web services. BT Technology , 22(1), 118–127. doi:10.1023/B:BTTJ.0000015502.09747.39

Deshpande, Y., & Ginige, A. (2001). Corporate Web development: From process infancy to maturity. In S. Murugesan & Y. Deshpande (Eds.), *Web engineering managing diversity and complexity of Web application development*. Germany: Springer-Verlag Berlin Heidelberg.

Doernhoefer, M. (2005). Surfing the Net for software engineering notes. ACM SIG-SOFT Software Engineering Notes , 30(6), 5–13. doi:10.1145/1102107.1102116

Finkelsteing, C. (2006). *Enterprise architecture for integration: Rapid delivery methods and technology*. Boston, MA: Artech House Publishers.

Ghanbary, A. (2006). Evaluation of mobile technologies in the context of their application, limitation & transformation. In B. Unhelkar (Ed.), *Handbook of research in mobile business*. Hershey, PA: Idea Group Reference.

Ghanbary, A. (2006). collaborative business process engineering across multiple organisations. In *Proceedings of the ACIS Conference, ACIS 2006*, Adelaide, Australia.

Ghanbary, A., & Arunatileka, D. (2006). enhancing customer relationship management through mobile personnel knowledge management (MPKM). In *Proceedings of the IBIMA International Conference*, Bonn, Germany.

Ghanbary, A., & Unhelkar, B. (2007). Collaborative business process engineering (CBPE) across multiple organisations in a cluster. In *Proceedings of the IRMA Conference, IRMA 2007*, Vancouver, Canada.

Ghanbary, A., & Unhelkar, B. (2007). Technical & logical issues arising from collaboration across multiple organisations. *Proceedings of the IRMA Conference, IRMA 2007*, Vancouver, Canada.

Goethals, F., & Vandenbulcke, J. (2006). Using Web services in business-to-business integration. In M. Fong (Ed.), *E-collaborations and virtual organizations*. Hershey, PA: IRM Press.

Gohring, N. (2005). Mobile data usage is on the rise. *IDG News Service*.

Gorton, I., & Liu, A. (2004). Architectures and technologies for enterprise application integration. In *Proceedings of the 26th International Conference on Software Engineering (ICSE'04)*. IEEE Computer Society.

Gustavo, A., Casati, F., Kuno, H., & Machiraju, V. (2004). *Web services: Concepts, architectures and applications*. Berlin: Springer-Verlag Publications.

Harding, C. (2005). *Is SOA a fad or silver bullet?* The Open Group.

Harrison, A., & Taylor, J. I. (2005). WSPeer – an interface to Web service hosting and invocation. In *Proceedings of the 19th IEEE International Parallel and Distributed Processing Symposium (IPDPS'05)*.

Hazra, T. K. (2007). SOA governance: Building on the old, embracing the new. Cutter IT Journal , 20(6), 30–34.

Horvath, L. (2001). Collaboration: The key to value creation in supply chain management. Journal of Supply Chain Management: An International Journal , 6(5), 205–207. doi:. doi:10.1108/EUM0000000006039

Hsu, H. Y. S., Burner, G. C., & Kulviwat, S. (2005). *Personalization in mobile commerce*. Paper presented at the IRMA 2005, San Diego, CA, USA.

Jammes, F., Mensch, A., & Smit, H. (2005). Service oriented device communications using the device profile for Web services. In *Proceedings of the 3rd International Workshop on Middleware for Pervasive and Ad-Hoc Computing MPAC '05*. ACM Press.

Jinyoul, L., K. Siau, and S. Hong (2003). Enterprise integration with ERP and EAI. Communications of the ACM , 46(2).

Keen, M. (2004). *Partners: Implementing an SOA using an ESB*. Armonk, NY: IBM Redbook.

Kirda, E., M. Jazayeri, C. Kerer, and M. Schranz (2001). Experiences in engineering flexible Web service. IEEE MultiMedia , 8(1), 58–65. doi:10.1109/93.923954

Knorr, E., & Gruman, G. (2007). SOA: Under construction. *Information Age.*

Kock, N., R. Davison, R. Wazlawick, and R. Ocker (2001). E-collaboration: A look at past research and future challenges. Journal of Systems and Information Technology , 5(1), 1–9.

Kock, N., & Nosek, J. (2005). Expanding the boundaries of e-collaboration. *IEEE Transactions on Professional Communication, 48*(1). Retrieved from http://cits.tamiu.edu/kock/pubs/journals/2005JournalIEEETPC/KockNosek2005.pdf

Lee, J., K. Siau, and S. Hong (2003). Enterprise integration with ERP & EAI. Communications of the ACM , 46(2).

Leymann, F., D. Roller, and M. T. Schmidt (2002). Web services and business process management. IBM Systems Journal , 41(2).

Lin, K. J. (2006). Serving Web 2.0 with SOA: Providing the technology for innovation and specialization. In *Proceedings of the IEEE International Conference on e-Business Engineering (ICEBE'06).*

Marjanovic, O. (2006). BPM – bridging the gap between business processes and technologies for process management. In *Proceedings of the ACIS Conference, ACIS 2006*, Adelaide, Australia.

*Microsoft Service Providers*. (n.d.). Retrieved October 11, 2005, from http://www.microsoft.com/serviceproviders/resources/bizresmws.mspx

Mugo, F. W. (n.d.) *Sampling in research*. Web Centre for Social Research Methods.

Murugesan, S. (2007). Understanding Web 2.0. IT Professional , 9(4), 34–41. doi:10.1109/MITP.2007.78

Nakamura, M., Igaki, H., Tamada, H., & Matsumoto, K. (2004). Service applications: Implementing integrated services of networked home appliances using service oriented architecture. In *Proceedings of the 2nd International Conference on Service-oriented Computing ICSOC '04*. ACM Press.

O'Reilly, T. (2005). *What is Web 2.0? Design and business models for the next generation of software*. Retrieved August 2, 2007, from http://www.oreillynet.com/pub/a/oreilly/tim/news/2005/09/30/what-is-web-20.html

O'Reilly, T. (2005b). *Web 2.0 compact definition*. Retrieved August 2, 2007, from http://radar.oreilly.com/archives/2005/10/web_20_compact_definition.html

O'Reilly, T. (2006). *Web 2.0 compact definition: Trying again*. Retrieved from http://radar.oreilly.com/archives/2006/12/web_20_compact.html

Omar, W. M., A. D. K. Abbass, and T. Bendiab (2007). SOAW2 for managing the Web 2.0 framework. IT Professional , 9(3), 30–35. doi:10.1109/MITP.2007.56

Pashtan, A. (2005). *Mobile Web services*. Cambridge, UK: Cambridge University Press.

Philipson, G. (2001). *Australian e-business guide*. Australia: McPherson's Printing Group.

Philipson, G. (2007). *Web 2.0 and SOA are 'two sides of the same coin.'* Retrieved from http://www.theage.com.au/news/perspectives/web-20-and-soa-are-two-sides-of-the-same-coin/2007/07/30/1185647825516.html

Preist, C. (2004). A conceptual architecture for Semantic Web services. In *Proceedings of the International Semantic Web Conference 2004 (ISWC 2004)*.

Puustjarvi, J. (2006). Using mobile Web services in electronic auctions. In *Proceedings of the 2nd IASTED international conference on Advances in computer science and technology, ACST'06*.

Reiersgaard, N., Salvesen, H., Nordheim, S., & Paivarinta, T. (2005). EAI implementation project and shakedown: An exploratory case study. In *Proceedings of the 38th Annual Hawaii International Conference on System Sciences (HICSS'05)*. IEEE Computer Society.

Rolstadas, A., & Andersen, B. (2000). *Enterprise modeling – improving global industrial competitiveness*. Amsterdam: Kluwer Academic Publishers.

Roy, J., and A. Ramanujan (2001). Understanding Web services. IT Professional , 3(6), 69–73. doi:10.1109/6294.977775

S'duk. R., & Unhelkar, B. (2005). Web services extending BPR to industrial process reengineering. In *Proceedings of the Information Resource Management Association, International Conference*, San Diego, CA.

Sanchez-Nielsen, E., Martin-Ruiz, S., & Rodriguez-Pedrianes, J. (2006). Web services II: An open and dynamic service oriented architecture for supporting mobile services. In *Proceedings of the 6th International Conference on Web Engineering ICWE '06*. ACM Press.

Schneider, G. P. (2004). *Electronic commerce: The second wave* (5th ed.). Florence, KY: Thomson Course Technology.

Schroth, C., and T. Janner (2007). Web 2.0 and SOA: Converging concepts enabling the Internet of services. IT Professional , 9(3), 36–41. doi:10.1109/MITP.2007.60

Sharif, A. M., T. Elliman, P. E. D. Love, and A. Badii (2004). Integration of the IS with the enterprise: Key EAI research challenges. The Journal of Enterprise Information Management , 17(2), 164–170. doi:10.1108/17410390410518790

Stacey, M., & Unhelkar, B. (2004). *Web services in implementation.* Paper presented at the 15th ACIS Conference, Hobart, Australia.

Tilley, S., Gerdes, J., Hamilton, T., Huang, S., Muller, H., & Wong, K. (2002). Adoption challenges in migrating to Web services. In *Proceedings of Fourth International Workshops on Web Site Evolution*. Washington, DC: IEEE Computer Society.

Toffler, A. (1980). *The third wave.* New York: William Morrow & Company Inc.

Unhelkar, B. (2003). Understanding collaborations and clusters in the e-business world. In *Proceedings of the We-B Conference,* Perth, Australia.

Unhelkar, B. (2004). Globalization with mobility. In [*th International Conference on Advanced Computing and Communications*, Ahmedabad, India.]. Proceedings of the ADCOM , 2004, 12.

Unhelkar, B. (2005). An initial three dimensional framework for mobile enterprise transitions. *Cutter IT Journal, 18*(8).

Unhelkar, B. (2005). Transitioning to a mobile enterprise: A three-dimensional framework. Cutter IT Journal , 18(8), 5–11.

Unhelkar, B. (2005). *Practical object oriented analysis.* Australia: Thomson Social Science Press.

Unhelkar, B. (2007). Beyond business integration – management challenges in collaborative business processes. *ICFAI Journal*.

Unhelkar, B., & Deshpande, Y. (2004). Evolving from Web Engineering to Web Services: A Comparative study in the context of Business Utilization of the Internet, *Proceedings of ADCOM 2004, 12th International Conference on Advanced Computing & Communications,* Ahmedabad, India.

Unhelkar, B., & Saddik, R. (2004). Web services extending BPR to industrial process reengineering. In *Proceedings of the Information Resource Management Association, International Conference*, San Diego, California.

*Web services overview.* (2005). Retrieved October 11, 2005, from http://www.acs.openlab.net.au/content.php?article.131

Yildiz, U., Marjanovic, O., & Godart, C. (2006). Contract-driven cross-organizational business processes. In *Proceedings of the ACIS Conference, ACIS 2006*, Adelaide, Australia.

Zimmermann, O., Doubrovski, V., Grundler, J., & Hogg, K. (2005). Service oriented architecture and business process choreography in an order management scenario: Rationale, concepts, lessons learned. In *Companion to the 20th annual ACM SIGPLAN conference on Object-oriented programming, systems, languages, and applications OOPSLA '05*. ACM Press.

# Chapter 3
# Global Collaborative Business

*I can't understand why people are frightened by new ideas. I'm frightened of old ones.*

John Cage (1912-1992)

## CHAPTER KEY POINTS

- Discusses the importance and relevance of collaboration in the context of a global business.
- Discusses which characteristics and traits of a collaborative global enterprise would make it successful.
- Discusses the strategic approach to global collaboration.
- Discusses the customer, supplier, employee and governance relationships for a global collaborative business.
- Discusses the various levels at which businesses collaborate.
- Discusses marketing issues in global collaborative business.
- Discusses the factors that affect and challenge the proposed collaborative business environment.

DOI: 10.4018/978-1-60566-689-1.ch003

## INTRODUCTION

This chapter starts with a discussion on global collaborative business. The initial discussion in this chapter is on why and how a global collaborative business is brought about. Our premise in the discussion in this chapter is that electronic collaboration is invariably associated with globalization. While an organization may not be specifically seeking global business, the moment the services of the organization are exposed on the Internet high-seas; it has to accept the possibility of trading independent of regional borders. The definition of globalization and collaboration between multiple organizations that interact with each other irrespective of geographical and time boundaries is a vital concept for all modern-day businesses. This concept is developed and expanded on in this chapter. While reiterating the basic importance of electronic and communications technologies in the emergence of this global collaboration, this chapter also underscores the challenges and risks associated with such a business. The discussion in this chapter forms the basis for understanding the models of collaborative business build later in Chapter 5.

## INTRODUCING GLOBAL COLLABORATIVE BUSINESS

A global business is the one that conducts its internal and external business processes irrespective of its geographical location. A global *collaborative* business is the one that collaborates with multiple other businesses with common interests, in order to provide for the needs of a customer, irrespective of their geographical location. This location-independence of collaboration is a critical ingredient towards globalization. A global collaborative business deals with global customers and global suppliers. Furthermore, a global collaborative business partners with other businesses that may themselves be spread out globally.

The Internet-based communications technologies have long been accepted as strategic to global businesses (Grove 1999, Gates 1999, Lan and Unhelkar 2005). These electronic communications technologies (Unhelkar 2008), further augmented by mobile technologies, provide unique opportunities for business collaborations.

As mentioned in chapter one, Gates expounded the concept of a digital nervous system (DNS) for an organization as an electronic-communication's based approach to creating the enterprise architecture and management of the business. The global collaborative business further extends and expands the concept of a digital nervous system to incorporate numerous business organizations. These global collaborative organizations not only manage their internal operational processes electronically, but also transition to electronic processes with external parties such as customers, suppliers, and competitors. This business use of the web that was presented in Chapter

1 (Figure 3) becomes increasingly complex as we reach electronic collaboration. Those organizations that need to move towards collaboration need to understand, plan and transition to collaborative business in a formal manner – again, through the processes, technologies and people as discussed in this book.

The reasons why an organization would want to collaborate electronically with other organizations at a global level are manifold. Electronic collaboration among multiple organizations is happening because not only are the organizations able to communicate with each other, but also able to offer and consume services as entire packages. Communications technologies make it possible for organizations to not only exchange messages and emails, but also define and exchange services. A service-based approach enables organizations to flag their offerings on the Internet and other organizations to locate and consume these services. The upcoming Web 2.0 technologies and their discussion (Murugesan, in press) provide further opportunities for electronic collaboration for multiple organizations.

When organizations form wider electronic alliances, however, it becomes imperative for them to also consider the issues related to physical alliances. This is especially true when the e-business alliance is global, spanning across geo-political borders. More often than not, in our experience, the technological capabilities of organizations to interact with each other also need to be supported by the physical capability to service clients and business partners. A global alliance effectively builds on the possibilities offered by two or more companies that are able to communicate electronically and have value to offer to each other. Usually, the underlying principle for electronic business alliances that also require physical alliance capabilities is that each member of the business alliance has something to offer that is complimentary to the other across geo-political borders. It may happen that one organization is a technically-savvy global aspirant that is trying to reach across borders. However, due to numerous factors such as social, cultural, legal and political, this organization is unable to transcend its borders. This is when the electronic commerce world facilitates formation of these alliances, as it is easier to communicate electronically across boundaries than it is to do so physically. However, it is important to understand that alliances, although easily conceivable through technology, require a corresponding understanding of the nuances of those alliances' physical aspects as well. While it is true that offering and consuming a Web Service (WS) can be independent of the location – in practice, however, when organizations collaborate, they aim to establish relationships that they can build on for future offerings. Despite the availability of WS, we find that businesses have not been able to successfully setup collaboration without delving into the physical aspects of those relationships. Therefore, whenever such alliances are formed, it is imperative that stakeholders and players in these partnering organizations quickly understand and establish working relationships that transgress the socio-cultural borders evident in physical alliances. Employees and managers, especially in large organizations, need to effectively adopt different cultures and working styles in order to benefit each other (Gupta 2000). In fact, there are number of benefits accorded to the electronic business alliances with a physical component in them that continues to promote the creation and sustenance of these alliances.

## CHARACTERISTICS OF GLOBAL ENTERPRISES

According to Bartlett and Ghoshal's (1998), enterprises need to understand, review and improve their core organization characteristics in order to succeed in the global market. This is particularly true when an enterprise has to collaborate with other enterprises which are also going global. In order to further understand the challenges faced by these enterprises, it is important to build and expand on a number of core characteristics of the organization from a collaborative perspective.

First and foremost, it is vital that the traditional organization structures are changed to a more process-based approach. The centrally-controlled, coordination-based, hierarchical approach to organization is unlikely to provide value in a collaborative global market. Therefore, starting right from the strategic planning of the organization, through to the methods of encouraging and rewarding the employees, the organization has to shift from a hierarchical to a process-based organization.

The products and services that are offered by global collaborative organizations are likely to be far less fixed or pre-determined. Customization is the key to glean the advantages of globalization, and that customization has to be available for every product and service that is offered by the organization. For example, a service offered by a travel company needs to include the possibilities of offering car and hotel rentals dynamically; the traveler is going to continuously change (upgrade, downgrade, add, delete) what he or she needs through the travels *as the travel progresses* through various regions. Collaboration needs to necessarily focus on being able to customize services and products dynamically, as that customization is one of the key differentiators for collaborating organizations (over their competition that may not be collaborating).

Globally-collaborating organizations also search for resources worldwide in raw materials and components, in order to build their own products. The need to collaborate from a resource and supply chain viewpoint is vital in order to use the potential offered by collaborations fully. Such collaboration would also bring about value to the organization in terms of reduction in transportation costs, greater bargaining power and use of legislations across various regions.

Decision-making in a collaborative organization will be also distributed – collaborative organizations need a suite of policies and procedures that provide the guidelines for their relationships which allows the collaborators to take certain decisions that are specific to a situation or a region. As a precursor to this, organizations need to develop electronic relationships that allow rapid sharing of information and knowledge which enables them to assist each other in winning new business or expanding the current one.

Collaborative organizations exhibit a different socio-cultural approach in dealing with internal as well as external organizational matters. There is likely to be substantial variation in the way organizations are managed when their products and services are put together through electronic collaborations and communications. The local enterprise culture will be influenced by the local customs and value systems, as well as those of the partnering organizations.

The complexity of global collaborative business demands astute senior management capabilities that are not based on the brilliance of that single individual but also on his or her ability to bring together decision makers across a spectrum of organizations, electronically interacting with each other to provide the products and services. Thus, senior management in a collaborative organization goes beyond just the process-based approach to managing an organization; it moves towards managing a group of organizations all of whom have equal say in the manner in which the customer is served. Effective coordination between the participating organizations can be achieved through a common technical as well as business language. This is not a formal language, but an understanding among the partners as to what is implied in a particular situation. Formal and informal communication skills and language capabilities are likely to play some role in these collaborations.

## STRATEGIC APPROACH TO GLOBAL COLLABORATION

Successful collaboration requires the implementation of strategic vision both within and across the organization. Strategic vision refers to what an enterprise expects to be its ideal image in the long-term. In the context of collaboration, strategy is the primary driver for the enterprise's planning and implementation. The guideline for such an envisioning process will be the planning of a strategic vision for the enterprise's future position. Development of a long-term strategy can vary from industry to industry but the vision in terms of collaboration is vital. Process owners should consider how their enterprises will shape up when they have to deal with collaborating partners and what sort of knowledge and skills they should have in order to develop, produce, service, market and consume the products and services globally. In addition, it is vital to identify who the collaborators are and how they differ from the competitors, as in a global collaborative environment, there is a very thin line between the two. Competitors and collaborators can change roles very quickly in electronic collaborations. Often – in fact – they are one and the same, at the same time.

Strategy, particularly organizational strategic frameworks, can be constructed based on three principal elements – goals, stakeholders and processes. Goal orientation, however central to all strategic approaches, needs to incorporate multiple factors in order to develop a suitable global-collaborative strategic vision for an enterprise. There is a need to analyze the trend of financial, commercial, legal and environment factors. There is also a need to fully understand the current capabilities of the enterprise – what it has to offer in terms of products and services and how these offerings fit in with the long-term future of the industry to which the organization belongs. Note that it is not necessary, in a collaborative strategy, for an organization to be unique in its products and services. This is because collaboration, especially global collaboration, opens up opportunities for uniqueness beyond the actual product or service. Rather, it delves into the possibilities of collaborating for advantages such as different legal, taxation or cultural systems and approaches.

Three types of stakeholders that need to be considered in global collaborations: owners, actors and clients. Owners are the ones who have the decision-making authority in the collaboration process. They are the ones who can effectively start and stop the process. Identifying owners in a collaborative business can be challenging; at times they can be the very senior management including the board of directors, at other times they may be the major stock-holders who take the decisions on collaboration. The challenge in enabling collaboration is to identify the individual or the decision-making body and deal with it during the steps in becoming a collaborative global organization. The consent and participation of the owner (decision-maker) of the business is vital as it undergoes transformation to a global collaborative business.

Actors are those who operate the system. Usually they are easy to identify. It is equally important to identify all categories of actors and make sure they are on-board with the strategic framework being conceived. Without the consent and cooperation of the actors the transformation to a collaborative organization will not happen.

Clients are beneficiaries of the contemplated strategic move to global collaboration. They are users of the system, customers of the users of the system and their customers in turn. They too must be identified and brought on-board. The clients need to see the value of a collaboration and consent to using the global collaborative features (processes) of the organization.

And finally, once we have identified the goal, and the stakeholders only then can we proceed to actually lay out the global strategic framework in terms of its processes that include internal operations as well as external interactions. Various actors, as process owners (e.g. the senior management and other decision-making agents) of an organization, are required to understand and develop the best strategic vision for their enterprises to collaborate with other enterprises. This requires them to carefully evaluate the capabilities for communication, the level of trust and agreements with other organizations that is required, and the trends of the entire future business environment in which the enterprise exists.

## Understanding of Current Organizational Situation

Firstly, the enterprise should understand its current position or situation in terms of global collaboration. All actors within the enterprise should agree on the offerings of the organization, including a listing of all present successful products and services. The current major markets and the domain of customer service in which the organization operates need to be noted. Similarly, existing suppliers who provide services and materials/products for the business operations are also listed. Furthermore, ascertaining the current situation of the organization also requires determining the organizational core values such as employees' expertise, knowledge, skills and goals/objectives. The management style and organizational structure of the enterprise can be modeled as well, as a help in understanding where the organization stands today. Finally, the existing rules and regulations of the environment in which the organization operates, as well as the government styles and approaches are also valuable in understanding the current situation of the organization.

## Evaluating Critical Factors in Global Collaborative Strategic Vision

After ascertaining the current position, the various process owners need to study the factors identified, evaluate them and understand their positive and negative influences. These critical factors are listed below. Evaluation of these global collaborative factors includes studying the characteristics of successful products or services, markets and consumer domains as well as enterprise's core capability and weaknesses. Furthermore, there is a need to also model and study the characteristics of future products or services, markets and consumer domains. The current and potential competitors need to be studied from the point of view of their possibility as collaborators. (Younessi and Smith 1995)

## Developing Preliminary Strategic Vision for Global Collaboration

After the critical factors have been determined, the process owners and the senior managers (actors) can start developing a preliminary global strategic vision. The purpose of this part is to find the driving forces that will influence organizational performance. Thereupon, the management team can determine the driving force that best represents the enterprise's advantage.

The development of preliminary strategic vision requires the creation of a future strategy – and that too in a reasonable time framework. There is a need to identify the potential champions who will drive the transformation to global collaboration. The identification and validation of a market that is globally dispersed and that would require multiple elements to its products and services can be vital during this exercise. The global competitive advantage and its requisites, as well as the potential for the enterprise's growth, scope and investment return objectives are all studied here. There are possibilities of fostering relationships among global customers. There is also the possibility of developing and using global human resources management systems to enrich the global employees' capabilities. Integrated global supply chain systems that would deal with multiple collaborating suppliers need to be identified and studied; so too the government rules and regulations that needs to be incorporated in global collaborative business policies.

The owners (decision-makers, senior managers) need to compare the future collaborative global strategic vision with the current strategic vision. This comparative study includes, for example, some basic questions such as:

- What are the differences between the two strategies?
- What sort of variations should the enterprises perform when they start new products, services, markets and consumer domains?
- Are there any differences in driving force? How are they going to effect the business operations?
- Do they have the same capability?
- How are they going to effect the business operations?

## Settling New Global Collaborative Strategic Vision and Mission Description

The outcome of the examination step is the number of critical factors that will become the significant key factors in assisting new global collaborative strategic vision development. When these factors are finalized, the development of new global collaborative strategic vision can commence.

The organizational mission description focuses on the enterprise's future idea, resource allocation, and the plan of long-term and actual business operations. The mission description is the epitome of the global strategic vision and it covers information of the enterprise's core values, driving force, future products and services areas, future markets and consumer domains, and competitive advantages.

A successful mission description should include the enterprise's objectives, products, markets and technology information, core values, business operation philosophy, public image and financial aim.

Critical issues in the strategy to transitioning to global collaborative organization may be discovered at this stage. These issues would usually cause the enterprises to modify the current systems, resources, expertise, skills or structural frameworks. After passing through the previous phases, the newly developed global collaborative strategic vision is now ready to be implemented. The strategic vision is transient; it should be maintained and modified in accordance with varying situations in the global collaborative business environment, market requirements and technology evolution.

## GLOBAL COLLABORATIVE BUSINESS ELEMENTS

The enterprise strategic thinking key elements discussed so far provide sound basis for understanding and developing the core characteristics or elements of collaborative business. The main elements of a global collaborative business are customers, suppliers, management, employees and government. This is also highlighted in global collaborative organization shown in Figure 1.

### Global Collaborative Customer

Customers are the most important entity of most organizations; it is imperative to understand and recognize their existing customers in terms of the characteristics, requirements, and their level of satisfaction as the organization transitions to global collaboration.

Firstly, each customer should be categorized in accordance with the level of importance. The important factors can be identified through the analysis of sales orders, the monthly sales total and the payment history. Customers determined as crucial are those who feature in a high monthly sales total with a correspondingly

*Figure 1. The Global Collaborative Organization*

large volume of sales orders and acceptable payment schedules (no delays). Secondly, customer service programs should be developed to fulfill the requirements and achieve the level of satisfaction, particularly for those identified as crucial customers. The construction of appropriate customer service programs should consider several factors including the location of customers, customers' access times, creating a value-added supply chain, and developing or enhancing appropriate business processes to facilitate customers. Each of these factors is briefly delineated as follows:

- **Location of customers:** Customers are located everywhere in the world. When investigating the location of customers, organizations mainly concentrate on the analysis of product distribution. However, there are other concerns that also need to be addressed in relation to the location. These include cultural diversity, taxation and regulation systems, distribution channels and methods of transportation.
- **Customers' access times**: Further to the location of customers, organizations also need to recognize the time of access of information by each customer. In the global business environment, customers place orders and request services at anytime as necessary. It is imperative for organizations to ensure the information requested by customers is made available as needed.
- **Creating a value-added supply chain**: In order to provide customers with additional benefits over the purchased products, the improvement and effective management of the company's supply chain can be seen as an appropriate approach. To achieve this, firstly, the organization has to clearly identify each and all components of the supply chain and indicate the relationships between them. Once the processes and flows of the supply chain are determined, the analysis and redesign of the supply chain takes place to identify the improvement and develop value-added components.
- **Developing or enhancing appropriate business processes**: Activities and operations in association with customers are accommodated by several of the company's business processes. These business processes generally include ordering, production scheduling, delivering, accounting, and after-servicing. The concepts behind these processes, as well as their functionality, should be built to maximize customer benefits and facilitate customers in any circumstances.

## Global Collaborative Supplier

Managing suppliers is as important as managing customers. In today's competitive marketplace, many companies depend on suppliers to deliver materials, goods, or services that can be transformed into valuable products to provide to customers.

Supplier relationships have become increasingly important to assure companies reaming in the competitive edge. Supplier relationship management can be seen as a subset of supply chain management, which pertains to understanding the important suppliers and maintaining strategic relationships. The Gartner Research group defines supplier relationship management as "the practices needed to establish the business rules, and the understanding needed for interacting with suppliers of products and services of varied criticality to the profitability of the enterprise" (2001). Furthermore, it is even more critical for global organizations to manage suppliers all over the world. Thus, effective global supplier relationship management is a part of global information systems. It provides supplier intelligence through the integration of the internal enterprise's information systems and data obtained from the external suppliers.

## Global Collaborative Employee

A global employee of a global organization undertakes a unique combination of virtual and physical work as she proceeds with transitioning to globalization. As the organization becomes global, the work of the employee moves towards being more knowledge-based, as opposed to task-based, and the processes that are used by the employees traverse different departments and even different organizations that are coming together under a global organization umbrella. It is interesting to note that the effect of globalization also redefines the set views of a job. For example, in global organizations, employees will be connected to each other and to the customers almost all the time (or certainly the time and place of their choosing), resulting in the vanishing concept of a 9am to 5pm job day. Finally, because of globalization, the concept of a well-defined career is also vanishing. For example, in the earlier days, a person could start a career in bank as a teller, move up to branch manager and then head a department. In a globalized bank, though, the well organized concept of a department, or even a branch, is diminishing. Therefore, the career paths of individuals in global organizations will be lateral, not vertical (Unhelkar 2002).

## Global Collaborative Governance

Electronic governance is a crucial and integral part of the globalization process. This is because a globalized organization is bound to go across its geo-political domain, and come across customers, business partners and employees belonging to different cultures, society and working under different governments. This requires the globalized organization to create and maintain electronic and physical links with the government bodies in that region. Some of the core characteristics of relationships of a global organization with governments include the ability to understand

and comply with legal and taxation issues, conform to the requirements of health, security and welfare of the employees and distribution of funds.

## FACTORS AFFECTING GLOBAL COLLABORATIONS

The reasons why businesses attempt to globalize have been discussed by number of authors in the past few years (Hartmann 1997, McMullan 1994). Based on numerous such discussions (Unhelkar 2003), the major reasons why businesses undertake global venture are identified as company maturity, current overseas trade, foreign market potential, exceptional overseas demand for the product, demand for look-alike product abroad, knowledge capitalization, knowledge sharing, market expansion, customer service enhancement, risk apportionment, outsourcing and legal and tax advantages. In the subsequent paragraphs, we will expand on the above points in the context of the organizational structures and transition processes of the organizations going global.

## Company Maturity

Getting into the global marketplace requires time, money and resources. If the enterprise does not have a good track record at home base or a history of stable performance, a global venture may strain its resources and complicate issues for its domestic operations and business activities (Hartmann 1997). It is very important that the enterprise should be sure that it is meeting the demand for its products and services in the domestic market before branching out into the global arena. The initial stages of the path to maturity in a global company originate from strength in domestic value added, import of resources and export of products. This maturity of organizations has been important even for virtual organizations in the dot com era. Most globalizing companies do not start that way, hence, based on Bhatia & Dey (2007), the maturity level are classified as a) engaging the key players; b) change readiness; c) current levels of remote global work; d) knowledge management in global context; and e) information management and security. Such maturity must be acquired through gradual development of ability to collaborate: first within the local business and with domestic customers and suppliers, then by international suppliers and customers, then local, regional and national host governments and other regulatory authorities. Needless to say, irrespective of technology, the development of the collaborative relationships is organic and essential.

## Current Overseas Trade

Orders from overseas customers suggest a potential market and point to a market niche that closer suppliers are not filling. The enterprise intent on expanding should try to understand their overseas markets and customers, and find out why they are buying the products they buy and, more importantly, why are they not being marketed the product or services that the organization is considering supplying. A comprehensive analysis of the overseas opportunity helps give the enterprise an opening to demonstrate its strengths to customers. It also acquires a clear view of the overseas market. If the result of visiting shows that the overseas competitors have insufficient ability in their own domestic marketplace, it may indicate a positive suggestion for going global.

It should be noted that the inability to serve a market may not necessarily be only a commercial or technological issue. The issue may be legal, cultural, social or behavioral. It may mot be that they cannot build it; it may be that they don't need it or they won't use it. Pork sausages in Jerusalem or French cognac in Mecca both have very limited markets.

## Foreign Market Potential

Conducting simple market research or reviewing competitors' financial statements would provide the enterprise an overview of the market other firms are servicing abroad. Collecting information about product origins from the overseas customers is another way of determining the market share of global competitors. In the global electronic environment, the companies have the opportunity to explore the foreign market and offer the desired products and services to them. In the proposed collaborative environment, the customer can easily reach these created products and services and proposed *CBPE* model can market for these products and services.

## Exceptional Overseas Demand for the Product

Some products draw the whole world's attention. Unfortunately, it is precisely the enterprises producing these products that make the biggest mistakes in their marketing plans. On the face of it seems that with such demand and attention, no firm supplying said market can go wrong in their marketing plans. It is, in fact, exactly this sort of market that requires the most astute marketing strategy. To begin, if demand is so high, the ability to supply probably is as well. The market is probably very competitive and as such the competition model approaches the economic concept of pure competition (e.g. as is the case with commodities). This type of competition drives margins down and the operating point approaches the confluence of marginal demand and marginal supply. Secondly, with such a market, the slightest change that is perceived to disadvantage the customer (a slight delay in shipping, non-uniformity of batches of supply, etc.) will cause the customer to change suppliers. There is very little loyalty that can be relied on in such markets. Marketing plans must strive for establishing market segmentation and developing a unique distinguishing feature. This is very difficult as any distinguishing feature may be precisely what the market needs to see for your product NOT to any longer receive the attention it once did.

## Demand for Look-Alike Product Abroad

A very important question the enterprise must ask itself is "Do our products have the sort of appeal that will eventually tempt someone to copy them?" If yes, and the enterprise does not take these products overseas, they will eventually be made by some foreign supplier who may even eventually intrude the enterprise's domestic market. Although many developed and developing countries have adopted copyright and intellectual property regulations, there is no guarantee to prevent imitation. For this reason, the enterprise needs to investigate the overseas markets in regard to its product's acceptance rate and the government's regulations. However, the *CBPE* could provide a competition for those products since the price or quality might be different from the existing local product.

## Knowledge Capitalization

When two organizations from different regions come together, they invariably bring rich knowledge and know-how in terms of products and services offered. Collaborations between people belonging to these organizations, reinforced by information flow, make it possible for them to share knowledge, thereby enhancing the overall pool of expertise in the organization. This can lead to benefits such as faster innovation of new products, reduced duplication of efforts, savings in research and development costs, and enhanced employee satisfaction. Being able to share and build upon knowledge in order to create a richer set of knowledge is one of the major advantages of global alliances. Electronic technology facilitates these alliances, but the physical interaction between people is what eventually brings the knowledge to fruition.

## Knowledge Sharing

In addition to creating new pools of knowledge, global e-business alliances also enable sharing of knowledge. On the social front, this is amply evident in fighting crime as well as the scourge of modern day – terrorism. This is because in this age of communication, it is sharing of knowledge that takes even higher precedence than the existence and capitalization of such knowledge. In terms of e-business alliances, sharing of knowledge in the domains of processes, designs, engineering models, customer data, and analytical techniques and so on, form substantial reasons for creation of such alliances.

## Market Expansion

Market expansion has been considered as one of the basic reasons for formation of business alliances. Business alliances between two or more organizations enable the partnering organizations to have access to each other's customers, suppliers and the general markets where the organizations have been conducting business activities. It is understandable then that formation of a business alliance requires creation of a local know-how among all participating businesses. It is equally understandable that for some partnering businesses that are coming for a different "geo-political" climate, the social and cultural aspect of the local know-how may itself be too idiosyncratic to be relevant outside the particular local market. For example, a computer chip manufacturer in Japan wanting to sell its products through alliance partners in Australia would want to understand the cultural and social nuances of the Australia-New Zealand region before embarking on the market expansion journey. Another common example is of a bank in Hong Kong wanting to expand its markets in the USA. It will have to adopt to the socio-cultural value systems of the American market, which may be dramatically different to, say, the Gulf market, in terms of lending policies and value systems. Despite the challenges of differing cultures, however, businesses eventually find that through formation of alliances they are able to sell in a market that they had no access to earlier. Thus, while alliances enable businesses to sell in a foreign market, they also make it almost obligatory to understand and leverage the cultural nuances of those markets. Leveraging different cultures is not just a business advantage, it is also a business imperative (Teitler 1999). Companies that develop best practices for managing culture capital find they are able to expand and supplement their e-business with physical growth. Without such best practices, however, they face the situation similar to the case study discussed by Unhelkar (2003b), wherein an Indian chemical manufacturing company rushes into its expansion in Australia and finds the going tough precisely due to lack of consideration to these socio-cultural factors.

## Customer Service Enhancement

While a sale across borders may happen easily using electronic commerce, it is not always easy to service the same customer across boundaries. In many post-sale scenarios, commonly experienced by customers buying groceries, even local customer care is uneven at best let alone customer care across global markets. Global markets increase the risk of customer dissatisfaction. "Customer service is often seen as a necessary evil," says Raul Katz, a vice president with Booz-Allen & Hamilton. Good managers realize that in their business, customer service would be one vital element in holding onto premium customers in the face of competition. An example of enhanced customer service through alliances was that of IBM, which set up alliances with 61 software companies in 2001, up from its 50 alliances in year 2000. The expectation of IBM, through these global alliances, was that they will add up to $2 billion in new revenues in year 2001. Mike Gilpin, vice president and research leader of Giga Information Group comments on these increasing partnerships that they: "allow IBM to solve a wider percentage of their customers' problems". Bryce (2001) adds: "They can grow global services, do more outsourcing deals and provide more strategic assistance to clients." This is because IBM's alliance partners are available to provide service for products that may have been sold across boundaries, in another country or region where IBM itself may not have had a physical presence. Thus, while e-business provides a single unified face to the customer, because of global alliances, personalized and even peculiar needs of customers can be satisfied by the local know how, expertise and physical presence of alliance partners. This not only results in wider customer base but also higher volume growth from the same customers.

## Risk Apportionment

Global e-business alliances are extremely helpful in spreading the risks to businesses arising, among other things, primarily due political instabilities. Global alliances provide excellent opportunities for strategic management of risks in businesses when they are operating out of unsure political climates. This, of course, requires that the issue of response to changing political circumstances in different cultures is properly considered and integrated in the global response strategies of these business alliances. In order that the management of a company keep track of all the changing technological, economic, political-legal, socio-cultural trends around the world, it is essential that they shift from a vertically organized, top-down type of organization to a more horizontally managed, interactive organization (Nuese et al. 1998). Horizontal structures are flexible, enable ordinary employees to play crucial role by interacting among themselves. They also enable spreading of risks due to vacillating external (in this context political) factors. Alliances with local players have a distinct advantage over traditional multinational company structures in this respect. For example, to gain access to China while ensuring a positive relationship with the often-restrictive Chinese government, Maytag Corporation formed a joint venture with the Chinese appliance maker, RSD (Adler 2001).

## Outsourcing

Although criticized in the current (year 2004) political charged climates of Australia and the USA, outsourcing plays a significant cause for business alliances, enabling alliance partners to capitalize on the unevenly distributed pools of skills and resources across the globe. By making it feasible for organizations to outsource certain routine work, typically to another country, there is potential for significant saving, as well as ability to provide service round the clock (due to time zones). This is invaluable, for example, in providing 24/7 call centers, which are made possible through the electronic and communication medium. However, outsourcing usually comes with its own limitations in terms of social communication problems, understanding of what is meant within the contractual terms, understanding the requirements and agreement on what constitutes a quality deliverable. Furthermore, when strategic work is outsourced (as compared with routine work), it brings even greater challenges of the need to understand the direct and implied meanings behind all types of communications. These are the situations where excellence in business processes, use of industry standard modeling tools and techniques by partnering organizations, as well as improving the overall communications between outsourcing partners can play a crucial role in the success of such alliances.

## Legal and Tax Advantages

Global alliances facilitate companies to research, produce and sell legally, by taking advantages of the local rules and regulations of the governments of the environments where they operate. For example, stem cell research may be considered unacceptable, unethical or even illegal in some regions, but may well be acceptable in others. Alliances, especially at global level, are able to take advantages of the regulations spread across the globe, in order to achieve their goals. Alliances in educational sector are common and popular examples of legal and tax advantages being used effectively in running a global business.

## LEVEL OF COLLABORATION

Global collaborations among different organizations influence both their internal and external processes. This calls for study of both intra- and inter-organizational factors that influence business activities and operations.

The external business activities and operations can be seen as the communication channels between the organization and other enterprises such as customers, suppliers, and competitors. External communication channels play a major role in the global collaboration strategy as a number of new business processes start emerging as part of the core business functions. These new processes extend the enterprise's organizational scope and change the organization's structure. Furthermore, inter-organizational technologies such as traditional EDI (Electronic Data Interchange), XML (Extensible Markup Language), VPN (Virtual Private Network), and Extranet provide the technological foundation to enable inter-organizational communications. The following subsections discuss the new emerging business processes including customer relationship management (CRM), supplier relationship management (SRM), supply and chain management (SCM).

## Customer Relationship Management (CRM)

Swift (2001) defines CRM as "an enterprise approach to understanding and influencing customer behavior through meaningful communications in order to improve customer acquisition, customer retention, customer loyalty, and customer profitability". The fundamentals of CRM function in an organization can be designed to fulfill the global customer satisfaction through a number of categories. These categories consist of the CRM strategy, sales force automation, marketing automation, customer support center, e-enabled CRM, and the supporting technology and infrastructure for CRM implementation.

- **CRM strategy**: should align with or be part of the global business strategy. It refers to the plan for developing comprehensive customer related functions by integrating people, process and technology to maximize relationships with all customers. The basic principles of CRM strategy may involve aligning the organization around customers, sharing information across the entire business, leveraging data from disparate sources to better understand the customers and anticipate their needs, and maximizing customer profitability.
- **Sales automation**: involves the use of a multi-channel selling system that might include the direct/automatic delivery of products or services to the customers. The objective is to make the customer the focus of sales efforts by integrating customer needs into service channels and product strategies through the use of network sensors, microprocessor intelligence, and wireless communication.
- **Marketing automation**: refers to the utilization of technologies to an organization's marketing process. The modern marketing strategy involves the combination of traditional offline and online media channels, and taking the advantage of the Internet and technology to drive the B2C (business-to-

customer) and B2B (business-to-business) processes. The marketing initiatives involved in the organization's CRM function including personalization, profiling and segmentation, telemarketing, e-mail marketing, and campaign management. These projects are designed to fulfill customers' requirements by providing the right products and services at the right time.

- **Customer support center**: refers to a single multi-channel gateway that integrates all customer contact points and provides necessary services. No matter what the presentation of the customer support center, whether it is a help desk, a call center, or an online support via email or chat, the key concept is to provide the services and support to customers at any possible point and to present the customer with a positive impression and experience of the organization.

- **E-enabled CRM**: refers to the customer management tasks for business activities and operations through the Internet. The e-commerce capabilities such as online shopping, marketplace (online auction sites), the process of online transaction and payment and e-commerce security need to be addressed. These capabilities can be essential to successful e-CRM depending on the organization's readiness to handle Internet trading and transactions through various methods.

- Supporting technology and infrastructure from CRM: in order to implement a thriving CRM system, the organization needs to apply the flexible information architecture and applications that will cope with the implementation of new business tasks as well as the resolution of technological issues. The new business tasks may include migration management, change management, and comprehending organizational culture and behavior change. The technological resolutions consist of the utilization of knowledge-based systems, data warehousing and mining, introduction of software applications outsourcing concepts or Application Service Providers (ASPs), the fundamental information systems connectivity, integration with back-end systems, and maintenance and upgrading plans.

## Supplier Chain Management (SCM)

Supplier chain management has become the most influential practice in improving business operations and increasing commercial profits today (Poirier 1999). The components of supply chain management embrace a large portion of entire enterprise operations and involve numerous business processes such as procurement, logistics, production, transportation, warehousing, delivery, and distribution. In order to construct and maintain an effective supply chain management system, these business processes are required to connect together with the integration of suppliers, retailers, distributors, and consumers to form a supply chain network (Figure 2).

In the global business environment, the supply chain network strategy is often the essential factor to reduce costs in material purchases, storage and logistics requirements, and product transportation and distribution processes. In other words, a successful global supply chain strategy requires the collaboration of global suppliers, transporters, distributors, consumers, and business units. To achieve this goal, enterprises need to introduce the concept of information sharing in the global supply chain network. Information sharing among all parties in the global supply chain network can be implemented through the traditional EDI technology, or through the contemporary Internet platform (Figure 3).

*Figure 2. Supply chain network*

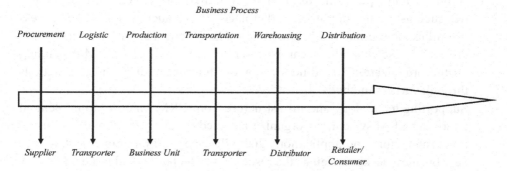

**Supply Chain Network Participants**

*Figure 3. Internet Information-Sharing Model for Global Supply Chain Network*

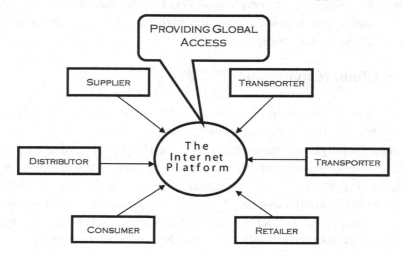

However, the major barrier to performing the information-sharing concept is the trust between the enterprise and other supply chain participants. It is believed that many enterprises treat their business information as top secret and would never share it with outsiders, including their trading partners. Thus, when developing the global supply chain management process, enterprises need to consider not only all contributors and business processes involved in the network, but realizing the problems may occur in establishing information sharing linkages among supply chain participants.

## Local: within the Organization

When talking about intra-organizational operations, people are predominantly referring to internal business functions. Most of these business functions are generic to any and every enterprise, while some of them are quite unique and dependent upon industry sectors. From this research point of view, I would like to focus on the generic business functions that apply to global organizations as well as non-multinational corporations, small and medium-sized enterprises. These functions work together, leading the enterprise to survive and prosper. In general, five business functions exist in any of the above-mentioned organization types. These functions are management and administration, human resources, finance and accounts, purchase and procurement, and sales and marketing.

## Management and Administration

The main tasks of the management and administration function consist of management of organization, corporate resources, corporate image, quality in all aspects, industrial relations, stakeholder relations, productivity, promotion of achievements, effective working relationships with external parties; liaising with political heads of sections or departments and administering services.

## Human Resources

Human resources refers to management of all the employees. This includes job analysis, position classification, employee training, employee selection, employee auditing and promotion, employee welfare, employee relations, work safety and sanitation, documentation and filing. The important tasks involved in human resources' function are the development of a human resources plan and strategy, providing a workforce; management of industrial relations, employee compensation and benefits, internal communications, employees' amenities, and personnel statutory obligations.

## Finance and Accounts

The finance and accounts function includes all the capital operations required by the entire enterprise activities. The major mission of financial activities is to deal with all the funds required by management, administration, sales, marketing, human resources, purchasing, procurement, and research and development; and to appropriately arrange the entire enterprise's financial resources.

## Purchase and Procurement

The purchase and procurement function consists of all activities in relation to obtaining and managing materials, services or products required to be involved in the production processes from suppliers or vendors. The key tasks may include the management of stores, inventory controls, procurement management, receipts management, investigation and analysis of purchases and procurement sources, and shipping and clearing management.

## Sales and Marketing

Sales and marketing refers to any transferring activities of products or services from producers to consumers. Sales activities are not only the traditional selling behaviors but also include the marketing mix or generally called "4P's" – production decision, pricing decision, promotion decision and place decision. Due to the rapid change in production techniques, many products have been supplied to the market efficiently. Many organizations have changed their operation philosophy from traditional production orientation to the modern marketing orientation. In other words, enterprises are now paying attention to all the sales techniques and methods, focusing on the consumers' requirements, designing acceptable products for consumers and reducing product costs in order to arrange reasonable and competitive prices. Some key activities of sales and marketing can be identified as surveying the market, selling products, managing products and sales outlets, promoting products, and providing sales support and after sales services.

## GLOBAL ISSUES IN PROPOSED COLLABORATIVE ENVIRONMENT

There are always some driving forces in each enterprise that lead the company towards its next stage. The concept of a driving force is the component that gives the enterprise momentum and drives the enterprise toward its expected direction.

Based on Robert Michel's (1988) important enterprise strategic areas, the key elements of driving forces are identified and classified into various categories. Figure 4 shows the required strategies for global enterprise.

## Enterprise's Global Strategy

Development of global strategic thinking and global strategic vision is a challenge even for an organization that operates its business only domestically. The senior managers also confront a difficulty in developing a global strategy. During the process of globalization, senior managers should compare the global strategy development with the company's current strategy in terms of global environmental factors, differences between global and domestic strategy and planning procedures provided by the subsidiaries and the entire enterprise.

## Global Environment Factors

Consideration of global environment factors is a preliminary and an essential step when a domestic company intends to expand its business and market into the overseas environment. These global environment factors, discussed earlier in this chapter, are the following: searching for sources globally, continuous development of new markets, scope of economy, trends in product-service consistency, lower costs in

*Figure 4. Enterprise strategic areas*

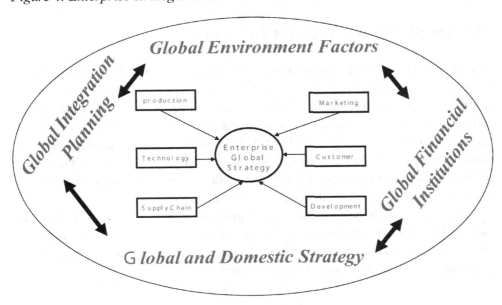

global transportation, government regulation, lower costs in telecommunications and equipment, trends in technology standards consistency, foreign competitors, increase of risks caused by exchange rate variation, the trend of expansion of customers from domestic to global markets, and rapid global technology transformation.

## Differences of Global and Domestic Strategy

Not all products are suitable in the global strategy. Some products must remain domestic due to the government regulations, local tastes and significant costs in transportation. For example, food, drink and concrete manufacturers are represented in this category.

However, those products that have the same characteristics, components or raw material requirements are the most likely to apply to global resource searching to find out how they can be operated in the global environment. Examples are computer and electronic manufacturing industries.

## Global Integration of Planning Procedures

Developing a global strategy is more complex than developing a domestic strategy because global strategy development is required to travel across borders and integrate the various subsidiaries and headquarters senior managers' opinions. Senior managers are from various countries or regions; their opinions and suggestions are critical in the process of global strategy development. Successful global strategy development must rely on the cooperation of each senior manager and the knowledge integration of subsidiaries and headquarters.

## Collaborative Global Product Viewpoint

From the product point of view in the proposed model of *CBPE*, a company's future products and services will greatly resemble its current and past products and services. Future products and services will be modifications, adaptations, or extensions of current products and services. Future products and services will be derivatives of existing products. Production capacity/capability – this company usually has a substantial investment in its production facility and the strategy is to "keep it running" or "keep it full." Therefore, such a company will pursue any product, customer, or market that can optimize whatever the production facility can handle.

From the customer point of view in the proposed *CBPE* model, the companies can continuously communicate with that user or customer to identify a variety of needs. Products are then made to satisfy those needs. A user-driven company places its destiny in the hands of that customer or user.

From the technology point of view in the **CBPE** model, the organization gains competitive advantage. It fosters the ability to develop or acquire hard technology or soft technology and then looks for applications for that technology. When an application is found, the organization develops products or services and infuses into these products or services a portion of its technology, which differentiates to the product.

From the supply chain point of view in the **CBPE** model, companies that have a unique way of getting their product or service from their place to their customer's place are pursuing a distribution method-driven strategy considering that natural resources are the key to company's survival.

From the development point of view in the **CBPE** model, companies that are interested in growth for growth's sake or for economies of scale are usually pursuing a strategy of size/growth. All decisions are made to increase size or growth. Whenever a company's only criterion for entering a marketplace or offering a product is profit, then that company is return/profit-driven.

## Electronic Finance: A Definition

Originally, e-finance is defined as the use of the Internet to deliver financial services to consumers, businesses, and financial institutions. The Internet has led to new forms of financial services delivery to the industry participants, who can either be financial institutions, individuals and/or businesses. A powerful example for one of these new forms is Internet banking. With advanced technology, banks, financial institutions customers or businesses may not have to attend the business 'bricks-and-mortar' branch to obtain their banking services such as fund transfers, bill payments, etc, as all of these types of activities may now be performed online. Based on the original definition, in the context of global business, e-finance is redefined as financial activities, functionalities, transactions, or services that global business may perform, conduct, or obtain through the Web in order to gain benefits.

## E-Finance' and Collaborative Global Business

With facilitation provided by Internet, e-finance may deliver global businesses and domestic business, as well as other industry's participants, numerous realistic benefits. Firstly, many companies are operating to provide funds and accept investments from businesses around the world. In fact, global businesses nowadays may either raise capital for their potential investments domestically and/or internationally. This was not the case just few years ago, when the potentials of the Internet were not sufficiently explored. For instance, an Australian investor can now invest his/her money in shares of a company based in the United States. It is also worth mentioning that prior to making investment decisions in any company, wise and knowledgeable individuals with surplus funds normally investigate the firm's financial health. This was previously accomplished by examining printed financial reports, produced by the company, and/or other related parties, which may have sometimes resulted in less-informed investment decisions. This is because that geographical distance existed between investors and companies made the information become less up-to-date, or often incomplete. This is has been overcome by publishing the financial information on the company's website, which can be accessed anytime or anywhere. E-finance's position is further favored when companies in one country list their firms with different stock exchange markets located in other countries. For instance, Telstra, an Australian telecommunications giant, has listed their company on the New York Stock Exchange (NYSE) since late 1997. It can be clearly seen that e-finance enables businesses in general and global businesses like Telstra to have access to wider financial sources around the globe. Furthermore, European and Asian banks, as well as a few American financial institutions currently offer A2A (account-to-account) funds transfer services, which are initiated over the Internet and enable customers to transfer funds freely from one account to another - whether their own accounts or others'- in real time. This certainly opens great opportunities for businesses involved in the e-business environment, especially global businesses. Specifically, it allows associated parties to accomplish their financial transactions at most cost-effective level. Huge savings will be realized for businesses operating globally, which have to conduct funds transfers and payments for their overseas operations and investments on regular basis. It is useful to indicate that not only activities such as investments, fund transfers and payments are now e-financeable, but so are services related to industries such as insurance, brokerage, securities services provision. These services might now be borderless obtained as well.

## Electronic Finance and Implications for Related Collaborative Parties

First of all, with the benefits and advantages that e-finance currently offers to financial institutions, it is believed that future of e-finance is promising. According to a World Bank report produced in mid-2001, e-finance will potentially continue to help the participants obtain financial services at lower prices. Lower costs will, in turn, allow consumers to have greater access to financial services. Due to this, profit margins of banks and financial institutions will certainly be narrowed in the future. This, in turn, will lead to establishment of greater and more aggressive competition among the industry players. The report also forecasted the sector's new entrants, using new technologies to provide low-cost services, will drive financial institutions to move online. In addition, there is no doubt that in the present dot-com era, businesses will move online and become involved in e-finance in order to exploit benefits offered by e-finance in particular and the Internet in general. Currently, enormous companies around the world are attempting to become financial portals that are one-stop websites that all customers financial needs can be met. However, such portals were not evidently available for global businesses and are expected to come to fruition in the near future. Moreover, it is expected that gradually, governments around the world will continue to address issues related to e-finance. For instance, many countries have not issued legislation and operational criteria for online banks; reviewed rules applying to parties play a direct or indirect role in providing financial services such as portals, etc. Favorably, however, the rules of e-finance are being harmonized with international standards in order to establish international best practices. Finally, one issue that must not be ignored regarding cyber-operations in general and e-finance in particular is security. Online security is one of the most sophisticated areas that governments, technologists, businesses and individuals wish to successfully resolve over time. In fact, realities of viruses spreading from computer to computer have made businesses become reluctant to undergo Internet-based fund-raising process. Certainly, efforts will be made in order to gradually construct a risk-free e-finance environment.

From the marketing point of view in the proposed CBPE model, the companies have "anchored" its business to a describable or circumscribable market type or category as opposed to a class of users.

## MARKETING IN GLOBAL COLLABORATIVE BUSINESS

Conventionally, customers were reached by broadcast and printed media. However, in the case whereby customers are spread out all over the globe, media of these types are no longer suitable, if not extremely costly. Nowadays, with exponential increase in number of individuals, businesses, organizations, etc using the Internet, the web is considered a giant market where organizations can sell goods to anyone, anywhere, and at anytime. With the Web store an enormous number of people are just one mouse click away from the business. In addition, the greater a number of customers is reached, the higher the revenue, and thus profit, will be generated. Based on this perception, marketers increasingly use the Web as a new platform on which marketing campaigns are run. Some organizations have implemented 'bricks-and-clicks' – a marketing strategy in which a company combines a physical presence with an online presence – approach to market their products and services.

## What is E-Marketing?

Throughout research conduction, e-marketing, Internet marketing, online marketing, cyber marketing, etc were found being used interchangeably. Also, there were a great number of definitions for the advanced marketing. Seltzer defines Internet marketing as "everything that affects visitor" to the Web sites. By 'everything', the independent Internet marketing consultant means the design, look, feel, content of the Web pages. It also includes the interactions with visitors or potential buyers; or those among themselves. Furthermore, the term comprises all activities and relationships that the Web page's owner has with other companies and individuals purposed to attract traffic to the Web site. On the other hand, according to Chartered Institute of Marketing (CIM), e-marketing is defined as "the way in which marketers increase sales or build brand awareness via the Internet, be it over their PC, TV, mobile phone or some other mobile device".

## Driving Forces for E-Marketing Implementation

There are four main factors among others that encourage marketers to use e-marketing. They are interactivity, cost-effectiveness, efficiency, and speed. Interactions are considered significantly useful in attracting customers, building their loyalty, favourably, without making a large investment. In addition to that, interactions between seller and buyers are perceived as one of the best ways to find out customer or consumer needs and wants. It would be extremely hard, if not impossible, to discover those needs and wants if the seller does not 'talk' with their existing and potential buyers. It would be even harder to satisfy the buyers based on unclear knowledge of what their need and want actually are. This most likely result in offering products and/or services, that are not, or least, required. With Internet's tremendous support, interactions with a massive existing as well as potential customers, clients, consumers, who may be located throughout the globe, might be accomplished without hassles. It is worth mentioning that the greater the mass interactions a certain seller can have with its buyers, the more solid the understanding of needs and wants will be. As needs and wants are understood, products and services will be produced accordingly in order to reach customer satisfaction at the highest possible level. There is also no doubt that interactions between seller and buyer are carried out almost instantly in the current Internet era. Not only that, their interconnection might also be accomplished in an efficient and cost effective manner through the use of present Internet technology. In fact, Milutinovic claims that it is significantly less expensive to keep a Web store than the real one. Lastly, but not least importantly, running marketing campaign on the Web also allows marketing decision makers be proactive about their marketing strategic planning. For instance, as online and offline marketing campaigns are combined to a single source of metric, Hewlett-Packard has been enabled to measure effectiveness of every campaign that the computer manufacturer runs. Accordingly, adjustments can be made in the real-time mode significantly more proactively than that in the non-Internet environment.

## E-Marketing's Brought-About Benefits for Global Business

There are numerous benefits that e-marketing may bring about for businesses in general and global firms in particular. First of all, e-marketing helps business improve consumer brand awareness more effectively than that achieved by conventional method. For example, by using parallel offline and online strategies, such global companies as McDonald's, Microsoft, and Unilever realised that they could increase awareness of their product's brand. Secondly, quick feedbacks regarding to the firm's products, services can be obtained easily, cheaply, and importantly, in a significantly quicker manner, through the Internet. These immediate feedbacks are extremely important for businesses running internationally, as wrong perception about any of these aspects of the business may easily result in or be converted in great loss or foregone opportunities. Also, the immediacy allows firms to make more informed strategic decisions in respect to critical areas of the business. In fact, quick feedback is one of main advantages that Intel gained by implementing its online advertising strategy. Thirdly, conducting marketing activities such as advertising online enables firms to keep track of customers and consumers interests in relations to a particular product or service. Again, this is useful for strategic decisions or customer satisfaction scheme. A giant computer network equipment producer, Cisco experienced this. Fourthly, with General Motors, one of the benefits that the car manufacturer could gain from its Internet marketing is improving how it learns about customers, which helped the global firm target its customers more accurately. The automobile producer also realised that online banner advertising did enable the company to extend its reach in global market. Fifthly, accountability enhancement was taken as the main benefit that online advertising can bring about for Orbitz.

## Future Direction of E-Marketing and Related Implications for Global Business

It is believed that e-marketing will be increasingly implemented by global businesses. According to research conducted by Forrester Research, by 2004, marketers will send as many as 200 billion emails. This finding is entirely consistent with research result produced by GartnerG2 (a division Gartner research group) that "additional marketing dollars will be spent online in coming years as both direct marketing - currently done largely through the mail - and branding campaigns currently conducted in print and broadcast make their way online". In Australia, online ads are growing, despite negative economic factors experienced recently. Interestingly enough, conventional advertising forms have figured a slight decline in spending. Based on these findings, the Internet will continue to be used as a marketing campaign carry-out platform. It was also forecasted that businesses will increasingly automate their business transactions via Web services. In addition, X Internet (i.e. Executable Internet) will be developed. The potential technology is potentially to upgrade the current static Web publishing with more responsive and personalised interfaces. Certainly, Web services and advances in Internet technology development will support the underlying firms in running their cyber marketing activities in even more effective ways. Interactions between buyers and sellers of goods and services are expected to have increasing trends since "the next generation of customers will have grown up with the Internet and feel much more at ease in using it for more interaction with business". Customer relationship management (CRM), which refers to activities undertaken by firms in order to develop and retain customers through increased customer satisfaction and loyalty, will be one of the areas that will continue being addressed, as, existing as well as future customers, consumers, buyers, clients, etc., will certainly have a great variety of substitutions for the products and services offered by competitors operating online. Furthermore, in the near future, organisations will launch their marketing campaigns not only via the Internet but also through mobile devices such as PDA (Personal Digital Assistant), Wireless Application Protocol (WAP) mobile phones, which allow users to have online access. Favourably, with development and deployment of wireless mobile technologies such as third generation (3G) (i.e. the technology is forecasted to change the world, deliver the bandwidth of as high as 2 mega bits per second, and being able to offer users additional mobile services, apart from voice traffic, such as video, multimedia, Internet searching and global roaming), users will be allowed to obtain high-speed quality information on any subject wherever they are and whenever they want it. This indicates that customers and consumers may also be reached 'on the move'; hence e-marketing's efficiency and speed are potentially improved further. Besides the bright and promising future of e-marketing, there are issues that need to be addressed. Firstly, like in the case of e-finance, online security problems will continue being rectified. Coupled with security, privacy is also aconcern in the Internet era. It remains no exception for e-marketing parties as well. In essence, in order to effectively drive people to a Website and place their purchase with it, these sensitive areas should be taken into careful consideration. Global businesses are expected to face competitive advantage ruin, as the Web enables small marketers to compete worldwide.

Although these ten strategic areas can be found in the enterprise, only one of them is strategically important to the enterprise and is the main imperative to drive the enterprise toward success. CEOs and senior managers should determine which area of driving force is the most appropriate one to represent the business nature of their enterprises, and develop their strategic planning process based on this specific driving force.

The outcome of the examination step is the number of critical factors that will become the significant key factors in assisting new global strategic vision development. When these factors are finalized, the development of new global strategic vision can commence.

The organizational mission description focuses on the enterprise's future idea, resource allocation, and the plan of long-term and actual business operations. The mission description is the epitome of the global strategic vision and it covers information of the enterprise's core values, driving force, future products and services areas, future markets and consumer domains, and competitive advantages.

A successful mission description should include the enterprise's objectives, products, markets and technology information, core values, business operation philosophy, public image and financial aim.

After the critical factors have been determined, the enterprise's CEOs and the senior managers can start developing a preliminary global strategic vision. The purpose of this part is to find the driving forces that will influence organizational performance. Thereupon, the management team can determine the driving force that best represents the enterprise's advantage. A number of essential processes should be carried out in this step. Focus on future strategy and set up a reasonable time framework.

- Develop a future driving force.
- Create a market and territory for future products and services.
- Develop competitive advantage and its necessary capability.
- Develop the enterprise's growth, scope and investment return objectives.
- Develop the relationships among global customers.
- Construct the global human resources management systems to enrich the global employees' capabilities.
- Develop the global integrated supply chain systems to enhance the related business operations.
- Incorporate the government regulations and required conditions into the business policies.

## ACTION POINTS

1. Identify and list the existing global business process of your organization
2. Work out a plan to model these existing global processes using a standard modelling approach

3.   Discuss, among various stakeholders, the relative importance of these processes from the point of view of collaboration
4.   Identify and describe the electronic alliance of your organization's global environment.
5.   Identify the global characteristic of your enterprise.
6.   Identify the various level of the global collaboration of your organization.
7.   Identify the global issues of your organization's business processes that could extent to the proposed *CBPE* model in this book.
8.   Based on the global strategic area, attempt to address the globalization strategy of your organization.

## REFERENCES

Adler, I. (2001, July). Merger mess. *Business Mexico*.

Bartlett, C. A., & Ghoshal, S. (1998). *Managing across borders: The transnational solution* (2nd ed.). Cambridge, MA: Harvard Business School Press.

Bhatia, A., & Dey, R. (2007). *Globalization of product development. How high-tech companies are disaggregating and globalizing their product development life cycle* [White Paper]. Retrieved October 20, 2008, from http://www.infosys.com/global-sourcing/white-papers/globalization-product-development-part2.pdf

Blake, R. K. (1985). Integrated networks: A realistic approach. Telephone Engineer & Management , 89(11), 64–69.

Bryce, R. (2001, August 29). IBM partners up. *Interactive Week*.

Deshpande, Y., Murugesan, S., & Hansen, S. (2001). Web engineering: Beyond CS, IS and SE evolutionary and non-engineering perspectives. In S. Murugesan & Y. Deshpande (Eds.), *Web engineering: Managing diversity and complexity of Web application development*. Springer.

Elliott, R., & Unhelkar, B. (2003). The role of Web services in e-business and globalization. In *Proceedings of the 4th International We-B Conference 2003*, Perth, Western Australia.

Gates, B. (1999). *Business @ the speed of thought: Using a digital nervous system*. England: Penguin Books.

Grove, A. (1999). *Only the paranoid survive: How to exploit the crisis points that challenge every company and career*. Westminster, MD: Bantam Doubleday Dell.

Gupta, A. K. (2000, March). Managing global expansion: A conceptual framework. *Business Horizons.* Retrieved from http://www.zdnet.com

Hartmann, E. J. (1997). Going international: How do you get there from here? Franchising World , 29(2), 30–34.

Lan, Y., & Unhelkar, B. (2005). *Global enterprise transitions: Managing a process.* Hershey, PA: Idea Group Publishing.

McMullan, W. E. (1994). Going global on startup: A case study. Technovation , 14(3), 141–143. doi:10.1016/0166-4972(94)90051-5

Michel, R. (1988). *The strategist CEO.* London: Quorum Books.

Moran, R. T., & Riesenberger, J. R. (1996). *The global challenge: Building the new worldwide enterprise.* UK: McGraw-Hill.

Murugesan, S. (Ed.). (in press). *Handbook of research on Web 2.0, Web 3.0 and X.0: Technologies and social applications.* Hershey, PA: Information Science Reference.

Nuese, C. J., J. E. Cornell, and S. C. Park (1998). Facilitating high-tech international business alliances. Engineering Management Journal , 10(1), 25–33.

Palvia, P. C., Palvia, S. C., & Whitworth, J. E. (2002). Global information technology management environment: Representative world issues. In P. C. Palvia, S. C. Palvia, & E. M. Roche (Eds.), *Global information technology and electronic commerce: Issues for the new millennium* (p. 2). GA: Ivy League.

Poirier, C. C. (1999). *Advanced supply chain management: How to build a sustained competitive advantage.* CA: Berrett-Koehler Publishers.

Swift, R. S. (2001). *Accelerating customer relationships: Using CRM and relationship technologies.* Upper Saddle River, NJ: Prentice Hall PTR.

Teitler, M. (1999). Alliances are not mergers: What problems should you expect? Nonprofit World , 17(2), 51–53.

Unhelkar, B. (2003a). Understanding the impact of cultural issues in global ebusiness alliances. In *Proceedings of 4th International We-B Conference 2003,* Perth, Western Australia. Retrieved from http://www.we-bcentre.com/web2003/

Unhelkar, B. (2003b, Jan-Feb). New beginnings: Case study on setting up Indian chemical engineering business in Australia. *Management Today.*

Younessi, H., & Smith, R. (1995). Utilization of a systematic business process re-engineering method as a tool to improve software process quality. *Software Quality Journal.*

Chapter 4

# Collaborative Business Process Engineering (CBPE) Model

*Our problems are man-made; therefore they may be solved by man. No problem of human destiny is beyond human beings.*

John F. Kennedy (1917–1963)

## CHAPTER KEY POINTS

- Introduces the *Collaborative Business Process Engineering (CBPE)* model as the core model for business collaboration.
- Discusses clusters versus collaborations as means for businesses to interact with each other using *CBPE*.
- Discusses the limitations and challenges in the way businesses currently collaborate.
- Discusses how *CBPE* helps multiple organizations to collaborate with each other irrespective of the knowledge of their physical whereabouts and their technological boundaries.

DOI: 10.4018/978-1-60566-689-1.ch004

# INTRODUCTION

This chapter describes the ***Collaborative Business Process Engineering (CBPE)*** model. This model is the core model for business collaboration and is the main contribution of this book to the literature on collaborative business. The descriptions of the technologies that facilitate ***CBPE*** were presented in earlier Chapter II. That discussion on the technologies as well as the underlying basis for collaborative environment discussed in the previous chapters is expanded here, together with the limitations of and expectations from the ***CBPE***. Most of the discussion undertaken in this chapter is based on examples; this is so because we believe that demonstrating the concepts of CBPE through the examples is best way to ensure the model gets applied in practice immediately. Furthermore, this chapter also discusses what we mean by a business cluster. This understanding of a business cluster also provides further clues to the challenges and limitations of the current as well as proposed collaborative environments. The identification and discussion of concepts and technologies such as Web Services (WS), Enterprise Application Integration (EAI), Service-oriented Architecture (SOA), Enterprise Service Bus (ESB), Mobile and Web 2.0 technologies also takes place in this chapter. This exploration of the aforementioned technologies, beyond what was mentioned in the earlier Chapter II, is undertaken here to enable us to utilize them in the collaborative business.

# DEVELOPMENT OF CBPE MODEL

The Collaborative Business Process Engineering (CBPE) model provides the basis for organizations to interact, innovate and integrate. The rapid evolution of the telecommunications industry has made it possible for businesses to collaborate electronically through their software applications and components. The development of an organization into a collaborative organization is based on the choice of a suitable website and applications, its document orientation, content and graphic design, budget and time constraints and the changing technology (based on Deshpande and Ginige, 2001). The capabilities of telecommunications, however, need to be further supported by appropriate processes that provide customers with effective product and service information.

The introduction of the World Wide Web opened the door of opportunities for many companies who were seeking to collaborate in a global environment. The Web made it easy for companies to expose products online. As companies strive to reduce expenditures by outsourcing jobs to locations beyond their boundaries, they also want to grow revenues by attracting international business. However, developing a process to deliver products in a timely fashion and ensure availability of items is the challenge.

This is where collaborative systems become important in the modern globalization scenarios. An effective and integrated IT solution will allow companies to ascertain and provide timely and accurate data on customer orders and/or demand that can be used by the collaborative system to plan and schedule the manufacture of goods or provision of services with minimal overruns or waste. However, there is concern about whether domestic and/or global sourcing can effectively manage CRM, SCM, and telecommunications. These concerns arise from the fact that, although technology has evolved, the question of whether it is possible to improve the process of globalization by merely improving functionality of the technology in the areas of many business systems such as CRM and SCM. We review these technology components and also discuss the underlying information and communications technologies that enable these systems to work. This is so because implementation of a correct telecommunications solution is a key element in successfully managing and meeting customer demand. A brief review of telecom technology and strategies help us understand the role they play in collaborative business processes and meeting customer expectations. The various drivers of the collaborative system can be categorized into business and technologies – as discussed below.

## Business Drivers

- **Globalization Climate:** Globalization has caused businesses to compete and distribute their products and services in different countries. In order to collaborate with international customers and partners, an integrated collaborative process is important in order for businesses to respond faster to market conditions.

- **Demanding Customers and Suppliers:** Due to the overflow of information and lower switching cost for products and services, customers require businesses to be faster, more reliable, and to provide better service. Second, suppliers require you to collaborate closely with them in providing customized product and services to customers.

- **Merger and Acquisition:** Merger activities triggered integration of best practices and processes in both companies' collaboration to eliminate process bottlenecks.

- **Increase in Operation Cost and Limited Working Capital:** Nowadays, working capital is scarce, and shareholders are often cautious with their investments; they talk about ROI (Return of Investment). As a result, businesses need to reduce their operating costs and fight for capital. For example, reducing inventories and WIP stocks are important for manufacturers and retailers.

- **Explosive Growth:** The expansion in your company requires management to integrate the collaborative processes in order to eliminate repetition of work and wastage in production in order to cope with the customer's demand.

## Technology Drivers

- **Explore New Technology Opportunities:** Businesses want to look into the opportunities of harnessing new technology, such as the Internet, Web services, e-business and e-collaboration in order to improve their collaborative models as well as processes.
- **Applications and Software Replacement:** This is another technology driver whereby a company's current business application does not deliver the required collaboration.

Collaboration enables businesses to communicate with each other in order to provide better services and products and improve management of the business itself. This is so because, through collaboration, businesses are able to share resources efficiently and effectively. However, Unhelkar (2003) has argued that when such collaborations are numerous and are not guided by underlying business principles, they tend to waste resources. This wastage of resources occurs as the collaboration between numerous potential customers, business partners and service-providers remains only at superficial level and may not get converted into real business. There is a need to forge collaborations that result in real business. There is also an equally important need to study these collaborations and clusters, and understand how technologies foster their formation.

## Business Clusters and Collaborations

Organizations trying to collaborate with each other tend to perform frequent transactions with each other. A logical classification or grouping of businesses that need to deal with each other on a more frequent basis than others leads to formation of groups of clusters of businesses. A "cluster" can be understood as an electronic segment of a group of organizations with some identifiable commonality. A "cluster" is usually a geographically proximate group of interconnected companies and associated institutions in a particular field, linked by commonalities, complementariness and perhaps eases of communication. The transactions between clusters of businesses are frequently conducted electronically. These electronic transactions are based on connections that use the information and communications technologies. Following are some well-known descriptions of the term "cluster":

- An industrial cluster is a set of industry sectors related through buyer–supplier relationships, or by common technologies, common buyers or distribution channels, or common labor pools (Porter, 1990).
- A regional cluster is an industrial cluster in which member firms are in close geographical proximity to each other. A more inclusive definition would be: regional clusters are geographic agglomerations of firms in the same or closely related industries (Enright, 1992, 1993).
- A concentration of firms involved in interdependent production process, often in the same industry or industry segment (Sforzi, 1992).
- A business segment consisting of several firms that have ongoing communication and interaction (Staber, 1996).
- Clusters are a group of businesses that are collaborating electronically, but which are grouped with an underlying logic or business purpose. (Unhelkar, 2003).

Understanding these electronic clusters and collaborations is an important factor for building a model of electronic collaboration.

## Limitation of Current Collaborative Environment

The above descriptions and definitions of clusters indicate that, in an existing environment of collaboration, a cluster as an electronic segment can only collaborate:

- *With parties that are using common technology:* This means that prior to the collaboration, organizations need to decide on the technologies that will be used in the collaboration. These technologies need to be common between the organizations.
- *With a common customer:* This means that the customer is already known to the organization. The fact that the customer is known, and so are the technologies, indicate that these clusters need to be set up "beforehand". The setting-up of electronic collaborations amongst businesses beforehand tends to indicate that these collaborations are static.
- *With using the common channels:* Channels are lines of communication that are used to connect the organizations. These channels could be in a mobile (or wireless) environment or the landline. In the current collaborative environment these channels are set in the same frequency (if mobile or wireless) and same path as that of a landline. These channels are preset for the known *static collaboration.*
- *With the known geographical proximity:* The current collaborative environment supports enterprises as long as their collaborative chain has already

been created. This chain depends on the "homogeneity" of the business environment, usually provided by a similar geographical region.

- *With related industries:* This means that the current collaborative environment is able to support transactions within industries that are related to each other. Collaborations between vastly different industries may not be supported by the current collaborative environment.
- *With organizations that have ongoing communication and interaction:* This means that the current collaborative environment is supporting the collaboration amongst the organizations that already have existing electronic transactions happening amongst them.
- *With similar legal framework:* Current collaboration requires legal commonality that enables conducting collaborative transactions with legal support especially if multiple geographical locations are involved.

## Expectations of the Modern-day Collaborative Environment

The expectations of the collaborative environment by the business world, and the technologies capable of delivering them, are discussed in the previous section in order to determine the need for the advent of the dynamic modern-day collaborative environment. These expectations of a dynamic modern-day collaborative environment can be summed up as follows:

- Collaboration is expected to happen between parties that may be using different technology. This implies that the organizations are using different platforms, operating systems, databases and related technologies.
- Collaboration is expected to happen when dealing with any customer, even when the customer is not known to the organization. The collaboration with unknown customer and organizations can be understood as a dynamic collaborative environment, since there is no need for prior set-up of transactions.
- Collaboration is expected to happen on various channels. There is no opportunity for prior setup of the channels in collaborating dynamically. The collaboration can occur at any time, even when organizations manage to locate and consume each other's services.
- Collaboration is expected to happen when the organizations are in far-spread and dispersed geographical regions. This means that the organizations are able to locate each other irrespective of the geographical boundaries or proximities.
- Collaboration is expected to happen amongst the organizations from any industries. This means a collaboration supporting multiple transactions, across multiple organizations in various industries, can occur by submission of a single application.

- Collaboration is expected to happen amongst the organizations that do not have an ongoing, pre-determined communication and interaction. This means that there is no prior contract and agreement. These organizations are not necessarily known to each other. They can get through on a collaborative platform to satisfy a need, or application, and disperse on the completion of that need.
- Collaboration is expected to happen amongst the organizations in different geo-political environments with varying legal frameworks.

The above section provides the expectations of collaboration in an environment when organizations are not necessarily known to each other. This book has identified these expectations as remaining unsatisfied through the formation of current clusters. This dissatisfaction was demonstrated in later sections of Chapter 1, wherein it was shown how the current environment does not support dynamic collaboration amongst multiple organizations. This is so because, while the existing collaboration model enables the customers to submit multiple applications to the various clusters, these are individual submissions by customers and business partners as they reach various organizations and their clusters for their specific products or services. Such individual pre-determined electronic submission does not capitalize on the full potential of the collaborative environment possible on the Internet. As against that submission of multiple applications, in the expected collaborative environment, the customer/client receives the desired services/products from multiple organizations by submitting only a *single* application that reaches these different organizations and the desired clusters.

This discussion thus far has highlighted various characteristics of a collaborative environment. The existing model of collaboration and the expected model of collaboration are now discussed with an example from the hospital domain.

## Example of Current Collaborative Environment

As discussed in Chapter I, Business-to-Business (B2B) can be understood as an existing collaborative environment. The limitations of this existing collaborative environment are demonstrated in Figure 1, which reviews an existing model of collaboration in more detail with an example from the real world. Figure 4.1 provides the pictorial illustration of the existing collaborative environment with a hospital application.

Figure 1 depicts an example considering a major disaster scenario wherein a Chief Medical Officer (CMO) of a Government hospital is in urgent need of 50 doctors and 300 nurses in the next 12 hours. Currently, this CMO must either make phone calls or send faxes to all the available hospitals to see whether they can satisfy this

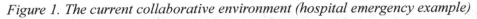

*Figure 1. The current collaborative environment (hospital emergency example)*

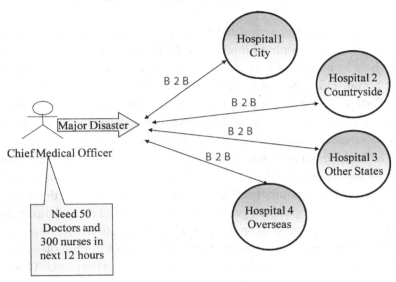

requirement. Alternatively, as shown in Figure 1, this request can also be submitted electronically, wherein the CMO will require multiple applications forwarded by him/her through the existing B2B connections to the various service-providers. Submission of such multiple applications can become very time-consuming. The connections between businesses must be "pre-fabricated". Furthermore, these requests may not reach the hospitals capable of providing the personnel at the right time if the connectivity is not correctly established. Thus, the CMO may have to contact each individual hospital manually, again and again, in order to find the availability of suitable required personnel.

The CMO of the Government hospital may have set up alliances or agreements amongst the various hospitals (for example, Hospital 1, Hospital 2 and Hospital n) beforehand. Such a B2B relationship can ease some of the pressure of contacting the hospitals manually. As mentioned before, this is, indeed, collaboration at a base "pre-determined" level. It should also be noted that all these hospitals need to be known to the CMO "beforehand" to help each other in major disasters.

The CMO might have already decided on the existing facilities and technologies, such as phone, e-mail and fax as contact mechanisms. They may even have a dedicated phone that can only be used in emergency situations such as major disasters. The CMO might have already calculated the time of transporting the personnel to the hospital in need of help. Thus, while there is collaboration amongst various hospitals in this scenario, it is all pre-determined, and worked out beforehand. These characteristics of static collaboration have been discussed in section 4.2.2 of this chapter.

## Example of Expected Collaborative Environment

Figure 2 demonstrates what is expected from a new collaborative environment. This example, based on the proposed model of *CBPE*, simplifies the whole process of calling for help by assigning a single message to a collaboration that is set up on an electronic portal. This set-up simplifies the channels of collaborations.

Figure 2 show that in the proposed environment the Chief Medical Officer submits only one request to the portal. The portal contacts all the hospitals, submits the application, creates the list of all the required doctors and nurses, their hospital resources and all the required information, and then forwards it to the Chief Medical Officer. Creation and use of a portal itself is not new, and has happened in the past. However, what is genuinely expected of this collaboration is that any number of hospitals from any region can get together to satisfy the need. Thus, there is an element of dynamicity that is happening in this collaboration. The important issue to note here is that Hospitals 1 and 4 might not be known to each other. However, the collaboration still takes place because they are known to the portal. This "knowledge" of the portal is not "pre-determined".

In the expected collaborative environment the hospitals should be able to interconnect through the CBPE-based portal, even though they may be using different technologies and may not have had prior contract for the collaboration. The CMO

*Figure 2. The simplified CBPE-based business process (hospital emergency example)*

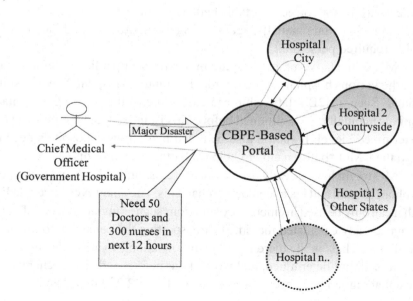

who is demanding the help is no longer restricted to "known" hospitals. Any number of hospitals that are capable of providing services and that can offer their services on the portal are in this collaboration. Collaboration takes place through the **CBPE**-based portal in a dynamic manner for a particular application or need.

The **CBPE**-based portal is responsible for identifying the most suitable channel for the collaboration. This collaboration may be via land-line or mobile channel. Mobility can enable this collaboration to take place anywhere and at any time.

This collaboration amongst the organizations that do not have ongoing, pre-determined communication and interaction can be understood as *dynamic collaboration*. This dynamic collaboration requires a formal model that would encompass wide-ranging issues from the core technologies that facilitate such collaboration through to social issues of trust and legal compliance.

## INFLUENCE OF WEB SERVICES ON DYNAMIC COLLABORATIVE ENVIRONMENT

As discussed, the core technology that facilitates dynamic collaboration is that described in Chapter II, Web Services (WS). WS, through the underlying XML, have changed the Enterprise Architecture (EA) and the business landscape. Web Services have been continually refined and, now, they play an integral part in bringing together various aspects of an enterprise's information systems. Formal incorporation of WS is accomplished through what is known as Service-oriented Architecture (SOA). Whenever we use SOA to amalgamate and integrate information systems in an enterprise, it leads to what we understand as Enterprise Architecture.

The Web Services operations are based on exchanging messages using the Internet communication protocols such as Hyper Text Transfer Protocol (HTTP). Extensible Markup Language (XML) is used for representing data that are exchanged among services in each operation. Web Services are often described as a component-based distributed architecture in which one application calls upon the services of another to perform a particular function. According to Gurguis and Zeid (2005), IBM considers the following standards as the base technologies for developing Web Services:

- *Simple Object Access Protocol (SOAP):* Implements the bind and use operation by containing an *Extensible Markup Language (XML)* message in a standardized envelope.
- *Web Services Definition Language (WSDL):* Implements the publish operation by defining abstracts interfaces and bindings.

- *Universal Description Discovery and Integration (UDDI):* Implements the find operation by providing a public registry that is accessed or queried for either searching or publishing.

Web Services become a simple SOA where applications are offered as services both within and across the enterprises (Curbera, 2003) with lower development costs (Huang and Chung, 2003; Chen et al., 2003; Maruyama, 2002). Web Services standards allow interfacing, publishing and binding of loosely coupled services available on the Web.

Web Services can easily live with distributed object computing middleware such as Common Object Request Broker Architecture (CORBA), Distributed Component Object Model (DCOM) and Enterprise Java Bean (EJB) technologies. Web Services technology is becoming the most attractive technology for interoperation. However, WS is still not mature enough, due to methodological factors, and its full potential is yet to be realized.

This book subsequently proposes a new dynamically collaborative environment. This proposed collaborative environment enables multiple organizations to collaborate with each other in order to serve a customer's electronic application. Figure 3 shows the functionality of the WS technology and the significance of this technology in the proposed collaborative environment.

Figure 3 depicts how the business application A1 submits an XML application. WSDL, on the left-hand side, defines the application and the UDDI publishes the application. On the left-hand side, the UDDI of the organization is capable of handling the submission of the application or service. The business application B1 has to locate the application. After location, the WSDL (on the right-hand side) consumes the application. This publishing and consumption of the required service happens in a global environment.

The portal presented in Figure 4 is equipped with all the explained technologies such as Web Services, Enterprise Application Integration, Service Oriented Architecture, Enterprise Service Bus (ESB) and also has the capability of connecting to mobile devices using Mobile Web Services.

In Figure 4, the proposed portal is equipped with the Web Services technology enabling the organizations A1...A5 to interact with each other through the proposed portal. In this portal multiple, organizations within the same industry are registered. When an organization is unable to fulfill the requirements of the specific application, the portal will forward the remaining part of the request to other organizations capable of handling the request until it is fulfilled. The Web Services technology (XML, WSDL and the UDDI) facilitates this new collaborative environment. However, the problem could be more complicated when an application requires multiple services from different industries.

*Figure 3. The Web services technology Source: Unhelkar (2003)*

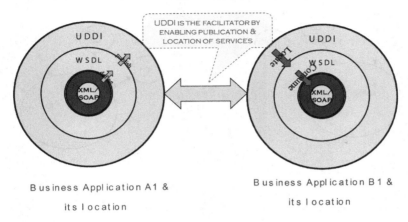

The proposed portal should have the capabilities of contacting multiple industries and connecting to multiple organizations. Figure 5 presents this increasing complex model, which is based on separate industries. The letter A could be a representation of the airline industry, while the letter B could be representative of the hotel industry.

Figure 5 demonstrates how the organizations within the same industry are interconnected, while different industries are not in collaboration with each other. Therefore, a mechanism is required to create the interconnection of these organizations in various industries. The next section presents the comprehensive model wherein the organizations from various industries are collaborating with each other.

*Figure 4. The portal equipped with WS for CBPE*

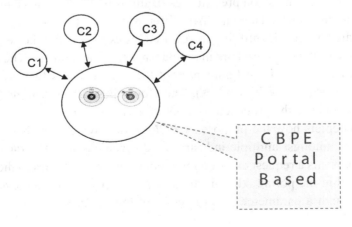

*Figure 5. The complex model of collaboration (different industries involved)*

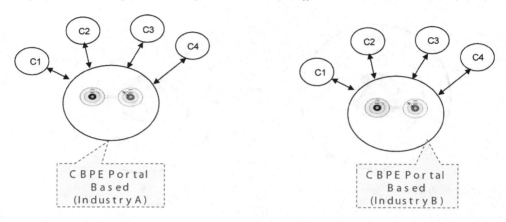

## INITIAL CBPE MODEL (TWO INDUSTRIES)

Having discussed, with specific examples, the limitations of and expectations from collaborations, now, the comprehensive model of *Collaborative Business Process Engineering (CBPE)* is described. Figure 6 presents this Collaborative Business Process Engineering model. Initially, the two industries shown in Figure 5 are used to demonstrate how these different industries interconnect to each other in the proposed *CBPE* model. This description is followed by the practical model of multiple unknown industries in the *CBPE* model.

The *CBPE* model, shown in Figure 6 is made up of two levels of portals. Both portal-levels are made up of corresponding "Directory Level 1" and "Directory Level 2".

The portal in level 1 is responsible for the collaboration between the industries, and the portal in level 2 is responsible for the collaboration of the organizations. The ovals named A1, A2 and so on present organizations while the ovals named IA and IB present the industries. There are two different levels of portals. The first-level one acts as an "engine" identifying the desired industries, while the second portal is the database of the registered organizations in a specific industry. The dark ovals on the right-hand side of the figure present the organizations that are not using interoperable systems (Web Services). Therefore, these organizations are unable to participate and use the proposed collaborative environment.

Figure 6 depicts how the proposed *CBPE* model creates the channels for the collaborations amongst multiple industries and organizations. The dashed line in the picture presents a request entering the model. The request goes to the directory of level 1 within the portal. All industries can be registered in the level 1 UDDI directory through a parameter. The directory at level 1 processes the request by

*Figure 6. The CBPE model with two industries*

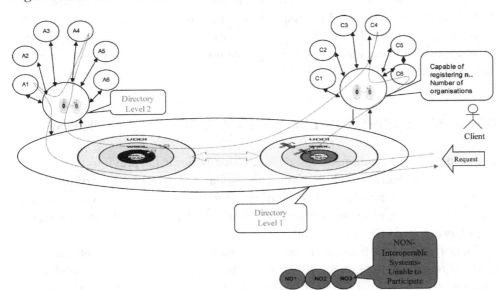

identifying the industries involved. The system then sends the request to directory level 2 portal in order to find the organization capable of handling the request, and submits the application.

The aforementioned proposed model has the capability of sending the application (request) to multiple organizations either in the same or different industries, until the overall process of fulfilling the request is completed. The response is then submitted back to the level 1 portal which informs the client of the final result. This model is also capable of performing another transaction by submitting the application back to level 1 to find the related industry for further processing at level 2. Alternatively, the process of submitting requests for various "sub-requirements" can continue through multiple industries until "cross-industry" applications have been fulfilled.

This arrangement in *CBPE* two-level portals helps in classifying the organizations as well as their relative industries. Such classification simplifies the publication and location of the submitted application.

Figure 6 also illustrates how the organizations that do not adapt to Web Services remain outside the model, unable to use or register in the system (dark-shaded organizations) that is based on the model. However, an organization or a client wanting to use the proposed system, but not registered, will still be able to use the system as long as it is using the Web Services (light-shaded organizations). Thus, the requirement of the *CBPE* model is not the need to "pre-register" but the need to be able to publish and consume services by using the WS technologies.

The application returns back to the client after the completion of the request, informing the finalization of the request by supplying all the related booking and transactions numbers. The dashed line in Figure 6 shows these dynamically created channels of collaborations across the organization and shows how the participants can collaborate without "pre-fabrication".

## COMPREHENSIVE CBPE MODEL (MULTIPLE INDUSTRIES)

The model of collaboration, discussed for two industries in the previous section, can be expanded to include multiple industries and an unknown number of organizations. Figure 7 presents this full model of the proposed collaboration when multiple industries and organizations are involved in the *Collaborative Business Process Engineering (CBPE)* environment.

The organizations that are using WS technology have the capability of sending their request to the system. A sample of these organizations is presented in the bottom-left-hand side of Figure 7. Please note that these organizations need not be registered in order to submit a request. However, the organizations that are not us-

*Figure 7. The complex model (multiple industries and organizations)*

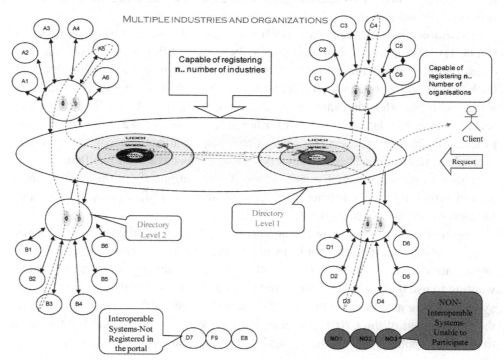

ing the interoperable system are not able to submit a request, receive a request or generally participate in the proposed model. These organizations are presented by the shaded circle in the bottom-right-hand side of Figure 7.

The UDDI directory in level 1 locates the required industry and processes the request through an engine. This *CBPE* engine then forwards the request to the relevant UDDI level 2 directories. The UDDI directory in level 2 then forwards the request to the relevant organizations. Various organizations are approached, one after the other, until the overall request by the customer has been fulfilled.

The level 1 and level 2 UDDI directories have the capability of registering numerous industries and organization. The implementation of the presented model is presented later in section 4.6 of this chapter.

Figure 7 (similar to Figure 6) is capable of handling the request when multiple industries and organizations are involved in the process of collaboration. The literature review in the Chapter II of this book discussed how, currently, there is no comprehensive model of collaboration in place. This study builds and describes a *Collaborative Business Process Engineering (CBPE)* model that is able to handle the complete collaborative model.

The *CBPE* model has the potential for practical application. This chapter also shows the practical or realistic aspects of the theoretical *CBPE* model. However, the technology has been a major cause in creating a dynamically collaborating electronic environment. Without the understanding of these technologies, it is not possible to create the *CBPE* model. Therefore, it is important to discuss the technologies separately, in the context of the *CBPE*. The next section discusses these various technologies and their influence on *CBPE*.

## The Strategic Application of the CBPE Model

The detailed planning and execution of a business collaboration initiative is not always simple, as there is a staggering amount of detail resulting from bringing numerous business processes together with many knowledgeable people to develop a successful outcome for an organization. However, at the strategic level, it can be made simple. In fact, at the strategic level, business collaboration is the process of ensuring that all critical business processes are available to meet the business needs under all agreed scenarios. The important factor is that an organization must be able to identify and to agree on what its critical business processes are. The best approach to understand this is determined through business impact analysis. Business impact analysis is a process to identify the impact of a concept, technology, method or decision (e.g. to go collaborative) on the core business processes of the organization. The key point is that the definition of critical business processes will differ from one organization to another, and it is reached through consensus of senior management. The followings demonstrate the strategic level of the analysis of the *CBPE* model.

- **Current Collaborative Situation:** Most organizations have some level of business collaboration. After all, their internal departments and staff are collaborating in the daily issues of keeping the business going. Identifying and documenting the collaborative capability is the first step.
- **Business Impact Analysis:** This is a standard consulting engagement that investigates and identifies critical business processes and the nature of their interconnections. The management needs to evaluate the impact of the collaboration on these critical business processes. For example, when a business offers a critical service that will now require sourcing of information from collaborating businesses, it becomes necessary to conduct a study of the impacts of collaboration on that critical service.
- **Risk Assessment:** This identifies the risks that may impact the organization, their severity, likelihood, and the ways in which thoses risks resulting from collaborations can be reduced.
- **Define Strategy:** Using the data collected during the first three steps, senior management then can determine the level of protection desired, the probable causes of an impact, and the resources they are willing to commit.
- **Define Solution:** Senior management can pass on its strategic requirements, together with the implementation and operational budget plans, to departments.
- **Select or Build Solution:** An organization can choose to build its own business solutions for collaboration, outsource, or use a mixture of both.
- **Document, Plan and Test:** A range of documentation needs to be prepared as part of the overall solution for collaboration. First, the description of the objectives, together with how these objectives will be achieved. Second, documentation for users needs to be made available. Great care needs to be taken to ensure that it is appropriately used in a collaborative environment. This means that it must be brief and straightforward. Finally, the plan must be tested on a regular basis, at least annually and more regularly, if the organization is undergoing change. There might be many general reasons why organizations do not wish to enter a collaborative environment. They include:
- Pressure to undertake other organization's work.
- Inability to see a return on investment.
- No obvious owner for the responsibility in the organization.

Some organizations delegate the task of implementing a business collaboration plan to the IT function. However, while this approach protects IT functionality, it isolates other critical business processes by leaving them vulnerable and unprotected. This is due to the fact that most organizations consider the cost rather than the long-term benefits of implementing a business collaboration plan. The challenge is to define the beginning and the end of the collaboration in the streamline of the business processes of the organization.

## DYNAMIC VS. STATIC COLLABORATION

Organizations are employing communication technologies to reach their business partners and customers. Currently, this trading is based on the emerging mobile communication technologies. The phenomenal growth of WS and Mobile Technology (MT) has created a new culture in the business world. The new technology of Mobile Web Services (MWS) has capabilities of text, voice and videoconferencing using wireless devices, as well as the ability to connect to the World Wide Web. Therefore, understanding Mobile Technologies, and the process of transitioning an organization to a mobile organization, is crucial to the success of business.

Pashtan (2005) indicates that Web Services can replace less flexible methods for information exchange. Pashtan (2005) also states that with Web Services multiple WSDL interface can be defined for accessing a service and multiple clients can make use of the provided access methods.

The application of WS has provided the opportunity to implement business processes that cross inter-organizational boundaries and that go beyond the simple exchange of information. Web Services deliver additional value to application integration, including a standard application for publishing and subscribing to software services, both local and remote. XML provides a common data-exchange format, encapsulating both data and metadata (Linthicum, 2004). The application and the use of mobile and Internet technologies require that people are organized into various common-interest groups. These groups are mentioned by Conners and Conners (2004) as varying from harmless fun groups (such as school sports groups) to serious military or political operations.

The expansion of MT also provides a robust basis for the organization's desire to reach wide customer and corporate bases. With the aid of mobile and Web Services technologies (MWS), the proposed application, demonstrated in Figure 8, will give the opportunity for multiple organizations to communicate with each other in single transactions or multiple transactions. As shown in Figure 8, the hospital, pathology, pharmacy or other related enterprises can collaborate and communicate with each other across organizational boundaries, to satisfy patient needs. The collaborating m-enabled WS have made it possible for service-providers to benefit all people involved in the process.

Figure 8 demonstrates how the business processes of multiple organizations could collaborate in a health-domain example.

Technically, with the aid of WS technology (especially XML) applications talk to each other irrespective of the differences in their operating platforms. The WSDL is an XML-based description of the services that are being offered. The WSDL defines services as collections of network endpoints, or ports. The Universal Description Discovery and Integration (UDDI) is a platform-independent, XML-based registry for businesses worldwide to list the services on the Internet. The ensuing use of the WS technologies in the model described as follows:

*Firstly,* the use of mobile devices enables physicians to monitor their patient's heart beat on their mobile devices, conduct a conference call, prescribe medications and have faster access to the patient's records.

*Secondly,* nurses will also have immediate access to the patient's records and the nurse is able to transmit it to the relevant area, enable a conference call with physicians on the move and check the patient's schedule on the move.

*Thirdly,* patients will benefit by having remote check-up devices enabling physicians to check on them faster, diagnose the sickness and prescribe medicine through their mobile gadget to the patient and relevant pharmacy.

*Fourthly,* faster receiving or ordering processes will be possible between hospital and suppliers, along with faster access to the recorded databases (hospital and

*Figure 8. Ccollaborative business processes (this example, hospital, pathology and pharmacy)*

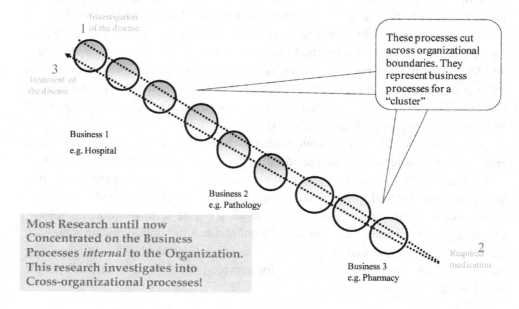

pharmacy's inventory) and more efficient access to the medicine available in the nearest pharmacy. These are the advantages of the constructed model that connects the hospital, pharmacy, pathology and other related organizations together.

These organizations that are brought together by this model could use entirely different platforms and frameworks. MT has its own characteristics and limitations that should be clearly identifiable to business enterprises when it comes to collaboration. Access to the wireless mobile Internet is not just an extension of the Internet into the mobile environment that would give the user access to the Internet while on the move. This access is about integrating the Internet and telecommunications technologies into a single system that covers the communication needs of all people. The current network architectures used in either the wired Internet or cellular networks would not be appropriate and efficient for the future wireless mobile Internet, even if we assume that the cellular network will provide the major infrastructure of the mobile Internet (Jamalipour, 2003).

The described advantages of Web Services have opened up opportunities for organizations to revolutionise their business processes. WS make software functionality available over the Internet so that programs can request a service running on another server (a Web Service) and use that program's response in a website, Wireless Application Protocol (WAP) services, or other applications. The possibilities are endless (Unhelkar et al., 2005). However, the organizational success depends upon their channels of communications.

## ACTION POINTS

1.  Identify the potential for collaboration for your organization by listing the potential partnering organizations that can help you deliver improved service to your customer
2.  List the clusters to which your organization can belong to – by listing the products and services offered by your organization together with the offerings of other organizations in similar cluster.
3.  Identify the current limitations and challenges that you face when you try to collaborate with other organizations.
4.  Identify the areas for strategic application of the CBPE model to your collaborative environment from the business point of view.
5.  Identify the benefits of performing the *CBPE* model in details for your organization and underline the collaborative cluster of the your organization that are capable to enter the *CBPE* environment.

# REFERENCES

Cabrera, L. F., & Kurt, C. (2005). *Web services architecture and its specifications: Essential for understanding WS.* Redmond, CA: Microsoft Press Corporation.

Chen, M., A. K. Chen, and B. B. M. Shao (2003). Implications and impacts of Web services to EC research and practice. Journal of Electronic Commerce Research , 4(4), 128–139.

Conners, J., & Conners, S. (2004). The impact of mobile technology on business planning. In *Proceedings of the IRMA 2004*, New Orleans.

Curbera, F., R. Khalaf, N. Mukhi, S. Tai, and S. Weerawarana (2003). The next step in Web services. Communications of the ACM , 46(10). doi:10.1145/944217.944234

Enright, M. J. (1992). Why local clusters are the way to win the game. *World Link, 5*, 24–25.

Enright, M. J. (1993). The geographical scope of competitive advantage. In E. Driven, J. Groenewegen, & S. Van Hoof (Eds.), *Stuck in the region?: Changing scales of regional identity* (pp. 87-102). Utrecht, The Netherlands: Netherlands Geographical Studies.

Ghanbary, A. (2006). Evaluation of mobile technologies in the context of their application, limitation & transformation. In B.Unhelkar (Ed.), *Handbook of research in mobile business*. Hershey, PA: Idea Group Publishing.

Ghanbary, A. (2006). Collaborative business process engineering across multiple organisations. In *Proceedings of the ACIS Conference, ACIS 2006*, Adelaide, Australia.

Ghanbary, A., & Arunatileka, D. (2006). Enhancing customer relationship management through mobile personnel knowledge management (MPKM). In *Proceedings of the IBIMA International Conference*, Bonn, Germany.

Ghanbary, A., & Unhelkar, B. (2007). Collaborative business process engineering (CBPE) across multiple organisations in a cluster. In *Proceedings of the IRMA Conference, IRMA 2007*, Vancouver, Canada.

Ghanbary, A., & Unhelkar, B. (2007). Technical & logical issues arising from collaboration across multiple organisations. In *Proceedings of the IRMA Conference, IRMA 2007*, Vancouver, Canada.

Gurguis, S. A., & Zeid, A. (2005). Towards autonomic Web services: Achieving self-healing using Web services. *ACM SIGSOFT Software Engineering Notes, 30*(4).

Huang, Y., and J. Y. Chung (2003). Web services-based framework for business integration solutions. *Journal of Electronic Commerce Research and Applications, 2*(1), 15–26. doi:10.1016/S1567-4223(03)00007-3

Jamalipour, A. (2003). *Wireless mobile Internet: Architectures, protocols and services.* Hobokon, NJ: J. Willey.

Linthicum, D. S. (2004). *Next generation application integration. From simple information to Web services.* Upper Saddle River, NJ: Pearson Education Incorporations.

Maruyama, H. (2002). New trends in e-business: From B2B to Web services. New Generations Computing , 20, 125–139. doi:10.1007/BF03037262

Pashtan, A. (2005). *Mobile Web services.* Cambridge, UK: Cambridge University Press.

Porter, M. E. (1990). *The competitive advantage of nations.* New York: The Free Press.

Sforzi, F. (1992). The quantitative importance of Marshallian industrial districts in the Italian economy. In F. Pyke, G. Becattini, & W. Sengenberger (Eds.), *Industrial districts and inter-firm co-operation in Italy* (pp. 75-107). Geneva, Switzerland: International Institute for Labour Studies.

Staber, U. (1996). Networks and regional development: Perspectives and unresolved issues. In U. Staber, N. Schaefer, & B. Sharma (Eds.), *Business networks: Prospects for regional development* (pp. 1-23). Berlin, Germany: Walter de Gruyter.

Unhelkar, B. (2003). Understanding collaborations and clusters in the e-business world. In *Proceedings of the We-B Conference,* Perth, Australia.

Unhelkar, B. (2005). An initial three dimensional framework for mobile enterprise transitions. *Cutter IT Journal, 18*(8).

Unhelkar, B. (2005). Transitioning to a mobile enterprise: A three-dimensional framework. Cutter IT Journal , 18(8), 5–11.

Unhelkar, B. (2005). *Practical object oriented analysis.* Australia: Thomson Social Science Press.

Unhelkar, B. (2007). Beyond business integration – management challenges in collaborative business processes. *ICFAI Journal.*

Unhelkar, B., and Y. Deshpande (2004). Evolving from Web engineering to Web services: A comparative study in the context of business utilization of the Internet. In [*th International Conference on Advanced Computing & Communications,* Ahmedabad, India.]. Proceedings of the ADCOM , 2004, 12.

Unhelkar, B., & Saddik, R. (2004). Web services extending BPR to industrial process reengineering. In *Proceedings of the Information Resource Management Association, International Conference*, San Diego, CA.

# Chapter 5
# Advanced Technologies and Architecture for Collaborative Business

*Nothing in life is to be feared. It is only to be understood.*

Marie Curie (1867-1934)

## CHAPTER KEY POINTS

- Discusses the technologies and information architectures that facilitate the collaborative business environment.
- Focuses on the concept of Service Oriented Architecture (SOA) and Web 2.0 technologies; and their role in bringing about a collaborative business environment.
- Evaluates the organizational restructures resulting from the use of SOA as a part of the Collaborate Business Process Engineering (CBPE) model.
- Reviews the impact of The Open Group Architecture Framework or TOGAF as a reference architecture in the context of *CBPE*.
- Discusses the influence of Enterprise Service Bus on the *CBPE* model.
- Extends the discussion on Mobile and Web 2.0 technologies from an architectural viewpoint on *CBPE*.

DOI: 10.4018/978-1-60566-689-1.ch005

## INTRODUCTION

This chapter discusses the role of information system architectures in *Collaborate Business Process Engineering (CBPE)*. Thus, in this chapter, there is an extension of the discussion on Service-oriented Architecture (SOA) from chapters 2 and 4, and its importance and relevance to *CBPE*. The SOA based architecture is extended and applied in a collaborative business environment. The technical platform of Service Oriented Architecture (SOA) provides an ideal mechanism to start building collaborative business processes, as it facilitates technical collaboration of different environments - as discussed in this chapter.

## TECHNOLOGIES FOR COLLABORATION

Web Services (WS) is discussed in the previous chapter as a core technology that enables collaboration amongst multiple business applications. Service Oriented Architecture (SOA) utilizes Web Services (WS) to provide the basis for information systems architecture that assimilates software components that belong to different organizations, governmental bodies and technical environments. As a result, information system architectures that incorporate WS-based applications facilitate global collaboration that can be dynamically created, consumed and dispersed. Technical communication through Web Services includes exchange of core data types, message formats and communication protocols – regardless of the specific platform or vendor specifications. This enhanced ability of information systems to connect and communicate with each other has lead to an important business question: "why restrict it within the organization?" The answer to this question opens up the doors for creation of collaborative software entities through application service-providers that open entirely new revenue generation streams for global industries and provide potentially unlimited global growth for organizations. These technologies also form the basis for a comprehensive architecture for the enterprise that includes the software systems, business processes, communications and people: the Enterprise Architecture (EA). The technologies discussed here are thus the fundamental technologies creating undertaking business transformations

## SERVICE ORIENTED ARCHITECTURE AND CBPE

Services are self-contained (and usually object-oriented) software components that have well defined interfaces. Information systems based on the concept of offering and consuming of services are considered service-oriented in nature. Therefore, a software architecture that comprises many self-contained services and which process data and information through the interfaces of these services is know as service oriented architecture (SOA). While SOA enables most software applications to easily offer and publish, as well as locate and consume services, this ability of SOA also has its effect on the way an entire enterprise is organized – leading to an understanding of service oriented enterprise (SOE).

The SOA approach breaks down large software applications and systems into sets and sub-sets of smaller, manageable components called services. These services then provide the building blocks of many different kinds of business applications and business processes. According to Hazra (2007), incorporating SOA in the organization's IT governance framework provides a systematic way to use services in customer-centric processes, enabling them to search for, discover and locate desired services in a consistent manner from the business.

Software components that are services lend themselves to reuse and integration in many different ways. The characteristics of these services with respect to a collaborative business model are:

a.  Self-contained so that they are able to process data and information within themselves
b.  Having a well-defined interface with the intention that inputs to and outputs from these services can be easily understood, and
c.  Available for communication – that is they are Internet enabled.

Services treat data and information as important inputs. These data and information are then processed and are available to other services that are calling them. The SOA concept has evolved from earlier component-based software development approaches – now with the extension of the ability of these components to communicate across different platforms and operational environments. The ability of executable services being made available across communication channels further promotes the idea of writing the code once and then using it everywhere else. Apart from the ability to communicate and thus enhance collaboration, this services-based approach also results in overall less software code, lower cost of developing and deploying software solutions and increased standardization. Architecting software systems based on services not only results in collaboration between many applications and components, but also helps source and share contents with a broad audience. As per Philipson (2007), the SOA approach together with the use of Web as more than mere communication tool (i.e. Web 2.0) creates ecosystems for communicating, connecting, collaborating and creatively expressing ideas and information in new and revolutionary ways.

SOA provides the platform for services or software components that are then tied together by a set of protocols, open standards and agreements for cooperation resulting in complete software systems. SOA thus provides the philosophy of encapsulating application logic in services with a uniformly defined set of interfaces and making these interfaces publicly available via a discovery mechanism. Thus, SOA can be considered as a technology for reusing components and utilizing existing software and data in order to create applications that would support the collaboration and coupling of remote resources. SOA applications through their ability to couple distant and varied resources are creative cause for even structural changes to the organizations (discussed later in Chapter VII).

The principles of SOA-based software designs are meant to provide robust basis for the collaborative business process engineering (*CBPE)* model. While using the techniques and design principles of SOA, *CBPE* goes beyond the dedicated B2B interactions and, instead, aims to create a collaborative environment where "any number of businesses, known or unknown to each other" can come online and transact electronically. Thus, *CBPE* is able to create dynamic services online and provide for their interaction (location and consumption) through one or more web portals. This creation of a web portal brings together and integrates web users and their various applications from the many different channels (such as Internet and mobile channels) on a loosely controlled platform. Such platform then forms the basis for the discovering, mashing and tagging of diverse resources on a ongoing basis that bring about efficient and effective cross-organizational collaboration. *CBPE* facilitates businesses to first come and "search" for the kind of services they want to consume. Furthermore, *CBPE* also encompasses the ability of businesses to promote themselves by "publishing" their services. Eventually, when a cluster of businesses get together and "dynamically" start publishing and consuming, and in fact create a business process "on the fly", based on what various types and sizes of businesses are offering, we have *CBPE.*

## Web 2.0 and CBPE

Tim O'Reilly, an activist for Internet standards and open-source software, has been promoting Web 2.0 (O'Reilly, 2005a). He came up with the concept of the Web 2.0 that defined an emerging second generation of the Web technology. According to Omar et al. (2007), the Web 2.0 technology provides an enhanced platform for enterprise application integration as well as consumer content generation, sharing and collaboration. This collaborative ability of Web 2.0 is vital for the utilization of *CBPE.* O'Reilly (2005a) predicts an improved and seamless user interaction and management of the Web environment and resources, guaranteeing required services and a flexible generation of user applications. Web 2.0 applications make the most of the intrinsic advantages of that platform: delivering software as a continually updated service that gets better with usage. Thus there is remixing and consuming of data from multiple sources, including individual users, as well as providing their own data and services in a form that allows users to use it the way they want to, creating network effects through an "architecture of participation", and going beyond the page metaphor of Web 1.0 to deliver rich user experiences (based on O'Reilly, 2005b).

The use of the Web Services technology in Web 2.0 provides the greatest benefit to the *CBPE* model. The interaction capabilities of the Web 2.0 are used by CBPE in order to create new collaborative opportunities on the Internet. Some of the specific Web 2.0 characteristics, that have also been discussed by Murugesan (2007) and that provide benefits to the *CBPE* model:

- **Blogs:** A Blog is a website on which people can enter their thoughts, ideas, suggestions and comments. The Blog technologies enable the users of the system to add their thoughts. These inserted thoughts can enable the system to provide better service in future. A Blog is a website, usually initiated and maintained by an individual with regular entries such as text, graphical, audio and video images and other media related to its topic. The ability for readers to leave comments in an interactive format is an important part of many blogs. Blogging benefit the *CBPE* by allowing the organizations to use blogs as focus on art, photographs, sketches, videos, music), audio which are part of a wider network of social media. The use of the Blog technology enables any kind of customer to collaboratively publish his/her opinion in CBPE. This is, of course, personal collaboration which can then be used by collaborative businesses. The communication of the system and the user provides higher level of Customer Relationship Management (CRM).

- **Really Simple Syndication (RSS):** RSS is an XML file that summarizes information items and links to the information sources. RSS enables the *CBPE* model to identify the source of the specific product and services through checking the popular source for the desired request. RSS, through CBPE, can keep accessing various industries and organizations to satisfy a request.

- **Wikis:** A Wiki is a simple yet powerful Web-based collaborative-authoring system for creating and editing content. Wiki supports linkage of external documents, simple navigation, simple templating, access for multiple users, simple workflow and built-in search features. Wiki technology can assist the *CBPE* model to create a collaborative authored discussion that encompasses collaborative channels across multiple organizations. Easy linkage of the application, easy conversion of the Wiki application to Hypertext Markup Language (HTML), easy linkages of the pages' title, easy control of the privileged applications and search by the associated keys are the necessary components of the *CBPE* model provided by Wiki technology.

- **Mashups:** A Web Mashup is a website that combines information and services from multiple sources on the Web. Mashup can be grouped into seven categories of mapping, search, mobile, messaging, sports, shopping, and movies. The *CBPE* is a collaborative system searching the portals for various organizational services and products that are offered. The grouping-up of Mashup technology of Web 2.0 supports *CBPE* to have better access to the services required in the pointed-out seven Mashup categories.

- **Google AdSense:** The organizations can place their advertisement by using the Google Adsence. The Google search engine technology serve advertisements based on website content, the user's geographical location, and other related factors. Contents on the advertisement automatically find the content of the relevant web page and delivers advertisements to the audience based on the site content. The products and services that are offered on the *CBPE*, can use this technology to reach the audience that are looking for these products and services.

- **Tagging ("folksonomy"):** Folksonomies are social software applications that allow non-expert users to collectively classify and find information. Some websites include tag clouds as a way to visualize tags in a folksonomy. is intended to make a body of information increasingly easy to search, discover, and navigate over time. Folksonomic tagging can be used in CBPE to label existing contents of the collaborative environment such as registered Web sites to bolg the entries.

- **Flickr:** Flickr has been cited as a prime example of effective use of folksonomy. Flickr permit photo submitters to organize images using tags, which allow searchers to find images concerning a certain topic such as place name or subject matter. In *CBPE,* flickr can facilitate to search engine to identify the desired products or services via affiliated images and their related tags.

- **BitTorrent:** BitTorrent client is any program that implements the BitTorrent protocol. Each client is capable of preparing, requesting, and transmitting any type of computer file over a network, using the protocol. BitTorrent protocol facilitate *CBPE* to share a file or group of files amongst multiple organizations. The file could contain metadata about the files to be shared and about the tracker, the computer that coordinates the file distribution.

- **Search Engine Optimisation (SEO):** Also known as search optimization is a web marketing activities that allows the process of editing and organizing the content on a webpage or across a website to increase its potential relevance to specific keywords on specific search engines. In *CBPE*, SEO can ensure that external links to the site are correctly titled in order to aim for achieving a higher organic search listing. Hence SEO target different kinds of searches, (including image search, local search, and industry-specific vertical search engines) the products and services offered in *CBPE* will be easily accessible.

## Web 2.0 and SOA

Web 2.0 and SOA are technically close to each other as both technologies enable services to communicate with each other. However, there are also some divergent elements in these technologies. For example, many Web 2.0 applications incorporate a social aspect, such as facilitating human interaction that may not be mandatory in SOA considerations. As a result, Web 2.0 applications successfully deal with human-readable content (such as text and pictures). In contrast, conventional SOA merely aims at interconnecting dispersed services and business functionality and only concentrates on facilitating seamless machine-to-machine collaboration. Therefore, SOA's biggest challenge appears to be the way in which the resulting business processes get utilized by the end-user. The consumer of a service is not required to have a detailed knowledge of implementation, implementation language, or execution platform of the service (Chen et al., 2006). The only concern of the consumer is how a service can be invoked according to the service interface. However, SOA-based architecture of collaborative applications is removed from the users and mainly in the domain of application developers and integrators. Web 2.0, as a complete eco-system for business collaboration is not only focused on remote execution of services and components but also concerned with presentation and user interface integration. Together, SOA and Web 2.0 are fully utilized by *CBPE* discussed here.

## CORE WEB SERVICES TECHNOLOGIES

The technologies of Web Services have provided immense interactive capabilities and, at the same time, have provided technical challenges arising precisely out of the need to interact. The collaborative software applications must be well-defined and meet the required standards for interaction. The W3C (World Wide Web Consortium) provides the necessary XML and related standards that can help implementation of Service-oriented Architecture in organizations. Such an SOA, however, is hampered by the lack of industry standards as each vendor attempts to push its own standard on the collaborative business applications. Without a common standard for interchange of data and applications that is also acceptable to the numerous tool vendors and subscribers, development of global businesses is thwarted. Thus, similar to the acceptance of HTTP, TCP/IP and HTML as standards for the original development of the Internet, the acceptance and definition of standards for the development of Web Services are critical to the ultimate success of globalization through WS. The Chief Technical Officer (CTO) of the company BEA, Michael Smith, pointed to this fact in his statement "If things aren't built on a solid foundation of standards that everyone agrees to, nothing will happen." (Mills, 2003). Yet, while the basic XML/XMI standards are increasingly being incorporated in software applications, according to Microsoft's Greg Stone, conventional standards can simply take too long. "There needs to be some commercial reality brought to bear that makes it happen much more quickly. If you think of other open, collaborative standards, they can go on for years" (Mackenzie, 2003a, 2003b).

Lack of common acceptability of standards amongst application vendors can, in turn, also lead to tough competition (or friction and in-fighting) amongst the companies that produce the software development tools for services; and this can happen despite the platform independent nature of Web Services. For example, there appears to be a stand-off between Sun and Microsoft over their respective J2EE and .NET toolkits – eventually leading to Microsoft abandoning the Web Services "Choreography" working group in March, 2003. Similarly, IBM's Websphere, Oracle's 9i Application Server and BEA's WebLogic, have long since competed for market share of their respective products that can help build Web-Services-based software applications for global businesses (Mackenzie, 2003c). Furthermore, the Universal Description Discovery Integration (UDDI) for publishing-locating-consuming services – a vital ingredient of WS – requires commonly acceptable standards, which also do not seem to be converging. An example of this disparity is the fact that Microsoft, SAP and Siebel, who used to maintain UDDI standards in the past, have discontinued their UDDI instances. Finally, the availability of robust content management systems and databases with relevant contents for global services directories and transactions is also a crucial technical challenge to the globalization of businesses with WS.

Internally, to a business, collaborations enable dispersed teams and also participating businesses to communicate, coordinate and cooperate with each other in order to consummate a task. These electronic collaborations increase the effectiveness and speed of interactions between organizations, thereby enhancing strategic decision-making and genuine operational agility (Barekat, 2001). However, there is a technical need to support the teams and decision makers through group-ware technologies that use the Internet for communication. For example, there are web-based chat tools, web-based asynchronous conferencing tools, e-mail, Internet-based list servers, collaborative writing tools, group decision support systems, and teleconferencing tools as discussed by Kock et al. (2001). Furthermore, there are also non real-time and real-time discussion, whiteboard, screen-sharing, file- and document-sharing and document management groupware products such as Lotus Notes, and intranet that contains groupware functions such as e-mail, document management, electronic conferencing (Shani et al., 2000). These communication mechanisms need to be continuously kept up and running technically for the management aspect of the collaborations to develop, and are a technical challenge to the management itself.

The security of collaborative transactions is another major technical challenge that needs to be satisfactorily resolved before collaborative business can flourish. This is so because security in collaborations requires coordination amongst applications of numerous businesses. The security of these collaborative business applications create greater challenges than normal application security hence these service-oriented applications would be in separate technical environments as well as different geographical regions. There is no doubt that the development of WS technologies has itself been much faster than the handling of corresponding security issues related to these technologies. According to Grance et al. (2003), organizations must frequently evaluate and select a variety of information technology (IT) security services in order to maintain and improve their overall IT security program and enterprise architecture. IT security services, which range from security policy development to intrusion detection support, may be offered by an IT group internal to an organization, or by a growing group of vendors.

In fact, security is considered crucial to Web Services' future success. The adoption of the WS technologies and their communications framework as a dependable means of doing business relies heavily upon the ability of the business applications to ensure safe and secured transactions; and industry bodies such as the WS-I (Web Services Interoperability) are in the process of creating a way for protocols to handle this problem themselves.

Finally, the speed of WS-based transactions and the availability of corresponding bandwidths are also a crucial technical factor influencing collaborative businesses. SOAP, being based on XML, is not technically efficient, as it requires applications to send quantity of data to successfully communicate with each other. As reported in the past, XML-based transmissions are seven times or more *inefficient* than a standard CORBA (Common Object Request Broker Architecture) message (Foreshew, 2003). Subsequently, bandwidth may become a considerable technical challenge for the future of Web Services development. Figure 1 demonstrate the discussion thus far and show how Web Services technology provides an opportunity for business to interact with each other.

Figure 1 shows the core web services (WS) technologies that also form the basis for business interactions. The three core technologies depicted in Figure 1, for each of the two businesses interacting with one another are the Extensible Markup Language (XML), the Web Services Description Language (WSDL) and the Universal

*Figure 1. Approaching business interactions with Web services*

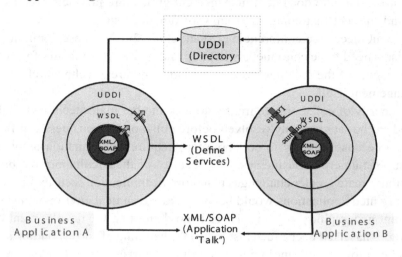

Data Discovery Interface (UDDI).

The Extensible Markup Language (XML) is a simple and flexible text format for message exchange that is based on the original Standard Generalized Markup Language (SGML) (ISO 8879). Originally designed to meet the challenges of large-scale electronic publishing, XML is now able to exchange of a wide variety of data on the Web and elsewhere (http://www.w3.org/XML/).

XML schemas needing advanced features and wrappers are put together with the Simple Object Access Protocol (SOAP). SOAP messages make use of extensible data schemas that are used for building documents and data which have multiple contexts. The application of the XML/SOAP messaging provides the opportunity to implement business processes that are complex and that go beyond the simple exchange of information. The request and response functionalities of WS are handled by the core technology of XML/SOAP that provides a data-exchange format that encapsulates both data and metadata. This ability of XML/SOAP allows the various applications and databases to exchange information irrespective of their platforms and technical environments.

Web Services Description Language, is the wrapper on top of XML/SOAP as shown in Figure 1. WSDL provides the basis for communication and understanding of what the service is meant to do. Building software services commence with the definition of what the service is and what the service does. WSDL is the starting point within SOA to provide a standardized means of building software services that can be accessed, shared, and reused across a network.

WSDL, according to the World Wide Web Consortium, is an XML format for describing network services. These descriptions are for one or more messages that contain either document-oriented or procedure-oriented information. While the operations and messages are initially described in an abstract manner, they are then bound to a concrete network protocol and message format in order for them to be understood and consumed. Related concrete endpoints are combined into abstract endpoint services (Christensen et al., 2001). WSDL is extensible to allow descriptions of endpoints and their messages regardless of what message formats or network protocols are used to communicate.

Universal Description, Discovery and Integration (UDDI) specifications define a registry service for Web Services and for other electronic and non-electronic services. A UDDI registry service is a Web service that manages information about service-providers, service implementations, and service metadata. Service-providers can use UDDI to advertise the services they offer. Service consumers can use UDDI to discover services that suit their requirements and to obtain the service metadata needed to consume those services (http://www.uddi.org/faqs.html).

UDDI discovers the prospective requester from the directory that is also an integral part of an organization. This specification allows for the creation of standardized service description registries both within and outside organizational boundaries. UDDI provides the potential for Web Services to be registered in a central location, from where they can be discovered by service requestors. Hence SOA services should be accessed, shared, and reused across a network. The UDDI directory provides the channels of access across the network.

## External and Internal Impact of Web Services

Figure 2 lists the impact of Web Service on an organization and its applications – both internally as well as the externally. This impact of WS is important to understand in order to have a complete picture of making a service-oriented architecture work (Barry, 2003).

Web Services allows different applications from different sources to communicate with each other without time consuming custom coding. This communication can take place within the internal as well as external applications of any organization. The management of internal operations typically internal business processes includes inventory management systems, payroll applications, HR systems and the likes. Having recognized the potential benefits of Web Services to internal departments, many organizations opt to undertake a complete redesign of their internal and external processes based on the Internet, and produce a more holistic approach to their operative business. It should be mentioned here, though, that due to re-alignment of the internal processes along with the external ones with the customers and suppliers, there is also a large component of B2B transactions in operative

*Figure 2. The internal and external impact of WS*

### External Impacts

Collaboration of external application

Rapid evolvement of standardization

Benefit Quality of collaborative Services

### Internal Impacts

Collaboration of internal application

Create holistic approach to operative business

Shift the business operation on the Internet

businesses. Finally, because of the ability of the business to shift all its operations on the Internet, these transactions are also going to have a component of business-to-government (e.g. taxation) in it.

SOA is architecture constructed based on internal and external processes of an organization. The Web Services technology is the most appropriate technology to develop SOA. Web Services represent the applications that organizations "Publish and Locate" on unknown and disparate platforms (Ghanbary, 2006). Web-Services-based technologies enable applications to "talk" with one another even across organizational firewalls, resulting in an opportunity for a cluster or group of organizations to simultaneously transition to web-based entities (Unhelkar and Deshpande, 2004).

## Web Services and Increasing Complexities of Interaction

Web Services (WS) provide ability for applications and, thereby, organizations to interact with one another. Figure 3 through to 5.6 depict this increasingly complex level of communication and interaction amongst various service components within and between organizations.

Figure 3 depicts how the individual internal departments of an organization perform independently of each other while there is no SOA in place. Figure 4 demonstrates two possible options for the internal departments of the organizations to adapt SOA.

*Figure 3. Services facilitate interactions amongst various departments of an organization – by interconnecting their applications*

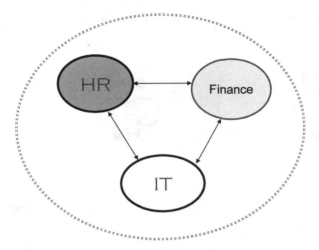

Option 1 (SOA-1) the interrelated cluster of individual departments communicates with each other while they are still independent of each other. Option 2 (SOA-2) proposes those interrelated clusters (that need constant communication) to partly integrate. There are numerous advantages and disadvantages. The advantages are sharing services, better quality, faster service and creating an opportunity for the future **CBPE** model. The disadvantages are that the departments are not independent and their tasks are shared across the organization, causing the complex issues of controlling the security, trust, management duties and control over the information and staff.

Figure 4 provides a similar concept, presenting the impact of SOA when multiple organizations collaborate with each other in a B2B environment.

Figure 5 shows how multiple organizations are collaborating in a B2B environment. This book identifies that the same advantages and disadvantages apply when these organizations are collaborating in B2B environment. Figure 5 demonstrates that internal departments of the organizations are also SOA-enabled. The full potential of the SOA is not yet extracted as far as the **CBPE** is concerned. The current SOA is not providing the full support for the expected model of collaboration, since the communications and the integration in the current organizations are limited and these organizations are not fully SOA-enabled.

Figure 6 depicts how the SOA can support the proposed **CBPE** model by SOA-enabling the organizations. Figure 6 shows the application of SOA in **CBPE** environment while the clusters of multiple organizations communicate in different situations. Figure 6 demonstrates how, in **CBPE**, the impact of the collaborations

*Figure 4. SOA-based approach facilitates communications within and between two specific Organizations*

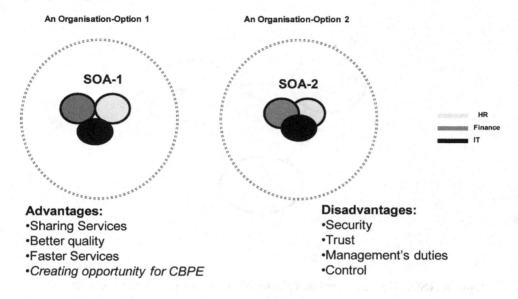

**Advantages:**
•Sharing Services
•Better quality
•Faster Services
•*Creating opportunity for CBPE*

**Disadvantages:**
•Security
•Trust
•Management's duties
•Control

*Figure 5. The business-2-business (B2B) communications provide specific connectivity between applications belonging to many organizations*

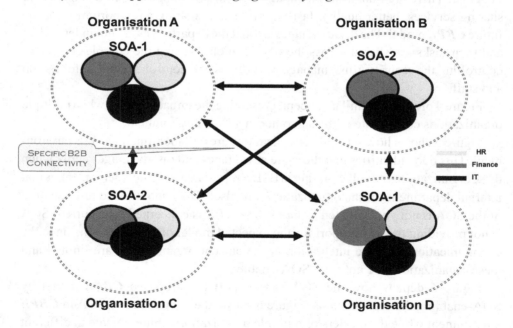

*Figure 6. Using SOA and extending CBPE leads to opportunities for communicating amongst multiple organizations*

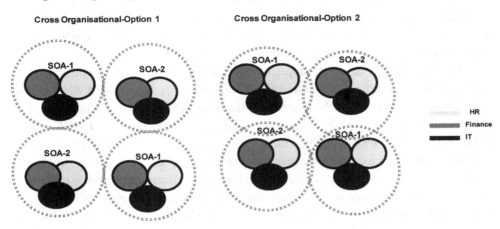

affect the whole structure's (internal as well as external) business processes when the internal as well as the external organizations are integrating in order to satisfy the requirements of the SOA.

The complexity evolves as individual departments are using numerous different applications on numerous different platforms. Thus, Figures 3, 4, 5 and 6 demonstrate the evolutionary influence of the SOA in the ***Collaborative Business Process Engineering (CBPE)*** model.

## INFLUENCE OF ENTERPRISE SERVICE BUS IN CBPE

An Enterprise Service Bus (ESB) is a software infrastructure that enables SOA by acting as an intermediary layer of middleware through which a set of reusable business services are made widely available. An ESB helps enterprises obtain the value of SOA by increasing connectivity, adding flexibility and speed, and providing greater control over use of the important service resources it binds.

A critical step for organizations is to align information technology (IT) systems using SOA with their business strategies. Such alignment provides an end-to-end enterprise integration and virtualized IT services. However, the SOA paradigm also needs to be extended to transmute organizational structures and behavioral practices (Bieberstein et al., 2005). ESB is a hub for integrating different kinds of services through messaging, event-handling, and business performance management (Luo, Goldshlager and Zhang, 2005). ESB does not implement an SOA. However, ESB incorporates the SOA. The wide range of mediation services provided by an ESB is a broader architecture pattern, which may be partly or wholly implemented, depending on the breadth of actual requirements.

According to Gilpin et al. (2004), any enterprise looking to implement SOA should evaluate what form of ESB would be required, and begin to take the initial steps to exploit this key emerging technology (http://www.forrester.com)

EAI comprises the computer applications enabling the computer applications of an enterprise to coordinate and consolidate each other. A successful *CBPE* model needs successful SOA when the internal applications of the organizations are capable of communicating. Figure 7 presents how the technologies support *CBPE* model and how the *CBPE* model enables them to have a successful SOA and EAI.

ESB is a bus which delivers messages from service requesters to service providers. Since it sits between the service requesters and providers, it is not appropriate to use any existing capacity planning methodology for servers, such as modeling, to estimate an ESB's capacity. There are programs which run on an ESB called mediation modules. The mediation modules' functionalities vary and they depend on how people use the ESB. This usage creates difficulties for capacity planning and performance evaluation.

According to Vaughan (2003), ESB is an open standards-based messaging means designed to provide interoperability between larger-grained applications and other components via simple standard adapters and interfaces (http://www.adtmag.com/). The infrastructure that underpins a fully integrated and flexible end-to-end SOA is called ESB (Schnidt et al., 2005).

*Figure 7. The relative impacts of supporting technologies on CBPE*

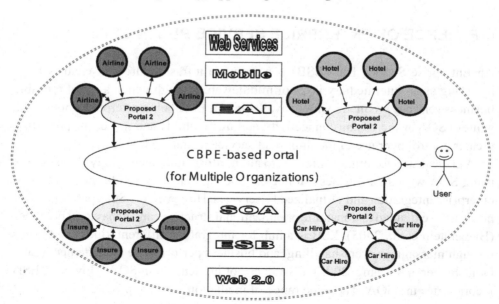

The ESB provides a new way to build and deploy SOA architectures. ESB is a concept that is increasingly gaining the attention of architects and developers, as it provides an effective approach to solving common problems such as service orchestration, application data synchronization, and business activity monitoring. In its most basic form, an ESB offers the following key features that are of interest to this discussion on ***CBPE***:

- **Web Services:** Support for SOAP, WSDL and UDDI, as well as emerging standards such as WS-Reliable Messaging and WS-Security
- **Messaging:** Asynchronous store-and-forward delivery with multiple qualities of service
- **Data transformation:** XML to XML
- **Content-based routing:** Publish and subscribe routing across multiple types of sources and destinations
- **Platform-neutral:** Connect to any technology in the enterprise, for example, Java, .Net, mainframes, and databases.

ESBs are the evolution of middleware infrastructure technology. In the past, developers used a variety of technologies to support program-to-program communication, such as Object Request Brokers (ORBs), Message-oriented Middleware (MOM), Remote Procedure Calls (RPC), and, most recently, point-to-point Web Services. These technologies are frequently grouped under the "middleware" category. ESBs are attractive to organizations today because they combine features from previous technologies with new services, such as message validation, transformation, content-based routing, security and load balancing. ESBs also use industry standards for most of the services they provide, thus facilitating cross-platform interoperability and becoming the logical choice for companies looking to implement SOA (http://dev2dev.bea.com/).

Many integration problems today are relatively simple in nature, requiring data synchronisation across two or more applications. For these types of problems, an ESB is a lightweight, cost-effective technology. ESB can be the backbone that transports and routes messages across an enterprise, as it is a standards-based integration platform that combines messaging, Web Services, data transformation and intelligent routing in an event-driven SOA. According to Chappell, vice-president and Chief Technology Evangelist at Sonic Software (CTESS), ESBs are being rapidly adopted within IT organizations across a wide variety of industries, solving real-world integration challenges in unique ways. According to Roy Schulte, The ESB is primarily concerned with the program-to-program communications necessary to support services-oriented interactions and combines messaging, transformation, and content-based routing into a single off-the-shelf product. ESBs have emerged because of the growing need for general-purpose enterprise communication back-bones. This is the whole concept of the enterprise nervous system gradually coming to life, step-by-step and without fanfare (http://www.sonicsoftware.com/).

The ESB model, in which there is a set of intermediary services that support the functions mentioned previously, is fundamentally more flexible and inherently more scaleable because it provides access to a core set of common functions without having to rewrite all of the applications that require those functions. Instead of one application simply consuming the services of another on an ad-hoc basis, proponents of the ESB model envision a network made up of collaborating services. Such network has repercussions for the *CBPE* model.

Based on Sherman, regular contributor to *Enterprise Architect*, ESBs support SOAs by implementing SOAP and leveraging Web Services Description Language (WSDL) and Universal Description, Discovery, and Integration (UDDI). In addition, ESBs make extensive use of XML-based content routing and transformation (http://www.ftponline.com).

The ESB influences *CBPE* because, based on an ESB, the choice of a platform can be made. This platform builds services from scratch based on provisioned via configuration rather than the coding. The ESB enables the *CBPE* to connect services, while just focusing on design for the maximum reuse. ESB provides a messaging bus and service platforms, making it relatively easy to hook up legacy systems and to manage the orchestration of the *CBPE*. The ESB also transforms and routes the messages in the proposed collaborative model of the *CBPE*.

## BUSINESS INTEGRATION WITH CBPE

One of the key challenges in modern-day business is the pressing need to 'integrate organizations' wide and varied software systems and applications (Figure 8). Further-more, large organizations such as banks and insurance companies have vast amounts of data that are embedded in their legacy systems. They have a need to expose this data and the corresponding applications in a "unified" view to the customer on the Internet – resulting in what is known as "business integration". However, as a result of this integration, and technical ability of applications to transact over the Internet, businesses are now readily able to offer and consume "services" across the Internet. Currently, there is limited literature on modeling and managing the challenges emanating from collaboration between varied businesses and applications.

Service interoperability is paramount. Although researchers have proposed various middleware technologies to achieve SOA, Web Services standards better satisfy the universal interoperability needs (Pasley, 2005). In order for multiple organizations to collaborate, many challenges are identified, such as: technological,

*Figure 8. Business integration with CBPE*

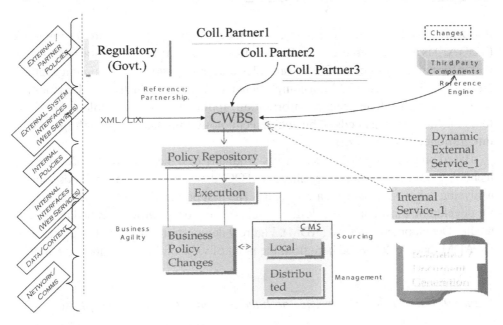

methodological and social factors resulting rational interactions between businesses. The good architecture takes place when the services of different applications have the capability to communicate. The previous statement leads us to the concept of SOA departing beyond the boundary of standard communications framework.

SOA is a design model with a deeply rooted concept of encapsulating application logic within services that interact via a common communication protocol (Erl, 2004). Web Services are used to establish this communication framework. WS basically represent a web-based implementation of SOA. Business process integration is part of enterprise integration solutions, which is why coordination services for business activities are utilized exclusively for the management of long-running business activities.

EA provides the "organizational policy" in terms of how SOA (made up of WS) is to be used by the various information systems of the organization. Thus, the implementation of EA leads to what is called Enterprise Architecture Integration (EAI).

An EAI sets the platform and plays an important role in enabling business processes to transcend various technological boundaries.

## INFLUENCE OF TOGAF IN CBPE

According to Rivett et al. (2005), The Open Group Architecture Framework (TOGAF) is a critical architecture for the effective and safe construction of business and information systems. TOGAF provides the Architecture Development Method (ADM). This TOGAF ADM is a comprehensive, detailed, industry standard method for developing EAI, and related information, application, and technology architectures that address the needs of business, technology, and data systems (http://www.integrationconsortium.org).

Based on Chase (2006), TOGAF was originally designed as a way to develop the technology architecture for an organization. TOGAF has evolved into a methodology for analysing the overall business architecture. The first part of TOGAF is a methodology for developing the architecture design which, as mentioned earlier, is called the Architecture Development Method (ADM). Figure 9 demonstrates the nine basic phases of the ADM that are discussed here from the point of view of their relevance to **CBPE**.

*Figure 9. Using TOGAF reference architecture for CBPE (the ADM phases)*

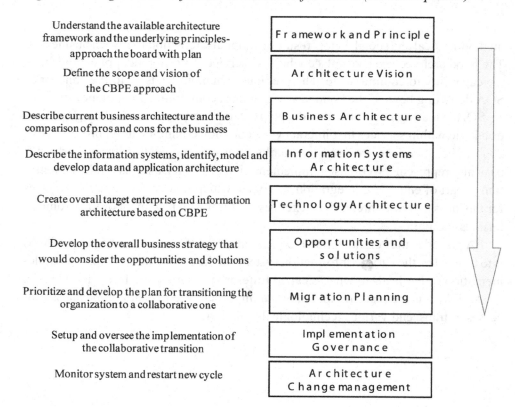

- **Preliminary phase: Framework and principles.** Get everyone on board with the plan. This phase has a significant influence in the *CBPE*. This phase in the *CBPE* enables everyone to participate in the collaborative environment. This phase facilitates to understand the available architecture framework and the underlying principles in order to approach the board with plan.

- **Phase A: Architecture vision.** Define your scope and vision to map your overall strategy. In *CBPE*, the scope and vision of the participating organizations must be clearly stated upfront. The *CBPE* maps the overall strategy in order to define the scope and vision of the *CBPE* approach.

- **Phase B: Business architecture.** Describe your current and target business architectures and determine the gap between them. This phase enables the organizations to realize the need for *CBPE*. After the business architecture phase, the organizations start to realize the initial benefit of the *CBPE* for the collaborative environment. In general, this phase describe current business architecture and the comparison of pros and cons for the business

- **Phase C: Information system architectures**Develop target architectures for your data and applications. The *CBPE* keeps records of all transactions and data throughout a well-defined Information Systems (IS) architecture. The actual creation of the IS architectures is left up to the architects. Description of the information systems, identify, model and develop data and application architecture are the primary functions of this phase.

- **Phase D: Technology architecture.** Create the overall target architecture that you will implement in future phases. In *CBPE*, all the recorded data will be implemented for the future phases and transactions. Web Services technology provides the base for technology architecture, also networks consecutively to create overall target enterprise and information architecture based on *CBPE*.

- **Phase E: Opportunities and solutions.** Develop the overall strategy, determining what you will buy, build or reuse, and how you will implement the architecture described in Phase D. The recorded data in *CBPE* supports the reuse of the services implementing better architecture for the collaboration. This phase enables the organizations to develop the overall business strategy that would consider the opportunities and solutions by implementing the *CBPE*.

- **Phase F: Migration planning.** Priorities projects and develop the migration plan. *CBPE* prioritizes the organizations and the customer's request. *CBPE* has the capability of cooperating with Phase F of the TOGAF by marking the organization that received the previous request. The next request will go to the next organization capable of handling it. This phase enable the *CBPE* model to prioritize and develop the plan for transitioning the organization to a collaborative one.

- **Phase G: Implementation governance.** Determine how you will provide oversight to the implementation. One of the functions of the *CBPE* manager is to provide an oversight to the portal implementation to setup and oversee the implementation of the collaborative transition.

- **Phase H: Architecture change management.** Monitor the running system for necessary changes and determine whether to start a new cycle, looping back to the preliminary phase. The communication within the different levels of the *CBPE* allows the monitoring of the systematic transaction and determines the new cycle if a customer desires to receive products and service from different industries.

These phases provide a standardised way of analysing the enterprise and planning and managing the actual implementation. The term "enterprise integration" (or "system integration") reflects the capability to integrate a variety of different system functionalities. The increase in demand for managing information has contributed to the focus on integrating business processes and data.

Traditionally, information systems are implemented to support specific functional areas. However, the advancement of information technology enables new forms of organizations and facilitates their business processes to collaborate even when these organizations are not necessarily known to each other. As organizations become more complex and diverse in the collaborative context, it becomes nearly impossible for organizations to implement their collaborative business concepts without enterprise integration.

The demand for flexible, efficient and user-friendly collaborative services is becoming more and more urgent as the competition in the current market-oriented arena is becoming more intense and fierce (Jostad et al., 2005). Enterprises have to be more dynamic in terms of collaboration with partners and even competitors. The SOA is a promising computing paradigm offering solutions that are extendible, flexible and compatible with legacy systems.

The successful architecture confirms that business requirements and information technology design are captured in models. The modelling technique of abstraction to separate business concerns from technology concerns (what the business system needs to do, versus its underlying computing platform) is also an important aspect of the success of the architecture.

Based on Miller and Mukerji (2003), the following issues could also be classified as critical factor for the success of the Service Oriented and Enterprise Architecture:

- The capture of business requirements
- The Platform-independent Model (PIM), by promoting the design of a business solution prior to selecting how it will be deployed
- The Platform-specific Model (PSM) adds to the PIM the details of a specific computing platform on which the business solution will be deployed
- The transformations (mappings) are performed on these models to progress from a higher level of abstraction to a lower level of abstraction
- The activities are based on internationally accepted standards

Most organizations have already realized that their information technology infrastructure is effectively a distributed computing system. The integration of information assets, and effective use of information, must be accessible across the department, across the company, across the world and, more importantly, across the service- or supply-chain from the supplier, to one's own organization, to one's customers. This means that Central Processing Units (CPU) must be intimately linked to the networks of the world and be capable of freely passing and receiving information, not hidden behind glass and cooling ducts or the complexities of the software that drives them (Miller and Mukerji, 2003).

## CONSIDERING THE INFLUENCE OF MOBILE TECHNOLOGY IN CBPE

Mobile devices have the capability to connect to the global network while they are connected to individual people, regardless of their location and time. Web 2.0 is capable of creating global connectivity using the experience of the prior technologies. Web 2.0 energizes IT-related entrepreneurs with a new approach. Web 2.0 serves different purposes based on the users' request. Based on O'Reilly (2005a), the differences between Web 2.0 and Mobile Web 2.0 are outlined in the followings:

- **Mobile Google:** Google mobile allows the perpetual connectivity to the mobile Internet to google mobile search engine, maps, Gmail, mobile Google talk, windows mobile Google calendar, mobile Google reader, mobile Google calendar and mobile Google docs.
- **Mobile Blogging:** Similar to blogging, Mobile blogging (moblogging) allows the user to publish blug entries directly to the web from a mobile phone or other mobile device. Camera-enabled mobile phones e-mail/MMS or SMS photos and videos as entries on a web site, or use mobile browsers to publish content directly to any blogging platform with Mobile Posting compatibility.

- **Mobile Search Engine:** Mobile search engine allows mobile users to retrieve information from mobile platforms and mobile handsets. Mobile Search is important for the usability of available mobile content for the same reasons as internet search engines became important to the usability of internet content.

According to Yamakami (2007), there are several critical issues for Mobile Web 2.0 in order to make it a new framework for the platform in the mobile Internet.

- Platform over multiple devices and execution environment
- Platform for any-time and any-place business
- Context-aware platform
- Super distribution of knowledge
- Leverage social networks

Web 2.0 gives a new perspective to the service engineering in the Internet. Mobile Web 2.0 provides the techniques and design principles facilitating the *CBPE* to locate and consume the desired available services, regardless of the location and time boundaries. Integration of the mobile Web users into mobile applications allows the users to have access to the additional features offered in Mobile Web 2.0.

Considering the new achievements in information technologies, companies are vulnerable if they do not respond to technologies such as mobile technology in a fast and proper way. Such systems as Mobile Supply chain Management (M-SCM) can further enhance the global SCM by reducing time and cost, increasing correct delivery and customer satisfaction, and providing for the global enterprise to do business at anytime and anywhere. As an example, the international logistics management focuses international ship delivery schedule management, time, place, and product quality management (Long, 2003).

The globalization era has created possibilities for interactive organizations to conduct business across different geographical boundaries. Enterprises in some countries can provide low labor costs, and some in different countries may have low material cost, or others in different countries may provide professional skills or idea product designs. However, all enterprises want to sell their products globally. The resultant ability of businesses and customers to connect to each other ubiquitously – independent of time and location – is the core driver of this change (Unhelkar, 2005). This change leads the traditional supply chain management to global supply chain management. Mobile technologies are thus a key influence in any effort towards the globalization of business (Unhelkar, 2004). The process of such m-transformation of an existing business into the mobile business via the adoption of suitable processes and technologies that enable mobility and pervasiveness has also been discussed by Marmaridis and Unhelkar (2005).

The evolution of mobile technology is considered in the context of the current discussion, in order to understand its origins and also to realize where it is heading. Mobile technologies form the basis of the "next wave" of software applications, resulting in "Global Businesses" that are unique in nature (Unhelkar, 2005a).

The uniqueness of mobile technology is that it has given organizations the freedom to conduct commercial transactions independent of both time and location. Established as an additional layer of technology on top of the traditional Internet, mobile networks ensure that information that is available through a physical computing device at a fixed location is now available at anytime and anywhere in a true "wireless" manner (Tarasewich, 2003).

Furthermore, due to the personalized nature of individuality of the mobile devices, it is possible for businesses to create various personalised business applications. According to Freeland, Mat-Amin, Teangtrong, Wannalertsri and Wattanakasemsakul (2001) and Godbole (2006), mobile computing is described as a vision of the creation of environments with information and computation, in which digital content, applications and services are made available in an integrated and personalized way to users, through a diverse range of devices and access networks. The ability of mobile applications to make their users location-independent is the major characteristic of the mobile technology. Accessing the applications from anywhere, and at any time, brings a new feature to the usage of mobility by businesses extending the potential usage of the traditional land-line Internet.

The growth of the Internet and the World Wide Web has had a significant impact on business, commerce and industry (Murugesan, Deshpande, Hansen and Ginige, 2001). The electronic commerce resulting from the popularity of the Internet offers a global market, potential cost savings, and provides unprecedented new business opportunities for organizations (Chung, Lin and Shim, 2005; Dutta, Kwan and Segev, 1998; Manecke and Schoensleben, 2004). The integration of mobile technology in business and commerce results in what is known as mobile business (m-business), which integrates the Internet, wireless devices and e-business together (Kalakota and Robinson, 2002).

The development of mobile business is referenced here in order to identify the potential of the mobile technology in the context of the *CBPE* model. The potential of the mobility in the context of the *CBPE* is to create a streamline of the engineered mobile collaborative business process for multiple organizations.

## ACTION POINTS

1.  List the technologies and architectures that play an important role in facilitating electronic collaboration in your organization
2.  Identify the impact of the emerging technologies on the internal as well as external departments of your organization
3.  List the advantages of the Web 2.0 technology for your organizational business processes
4.  List the advantages of the SOA technology for your organizational business processes
5.  Identify how SOA restructure the internal departments of your organization
6.  Identify the impact of SOA in your organization's collaborative business processes
7.  Identify the various phases of TOGAF-ADM and explain the impact of TOGAF on the business processes of your organization
8.  List the advantages of the Enterprise Service Bus and identify its potential for your organization

## REFERENCES

Barekat, M. (2001). The real time-enterprise [r]evolution. Manufacturing Engineering , 80(4), 153–156. doi:10.1049/me:20010404

Barry, D. K. (2003). *Web services and service-oriented architecture: The savvy manager's guide.* San Francisco: Morgan Kaufmann Publishers.

Bieberstein, N., S. Bose, L. Walker, and A. Lynch (2005). Impact of service-oriented architecture on enterprise systems, organizational structures and individuals. *IBM Systems Journal, 44*(4).

Booth, D., Haas, H., McCabe, F., Newcomer, E., Champion, M., Ferris, C., & Orchard, D. (2004). *Web services architecture.* Retrieved March 5, 2006, from http://www.w3.org/TR/ws-arch/

Chase, N. (2006). *Introducing the open group architecture framework, understanding TOGAF and IT architecture in today's world.* Retrieved April 3, 2007, from http://www-128.ibm.com/developerworks/ibm/library/ar-togaf1/

Christensen, E., Curbera, F., Meredith, G., & Weerawarana, S. (2001). *Web services description language (WSDL) 1.1*. Retrieved October 12, 2006, from http://www.w3.org/TR/wsdl

Chung, J. Y. (2005). An industry view on service-oriented architecture and Web services. In *Proceedings of the 2005 IEEE International Workshop on Service-Oriented System Engineering (SOSE'05)*. IEEE.

Dutta, S., S. Kwan, and A. Segev (1998). Business transformation in electronic commerce: A study of sectoral and regional trends. *European Management Journal, 16*(5), 540–551. doi:10.1016/S0263-2373(98)00031-0

Erl, T. (2004). *Service-oriented architecture: A field guide to integrating XML and Web services*. Upper Saddle River, NJ: Pearson Education, Inc.

Foreshew, J. (2003). SOAP too slow for capital markets. *The Australian*.

Freeland, M., Mat-Amin, H., Teangtrong, K., Wannalertsri, W., & Wattanakasem-sakul, U. (2001). Pervasive computing: Business opportunity and challenges. In *Proceedings of the PICMET '01. Portland International Conference on Management of Engineering and Technology*, Portland, OR.

Gilpin, M., Vollmer, K., & Peyret, H. (2004). *What is an enterprise service bus?* Retrieved February 16, 2007, from http://www.forrester.com/Research/Document/Excerpt/0,7211,35193,00.html

Godbole, N. (2006). Relating mobile computing to mobile commerce. In B. Unhelkar (Ed.), *Mobile business: Technological, methodological and social perspectives* (Vol. 2). Hershey, PA: Idea Group Publishing.

Grance, T., Hash, J., Stevens, M., O'Neal, K., & Bartol, N. (2003). *Guide to information technology security services, recommendations of the national institute of standards and technology*. National Institute of Commerce Special Publication.

Hazra, T. K. (2007). SOA governance: Building on the old, embracing the new. Cutter IT Journal , 20(6), 30–34.

Integration Consortium. (n.d.) Retrieved October 5, 2006, from http://www.integrationconsortium.org/docs/W054final.pdf

Jostad, I., Dustdar, S., & Thanh, D. V. (2005). A service oriented architecture framework for collaborative services. In *Proceedings of the 14th IEEE International Workshops on Enabling Technologies*: *Infrastructure for Collaborative Enterprise*.

Kock, N., R. Davison, R. Wazlawick, and R. Ocker (2001). E-collaboration: A look at past research and future challenges. Journal of Systems and Information Technology , 5(1), 1–9.

Long, D. (2003). *International logistics – global supply chain management*. Amsterdam: Kluwer Academic Publishers.

Luo, M., Goldshlager, B., & Zhang, L. J. (2005). Designing and implementing enterprise service bus (ESB) and SOA solutions. In *Proceedings of the IEEE International Conference on Service Computing (SCC'05)* (Vol. 2).

Mackenzie, K. (2003). Web services put to work for food safety. *The Australian.*

Manecke, N., and P. Schoensleben (2004). Cost and benefit of Internet-based support of business processes. *International Journal of Production Economics*, *87*, 213–229. doi:10.1016/S0925-5273(03)00216-0

Marmaridis, I., & Unhelkar, B. (2005). Challenges in mobile transformations: A requirements modeling perspective for small and medium enterprises SMEs. In *Proceedings of the mBusiness International Conference*, Sydney, Australia.

Miller, J., & Mukerji, J. (2003). *Model driven architecture (MDA) guide version 1.0.1*. Retrieved October 5, 2006 from http://www.omg.org/docs/omg/03-06-01.pdf

Mills, G. E. (2003). *Action research: A guide for the teacher researcher.* Upper Saddle River, NJ: Merrill/Prentice Hall.

Murugesan, S. (2007). Understanding Web 2.0. *IT Professional*, *9*(4), 34–41. doi:10.1109/MITP.2007.78

O'Reilly, T. (2005a). *What is Web 2.0? Design and business models for the next generation of software*. Retrieved August 2, 2007, from http://www.oreillynet.com/pub/a/oreilly/tim/news/2005/09/30/what-is-web-20.html

O'Reilly, T. (2005b). *Web 2.0 compact definition*. Retrieved August 2, 2007, from http://radar.oreilly.com/archives/2005/10/web_20_compact_definition.html

O'Reilly, T. (2006). *Web 2.0 compact definition: Trying again*. Retrieved from http://radar.oreilly.com/archives/2006/12/web_20_compact.html

Omar, W. M., A. D. K. Abbass, and T. Bendiab (2007). SOAW2 for managing the Web 2.0 framework. IT Professional , 9(3), 30–35. doi:10.1109/MITP.2007.56

Online, F. T. P. (n.d.) Retrieved February 16, 2007, from http://www.ftponline.com/ea/magazine/spring/columns/architectstoolbox/

Orchard, D. (2004). *Web services architecture* (W3C Working Group Note 11). Retrieved February 10, 2007, from http://www.w3.org/TR/ws-arch/#introduction

Pashtan, A. (2005). *Mobile Web services*. Cambridge, UK: Cambridge University Press.

Pasley, J. (2005). How BPEL & SOA are changing Web services development. *IEEE Internet Computing, 9*(3), 60–67. doi:. doi:10.1109/MIC.2005.56

Philipson, G. (2001). *Australian e-business guide*. Australia: McPherson's Printing Group.

Philipson, G. (2007). *Web 2.0 and SOA are 'two sides of the same coin.'* Retrieved from http://www.theage.com.au/news/perspectives/web-20-and-soa-are-two-sides-of-the-same-coin/2007/07/30/1185647825516.html

Rivett, P., Spencer, J., & Waskiewkz, F. (2005). *TOGAF/MDA mapping* (Document No. W054). The Open Group.

Schneider, G. P. (2004). *Electronic commerce: The second wave* (5th ed.). Florence, KY: Thomson Course Technology.

Shani, A. B., J. A. Sena, and M. W. Stebbins (2000). Knowledge work teams and groupware technology: Learning from Seagate's experience. Journal of Knowledge Management , 4(2), 111–124. doi:10.1108/13673270010336602

Sonic Software. (n.d.) Retrieved February 16, 2007, from http://www.sonicsoftware.com/solutions/learning_center/books/enterprise_service_bus/index.ssp

Tarasewich, P. (2003). Designing mobile commerce applications. *Communications of the ACM, 46*(12), 57–60. doi:10.1145/953460.953489

Universal Description Discovery Integration. (n.d.). Retrieved October 12, 2006, from http://www.uddi.org/faqs.html

Vaughan, J. (2003). *What is an enterprise services bus? Application Developments Trends*. Retrieved February 15, 2007, from http://www.adtmag.com/article.aspx?id=7561andamp;page=

World Wide Web Consortium. (2003). *Extensible markup language (XML)*. Retrieved October 12, 2006, from http://www.w3.org/XML/

Yamakami, T. (2007). A third service evolution dimension in Web 2.0 and real world integration inspired services in 3G mobile data communications. ICMB, 2001(61).

Zurko, M. E., & Wilson, D. (2005). *Using history, collaboration, and transparency to provide security*. Retrieved October 10, 2007, from http://www.w3.org/2005/Security/usability-ws/papers/19-zurko-history/

# Chapter 6
# Collaborative Web Based System (CWBS)

*When I am working on a problem I never think about beauty. I only think about how to solve the problem. But when I have finished, if the solution is not beautiful, I know it is wrong.*

Buckminster Fuller (1895-1983)

## CHAPTER KEY POINTS

- Applies the process-model in practice for a *Collaborative Web Based System (CWBS)*
- Discusses the technical basis for the CWBS for business collaboration.
- Identifies and discusses the Business Process Management Notation (BPMN) that is used for modeling the processes for *CWBS.*
- Discusses the software architecture (based on the *CBPE* concept) for *CWBS.*
- Demonstrates, through an example use case related to memberships, how collaboration occurs in *CWBS*.

DOI: 10.4018/978-1-60566-689-1.ch006

- Demonstrates, by extending the above example, the placement of prospective members of a system in the right directory within *CWBS*.
- Explains how the customer requests can be accepted and processed in a collaborative manner within *CWBS*.

## INTRODUCTION

This chapter describes the modeling of the *Collaborative Web Based System (CWBS)*. This *CWBS* is the means by which the *CBPE* model, discussed earlier in this book, is practically implemented. The focus of this chapter, however, is on the models of collaborative business processes that can be implemented in CWBS. The software architecture aspect of the CWBS is based on the detailed discussions of technologies in previous chapters 2, 4 and 5. The models in this chapter are based on the Business Process Modeling Notation (BPMN) and the use cases are based on the specifications of the Unified Modeling Language (UML). These notations and the ensuing process models are important when organizations try to collaborate with each other. These process models show, visually, how the interactions amongst multiple organizations will take place from a business viewpoint. Subsequently, these process models need to implemented in the CWBS using appropriate technologies. Each collaborating organization can decide to use its own technology – however, the interaction between the organizations need to be based on web services (WS) that ensure that the specific technical environment does not impede business transactions.

## CREATION OF A CWBS BASED ON CBPE

There are four major inputs that go in the creation of a *Collaborative Web Based System*. These are shown in Figure 1 as:

(a) The concepts and theory of *CBPE* and business collaboration as discussed thus far in this book, which provides the foundation for why organizations should collaborate

(b) The modelling of business processes using a modelling standard – BPMN in this case, which provides the visual basis for carrying out activities geared towards satisfying customer needs

(c) The concept of Services Oriented Architecture (SOA) and Web Services (WS) – as discussed in Chapters 2, 4 and 5, that provides the basis for software architecture for CWBS that is independent of technological environments within the organization, and

*Figure 1. The creation of a CWBS*

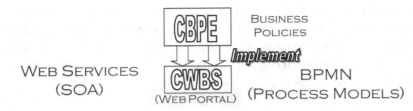

CONTENTS

(d)　The sourcing, updating and management of contents from multiple vendors that provides input into the collaborative processes as well as highlights the challenges associated with creating and implementing enforceable contracts between the vendors.

These four aspects of **CWBS** are discussed in detail in this chapter. The background to that discussion, however, is an understanding of how **CWBS** is related to, and based on, **CBPE** – the process model itself.

## CBPE and CWBS

The discussion on **CBPE** provides the basis for the creation of a system that can be used by one or more organizations in order to implement those collaborative processes. The **CWBS**, as discussed here, is the starting point for such implementation of a **CBPE**. When fully developed, a **CWBS**, unlike a stand-alone or single purpose software application, is a collaboration of many different software services and components. Furthermore, these components are not just statically linked with each other; rather, they are put together dynamically, which means these software components come together to satisfy the specific needs of a collaborative business process at a particular point in time, and then they disperse.

As shown in Figure 1, the **CBPE** dictates what is to be extracted and orchestrated from the **CWBS**. Each collaborate business processes is subject to the policies and procedures of the organizations participating in the collaboration. Since many different organizations are likely to collaborate with each other, a **CWBS** would be subject to many different business policies and procedures. Eventually, a **CWBS** will execute on a web portal as shown in Figure 1. However, the ownership, management and business model for the operation of such a web portal still remains a challenging issue in collaborative business. This is so because some organizations are keen to 'own' the collaborative portal, which leads to other potential participants from shying away from that portal. Alternatively, if a third-party web portal is maintained for collaborative business processes, then the ownership, maintenance and business model for that portal becomes a challenge – especially as the collaborating organizations can be geographically widely dispersed.

## BPMN AND CWBS

The Business Process Management Notation (BPMN - http://www.bpmn.org) is used as a tool for modelling the technical implementation of the *CBPE* model. It is worth understanding, briefly, what is BPMN and how it can help us model collaborative business processes. This is so because a business is a collection of processes that are increasingly complex, full of deeper interactions across systems and dependent on more collaborative activities. The Collaborative *Web-based System (CWBS)* which is the technical implementation of the *CBPE* requires extensive modelling of its business processes. BPMN is helpful in creating process models in a standardized manner. This standardized process modelling is helpful in understanding in detail, the creation, instantiation and management of the business processes. This overall activity of modelling and managing business processes is called Business Process Management (BPM). BPM encompasses methods, techniques and tools to design, enact, control, and analyse operational business processes involving humans, organizations, applications, documents and other sources of information (Aalst et al., 2003). BPM includes carrying out of appropriate process analysis by modelling new processes, demonstrates the operation of those engineered processes and provides facilities for reuse of those business processes.

From the technical point of view, the main objective of BPM is to provide a computer-based solution for management of processes that involve entities such as persons, activities and systems that all operate in tandem to fulfil particular business goals. (Yildiz et al. 2006).

According to the Notation Working Group Membership, (2001) Business Process Modelling Notation (BPMN) provides businesses with the capability of understanding their internal business procedures in a standardised graphical notation and gives organizations the ability to communicate these procedures in a standard manner. Furthermore, the graphical notation facilitates the understanding of the performance collaborations and business transactions between the organizations (http://www.bpmn.org).

BPMN is the standard for modelling business processes and Web Service processes, as put forth by the Business Process Management Initiative (BPMI – bpmi.

org). BPMN is a core enabler of BPM, a new initiative in enterprise architecture, which is concerned with managing change to improve business processes.

The BPMN demonstrates the interaction amongst all parties involved with a step-by-step process. These BPMN diagrams graphically present the chain of activities within a business process. According to White (2005), the characteristics of BPMN can be classified as follows:

- Be constrained to support only the concepts of modeling that are applicable to business processes.
- Be useful in illuminating a complex executable process.
- Be unambiguous. There should be a mapping from one or more BPMN notation instances to an execution-level instance (www.omg.org).

BPMN also offers technical business process diagrams, which represent the activities of the business process and the flow controls exactly the way they are performed. The advantages make the BPMN a tool for the test and validation of the proposed model.

A standard BPMN provides businesses with the capability of understanding their internal business procedures in a graphical notation and gives organizations the ability to communicate these procedures in a standard manner. Furthermore, the graphical notation facilitates the understanding of the performance collaborations and business transactions between the organizations.

Later, in this chapter, we also present the use cases that document the involved interactions between the users and the system. This interactions are what are modeled in the BPMN diagrams. Use cases were first described by Jacobson et al. (1992) in their objectory processes. These use cases can be shown in a diagram called the use case diagram. According to Unhelkar (2005b), use case diagrams provide a visual overview of the requirements of the system. The use case diagram provides a comprehensive high-level view of the requirements modeling workshops as they are able to visualize where they fit the system.

## SOA AND WEB SERVICES IN CWBS

*CWBS* is a system that also needs a software architecture in the background for it to be effective. Such software architecture involves the description of components from which systems are built, interactions among those components, patterns that guide their composition, and constraints on these patterns (Shaw & Garlan, 1996). Ideally, each software component needs to be defined and designed independently – enabling reuse and improved quality of the component within different contexts.

The characteristics of software architecture for the *CWBS* are:

- This software architecture would provide a high-enough level of abstraction of the CWBS system, enabling it to be viewed in its entirety
- The software architecture provides the constraints to the business processes involved in the collaboration.
- The information structure that must support the functionality required for the *CWBS*. This requires the dynamic behavior of the system to be taken into account.
- The software architecture must cater to the non-functional requirements of *CWBS*. These requirements include the software performance, security and reliability requirements associated with current functionality, as well as flexibility or extensibility requirements associated with accommodating future functionality at a reasonable cost to change.
- *CWBS* can potentially benefit from a variety of architectural styles (patterns) that can be utilized to analyze, model and construct a system. Each style has capabilities that are suitable for use in their specific areas and that can help in modelling complex interactions and reuse.

## Collaborative Web Based System: An SOA-Based Architecture

Having highlighted the importance of a good system architecture, we proceed here with discussion on the system architecture that is specific to *CWBS*. The *CWBS* system architecture deals with understanding, modeling and improving the process of capturing, analysing and presenting information to a collaborative group of users. Thus, the system architecture for *CWBS* needs to consider the collaborative nature of the business, its partnering systems, and the groups of customers involved in dealing with the business. For example, this system architecture has to consider the messages – typically service messages – and their orchestration that would make up the collaboration. Architecture developed for a single business is, therefore, relatively simple and different to a collaborative system architecture.

As mentioned in the previous section, system architecture is considered as an abstract view of the organization in terms of business processes. It could be interpreted as the senior executive's vision of the business in the context of information systems. Therefore, the *CWBS* system architecture needs to incorporate the visions and the ensuing policies of the decision makers of the collaborative organization. This architectural requirement is required of the functional architecture, network architecture and software architecture.

The general functional architecture in global collaborative information systems is based on the processes that transcend the system boundaries. The ever evolving strategies and business operations need to be incorporated in the information systems – and that is facilitated by the functional architecture. The functional architecture, thus, provides models for the implementation of the *CWBS* that are also flexible and that lend themselves to change. The flexible models for collaborative information systems enable business operations within and across the organization as they consider business activities beyond a single organization. The system architecture considers the activities going beyond one organization explicitly during the development phase of the *CWBS* in most cases. However, in addition, there is also a need to make provision for future activities – and assumptions to that effect need to be reflected in various components in the architecture.

In addition to the software components being incorporated in the system architecture, the architecture for *CWBS* also aims to understand the various roles and users involved in the collaborative organization. This consideration of the users helps the organization to ensure that the developed *CWBS* meets the objectives of the business visions and facilitate users to accomplish daily business activities – especially in a global collaborative business environment. This is so because in global collaborative information systems, business units and the business users are dispersed globally. Business users also appear from different backgrounds, cultures, and have quite distinct social expectations. In order to make sure each user carries out business tasks smoothly, understanding the potential roles of users is suggested as the essential primary stage in the architecture of *CWBS*.

Another important part of system architecture is to decompose business processes into smaller functional units. In global collaborative information systems development, a single business process may be operated through multiple business units (such as subsidiaries or branches). Applying the system decomposition method to partition business processes into functional units and identifying the interface/interaction between functional units could reduce the complexity and confusion in the system architecture design phase. Moreover, it helps the organization to identify any unnecessary functions that could be eliminated or reengineered as well as enhancing certain valuable functions.

Network architecture deals with the technical communication components of the information systems. Such architecture provides the basis for communications between various software components that are needed for collaborative business processes. The essential components of the network architecture are the physical wires (or wireless) connections and the supporting computing hardware. Collaborative web based systems are facilitated by provision of the commonly understood network cables, computer hardware and also the corresponding operating systems.

## COLLABORATIVE WEB BASED SYSTEM (CWBS) IN PRACTICE

The *CWBS* discussionthus far is on the various inputs and the approach to creating the system. This system, as mentioned earlier, is a loose collection of services (software components) that are themselves dynamically changing depending on the needs of the consumers and what the vendors have to offer. Thus, the database technologies, networks and communication technologies and the application services are all put together to create a *CWBS*. The advantage from such a *CWBS* in practice is not for one particular organization but from a conglomerate of organizations using these services.

The practical competitive advantage derived by the group of organizations getting together on the *CWBS* is that it opens up opportunities to streamline their collaborative processes, reduce costs, increase customer satisfaction, and enhance their planning abilities. The benefits of *CWBS* in practice can be categorized into the following: content, financial, customer, planning, production, and implementation. Each of these benefits is further discussed in the following subsections.

### Contents in CWBS

Contents for *CWBS* are made up of different size and type of data including text, video, television and various other multimedia contents. These contents are sourced from the collaborating businesses that want to vend their contents and services; at the same time, there are also many collaborating businesses that come to a portal in order to derive services.

*CWBS* facilitates communication, transactions and different valued added services in order to serve the consumers. This is because the advantages of transitioning to a collaborative environment are also not unfounded. Some of the main benefits that we see stemming from a successful participation in *CWBS* are as follows:

- Better information flow between systems since the *CWBS* provides access to the necessary information available to the people who need them.
- Improved customer projected image, since the adoption of collaboration enables the business to serve the customer in a personalized manner by adding to the projection of a forward thinking and dynamic image of the company.
- Rapid and dynamic customization of products and services being offered by the organization.

# Financial

One of the core benefits of driving efficiency through the collaboration is cost reduction. *CWBS* allows the organization to maximize profitability through reduced customer service administration and storage costs. Less staff is required to maintain the products or services and details can be made available to customers directly without human intervention.

Another benefit is the improvement and reliability of financial information. Collaborative systems maintain centralized databases that are linked to other enterprise systems (e.g., ERP, CRM) providing integrity, consistency, and real-time data access to managers so that they can manage the supply chain with an organizational perspective.

# Customer

*CWBS* through customer portals, provide customers with an instantaneous and holistic view of the progress of their transactions within the organization. This level of service (coupled with benefits derived from production) results in higher customer satisfaction levels and, in turn, improves the firm's ability to attract new customers and, more importantly, retain them.

The ability to capture customer transactions and preferences online provides the organization with the facility to track their behavior and, in turn, customize products and services to cater to them (Bragg, 2002). Because of the level of workflow automation and inventory statistics, organizations are able to provide accurate estimates of when orders will be filled at the time of ordering. This is known as capable-to-promise (CTP) capability.

# Planning

Companies with collaborative systems have the ability to mathematically and graphically observe the performance of the business processes. Collaborative systems provide the organization with the capabilities to derive more accurate demand planning with improved precision, create shorter planning and production cycles, establish one central data repository for the entire organization, and facilitate enhanced communications through rapid information dissemination (Bragg, 2002; Gledhill, 2002).

## Production

*CWBS* provides the ability to holistically manage the collaboration of multiple organizations, allowing managers to respond dynamically to any situation that may arise so as to minimize its impact on production.

By measuring the level of inventory and analysing turnover, supply chain systems can improve turnover by reducing the need for safety stocks and the risk of retailer out-of-stocks. Inventory items need to be numbered consistently in order to facilitate measurement and tracking.

*CWBS* measure the performance of the collaboration of multiple organizations through the generation of various collaborative portal levels. This allows process quality issues to be tracked and rectified, isolates bottlenecks in the process, and measures lead times so they can be aligned with available capacity in order to maximize plant utilization.

## Implementation

Consultants promise responsiveness and Plug & Play integrations. However, documented examples of collaboration failures by organizations are evidence that the implementation of collaborative systems is not as easy as vendors claim. Collaborative software requires a significant degree of customization in order to integrate the software to the rest of the organization. Customization to enterprise software comes with great risk and significant cost for ongoing maintenance.

Organizations need to take strategic view of collaborative systems. More so, they tend only to focus on transactions systems (e.g., inventory control, order processing, etc.), which provide little visibility of the enterprise. In a majority of implementations, analysis has focused on the technical aspects of integrating systems with the remaining architecture. One area that has been neglected is the effect on business processes. Organizations expect staff either to just accept change or to customize the software.

Cross-borders logistics, culture, language and economics, and regulatory climate are just some considerations that can affect the integration of business processes between regional offices and external organizations, creating communication issues throughout the collaboration. One ill-performing participant in the collaboration will affect the performance of the systems.

Many implementations have been classified as failures because of collaborative system's perceived inability to reap benefits and produce cost savings, as expected. However, in many cases, it is the initial analysis of cost and benefits that has been flawed.

The implementation and support of collaborative systems can be rather complex and, therefore, demands sophisticated resources and incremental implementations. Unfortunately, during the planning and analysis phases of implementation projects, organizations have failed to properly appreciate the level of complexity involved, resulting in significant under resourcing.

Due to the extent of failed collaborative system implementations, it is imperative to construct an appropriate analysis and development methodology that can be adopted as the roadmap for enterprises flourishing in collaborative systems development and operations. The following proposed methodology has been applied in developing the *CWBS* from recognizing problems and analyzing requirements to the implementation and operation. The development of the *CWBS* embraced the following phases:

1. Identifying the collaborative nature of the information management structure within *CWBS* that is, in principle, made up of numerous information systems;
2. Identifying software components that need to be connected to each other over physical networks and operating systems;
3. Ensuring detailed modelling of appropriate collaborative business processes that can be implemented and configured with *CWBS*;
4. Establishing, defining and modelling the interfaces amongst various software components of *CWBS*;
5. Modeling and developing new collaborative business processes across multiple organizations that can be implemented in *CWBS*;
6. Confirming strategic alignment of the business vision and subsequent policies and procedures within the software elements of *CWBS*;
7. Making provision for future changes to business processes that need to reflected in the implementation of *CWBS*;
8. Quality assurance of the *CWBS* by following the known principles of software quality assurance (discussed later in this book).

Given the global nature of collaborative systems and their level of required integration, a common ICT (information and communication technology) infrastructure must be able to extend around the globe, to support open and rapid communication, and to integrate easily with the architecture of not just the organization but also the architecture of customers and suppliers.

The enterprise's information systems architecture must be properly analyzed to ensure that it satisfies the needs of collaborative systems and can support security boundaries, largely distributed database operations, and event-driven applications. The architecture needs to be durable, flexible, and embedded with the appropriate middleware in order to integrate as easily as possible (Zieger, 2001). It also must be sufficiently robust in order to cater to firewalls and other security measures and have 24/7 global access and redundant systems and processes in order to handle events when collaborative systems need to be off-line for maintenance, emergency, and recovery purposes. In accordance with these criteria, the Internet-based structure can be considered the most appropriate platform to satisfy these requirements. Nevertheless, participants in collaboration have various capability and maturity levels in information management structure. Hence, prior to adopting the Internet technology for integration, the existing information management structure of each participant must be determined. One of the most critical functions of supply collaboration is to ensure the effective integration of information and material flows through the system.

These components also are considered the connecting components (or connecting business functions) among participants in the collaboration. These components include order management, customer service, invoicing, forecasting, distribution requirements planning (DRP), warehouse and inventory management, manufacturing planning, production control (MRPII), and integrated logistics. In order to enhance the collaboration, it is important to understand what happens currently. Generally, collaborative business processes may include the procurement, production, ordering, delivery, and inventory paths, both within the company and external parties.

Each process then should be prioritized and broken down into its sub processes, identifying each of its sources, outputs, transformations, timings, resources utilized, and requirements. This also would be an opportune time to gather metrics concerning each of the processes in order to establish a baseline for identifying problems and to measure future process improvement.

Once architectural issues have been resolved and data requirements have been determined, a structure needs to be established to enable common linkages between data providers and data recipients of the collaboration (i.e., customers and suppliers) and linkages within collaborative processes. This will require the need to ascertain whether there are any missing links and to determine how the data required will be sourced or provided and in which format.

## Impediments to CWBS Growth

There are several potential challenges to *CWBS* growth in emerging economies. Solutions providers that aggressively bring to market half-baked products that have not undergone stringent security testing would discourage consumers from paying from their computers. Privacy of the users can lead to a backlash. An unchecked 'push' model and consequent spamming can lead to rejection of the service offering. Quality of Service is a serious concern in *CWBS* operation scenarios, and delays in confirmations of transactions reaching the subscribers can lead to adoption problems. Timely enactment and enforcement of transactions are also essential to give the various stakeholders the comfort level needed for collaboration. These are some potential obstacles to widespread the adoption to the contents of *CWBS*, but hopefully players in the value chain are cognizant of these challenges and their responsibilities, and will hopefully work together to mitigate these risks.

## Developing New Business Processes

After conducting a detailed analysis of existing collaborative business n processes and identifying any inefficiencies and/or gaps in the process, a proposal should be created for the design of new processes. Not only should new processes cater to anticipated ISCM processing, but they also should be sufficiently visionary in order to accommodate other strategic initiatives (i.e., CRM, Supplier Management, and Knowledge Management).

The new collaborative environment should be modeled in a manner so that collaboration blueprints can be generated. Tyndall et al. (2002) suggest an iterative approach to process design, whereby a process is broken down into stages and then defined, analyzed, executed, assessed, and then redefined. This cycle continues until the appropriate performance expectations have been achieved. This process can become quite complex and convoluted, once organizations begin to incorporate backend systems and the processes of other organizations. Based on metrics determined during the initial business process review, goals should be set for process improvement.

The software architecture is constructed mostly in a Web-based environment that involves HTTP, server-side Java, and XML. ISCM systems are generally no different than other business applications but still require some interfacing with old technologies, such as aging ERPs and legacy systems (Zieger, 2001). The following section presents the proposed model of the *CWBS* as far as the developed business processes of those organizations (entering the expected collaborative environment) are concerned. Specific business processes considered are:

- Data structure.
- Services and applications.
- System interface.
- Registration of the prospective member
- Registration in the directory.
- Process product or service request.

## CWBS ARCHITECTURE

The discussion thus far provides a detailed basis for understanding, modeling and application of *Collaborative Web Based System (CWBS)* originated from the theoretical concept of the *CBPE*. The definitions and description of what comprises a collaborative system seems to depend on the perspective of the enterprise, the architect and the value it adds to an architecture work. *CWBS* deals specifically with collaborative business process issues that arise when an application needs the collaboration of multiple organizations specifically when these organizations are not necessarily known to each other. Technology facilitates this dynamic collaborative environment based on correlating data structure, services, application and the designed interfaces.

### Data Structure

The architecture of the business deals with the data and the corresponding model which need to be integrated into the system. The information architecture is addressed in the initial stage of the System Development Life Cycle (SDLC) commonly recognized as "problem space".

In order to design the accurate information structure for *CWBS*, the challenges of the business, their requirements, their interactions with external and internal parties and their constraints need to be addressed. The architecture is modeled here in order to communicate the requirements throughout the project. Figure 2, 3 and 4 presents the modeling of these business requirements in a BPMN diagram. These business architectures define the enterprise business model and process cycles and timing also by showing the integrated functions into the system.

Chapter 4, earlier in this book, presented a detailed discussion of the use of the emerging technologies in proposed collaborative environment as the provision of solution to the problem (implementation of a system capable of collaborating across multiple organizations) requires detailed understanding of the technologies. The provided solution helps the user to easily understand and use the interface and components.

The requirements models in the problem space, and the designs in the solution space are either expanded or tempered, based on the constraints in both organizational and technical level. These constraints result in a background or technological architecture, which is also a consistent set of ICT standards, which provide the infrastructures to support the aforementioned *CWBS* architecture.

The non-functional requirements of the system such as security and speed, for example, are tempered by the network infrastructure of the organizations and the way their business processes are broadcasted. The structure of data is based on an

*Figure 2. Business process: Register prospective members*

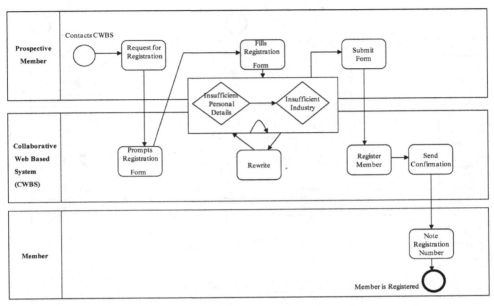

*Figure 3. Business process: Place the registration in the directory*

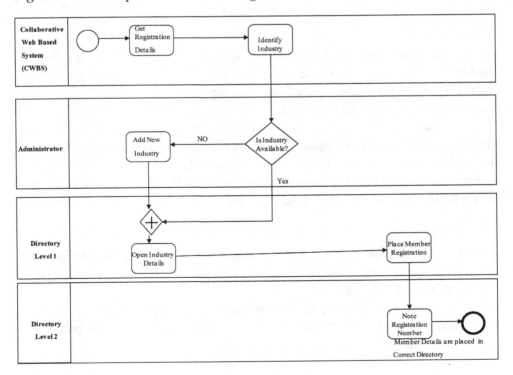

*Figure 4. Business process: Process service or product request*

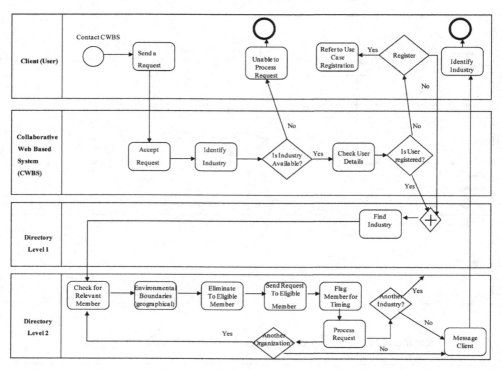

understanding and applying the constraints at the problem and the solution level of the SDLC. This application of the constraints is achieved by identifying and refining the requirements of the stakeholders, developing views of the architecture that show how the concerns and the requirements are going to be addressed.

Thus, data structure provides a strategic context for the evolution of the collaborative systems and strategies in response to the constantly changing needs of the business environment. Furthermore, a reliable data and business architecture is achieved through the right balance between IT efficiency and business innovation. The advantages that result from a reliable data and business architecture are as follows:

- An efficient collaborative operation that is prepared for the possible changes of the requirements, and that provides excellent interoperability amongst its systems and networks.
- A common and robust security policy that applies to *CWBS*.
- Create flexibility for *CWBS* which is easily adoptable by the participant organizations.

- Simplification of the complex *CWBS*.
- Provide for future growth of *CWBS* in response to the future needs of the participated businesses.

*CWBS* applications architecture suggests that the database architecture to pool the data in one common database, as far as possible. This pooling of data in a common source enables streamlined process-flows and process architectures which are able to handle the information in a consistent manner. *CWBS* architectures also facilitate reuse through use of design patterns. Furthermore, this application architecture needs to handle the replication of events on each client device. Creation or modification of events needs to be synchronized on each transaction.

## Application and Services

*CWBS* enables the businesses to enter a dynamic collaborative environment serving the specific services of the business required by their customer. These personalized services are then offered in the electronic collaborative environment. This is so because; the ensuing *CWBS* provides opportunities for the business to interoperate with the business processes of the other organizations. These collaborative business processes, applications and services are offered by *CWBS* architecture.

The need to consider the fundamentals of collaboration in a formal architecture, and the need to translate the advantages, namely dynamic collaborative environment, into flexible enterprise applications have never been so high. Such application of an architectural framework brings together, in a cohesive manner, the specifications and the details of all interfaces, applications, networks, databases and security aspects of the enterprise. Thus a collaborative business process cuts cross multiple systems and multiple functional groups within multiple enterprises. However, *CWBS* remain as a common platform for creation of collaborative business applications. The *dynamic collaborative nature* and *static system nature* of the *CWBS* allows the applications and services to connect at every step of the application execution either to get some information or authenticate the transactions.

## Interfaces

*CWBS* application architecture needs to interface with the various networks and middleware that will be used in its deployment. For example, when an application is submitted that needs to collaborate with multiple organizations, this application needs to reach various organizational networks and middleware in order to satisfy the requirements of the original submitted application. The location of the execution of the application, the involvement of third-party deployments and security also need to be considered in *CWBS* applications architecture.

The interface of these applications needs to be designed in such a way as to enable their access and coordination between network operators and service providers. Collaborative applications need to be designed keeping the "workflow" in mind. The mapping between the content management systems and the actual application will include availability and processing of data related to all business activities of the organizations collaborating with each other.

## Registration of Prospective Members

We consider here a couple of collaborative business processes within the CBWS context. Consider, for example, the registration process of users or members to a collaborative business. We use the concept of use cases (from the UML) and the BPMN diagrams for modeling the business process of a prospective member who wants to register himself or herself in a collaborative system. The prospective members, such as user, person (for example, doctor or patient) and organizations (such as a hospital or a medical association) could connect to the *CWBS* to register. The *CWBS* does not classify them as members until the registration is completed.

A prospective member connects to the *CWBS* and requests to register in the system. The *CWBS* prompts the appropriate member registration form to the prospective member to enter the relevant details. If the information is insufficient or incorrect, the prospective member is asked to input correct details.

Then, the *CWBS* prompts for the registration form to be submitted and the prospective member submits the registration form. At the end, the *CWBS* registers the prospective member by sending a unique registration number. The system recognizes the prospective member as a member and allows the client to log out of the *CWBS*.

Table 1 presents the detailed technical issues involved in the registration of the members. The system recognizes them as prospective members until the last process, when they are officially registered in the system. The system might issue them with a Member Identification Number (MIN) and recognize them as a member. The following BPMN depicts the pictorial illustration of the use case adopted from Unified Modeling Language (UML).

As depicted in Figure 2, the developed system is ready to accept registration of all prospective members. A prospective member could be any one of the following persons: user of the system, doctor, patient; or an organization such as police, insurance company, pharmacist, hospital, health-care system or any other organizations. Hence, this is the practical implementation of the *CBPE* model. The registration of the prospective members is not shown in the figure.

*Table 1. Use case: Register prospective member*

| Use Case: | Register prospective member |
|---|---|
| Actors: | Member, Collaborative Web Based System (*CWBS*), prospective member |
| Description: | Prospective member is registered in the *CWBS*<br>Please note that this is a generic use case. Different prospective members could come in to register. |
| Pre-condition: | Prospective member is using Web Services.<br>Prospective member is willing to work through the *CWBS.* |
| Post-condition: | Prospective member is upgraded to a member. |
| Type: | Complex |
| Normal Course of Events: | 1. Prospective member connects to the *CWBS* and requests to register in the directory level 1.<br>2. *CWBS* prompts the appropriate member registration form to the member.<br>3. Prospective member enters his/her details in the registration form (A1)(A2).<br>4. *CWBS* prompts that the registration form is to be submitted.<br>5. Prospective member submits the registration form.<br>6. *CWBS* registers prospective member sending a unique registration number.<br>7. Member logs out of the *CWBS*. |
| Alternate Course of Events: | A1: Information entered is insufficient or incorrect. Prospective member is asked to input correct member ID.<br>A2: It is crucial for the prospective member to fill in all details specifically identifying the relevant industry |
| References | • A prospective member could be any one of the following persons: doctor, patient, police, insurance company, pharmacist, hospital, healthcare system who/that is not yet registered with *CWBS*.<br>• When any of the following categories of industry/person registers with *CWBS*, it/s/he is classified as a member. |

## Managing the Registration Contents

The following section demonstrates when the *CWBS* places the registration in the allocated directory in order to avoid the pollution of the directories. The *CWBS* identifies the relevant member industry from the registration form. The *CWBS* identifies the industry's registration by informing the administrator for further direction if the industry does not exist. The directory level 1 receives an identification number from that specific member and the *CWBS* registers the member details of the member in directory level 2. Finally, the system stores the member details in the database. This is an automated process, and the only instance of human–actor involvement occurs when the specified industry is not available in *CWBS*.

Table 2 presents the use case of the technical issues involved in placing the member registration in the right directory before the pictorial illustration of the

*Table 2. Use case: Registration in the directory*

| Use Case: | Registration in the directory. |
|---|---|
| Actors: | Directory level 1, directory level 2, administrator. |
| Description: | When the *CWBS* place the registered members in the right place in order to locate and consume them. |
| Pre-condition: | Registration has taken place. |
| Post-condition: | Directories communicates with each other. |
| Type: | Very complex. |
| Normal Course of Events: | 1. *CWBS* identifies the relevant member area from the registration form (A1). 2. Directory level 1 receives an identification number from that specific member. 3. *CWBS* registers the member details of the member in Directory level 2. 4. Member's details are stored in the database. |
| Alternate Course of Events: | A1: If the industry does not exist in the directory level 2, the *CWBS* informs the administrator for further direction. |
| References | This is an automated use case. The only instance of human–actor involvement occurs when the specified industry is not available in *CWBS*. |

BPMN in Figure 3.

Figure 3 illustrates how an automated process places the member details in the right place for the uncomplicated publish/locate process. The difference between the process shown in Figure 3, and a non-collaborative business process would be that the non-collaborative business process would *not* have the directories.

## Process Service for Product Request

This section is a further illustration of the nature of the *CWBS*. The channels of identifying a desired organization are based on directories in which the products and services they offer are stored. The process is triggered when a client submits a request (an inquiry) to the *CWBS*. It is very important that the user is using the Web Services. The *CWBS* accepts the request and identifies the member's relative industry/industries based on the submitted request.

The *CWBS* prompts an optional form requesting details of registration if the Client is not a member. The *CWBS* prompts a message denying the request when there is no prior registry of the organization capable of handling the request. The *CWBS* finalizes the appropriate checks and submits the application to the directory level 1. The directory level 1 identifies the industry and submits the application to suitable level 2 directory to identify the organization capable of handling the requests. Then, the *CWBS* eliminates the organizations that do not meet the environmental boundaries (geographical, budget, member optional preferences). The *CWBS* follows eliminations of the capable parties that have received the most recent requests. In the next stage, the *CWBS* processes the client request and collaborates with selected members regarding the request.

Right at this stage, the system flags the members involved in the process who are not to receive the next query. The application returns back to level 1 and if other industries should be involved in the request, the *CWBS* goes through the process of locating them in order to complete the request. Finally, the *CWBS* prompts a message to the client, informing him/her about the outcome of the requested application, and allows the user to log out.

Table 3 presents the use case of the technical issues involved in processing an application submitted by a member (or non-member using the required technologies) before the pictorial illustration of the BPMN in Figure 4.

Figure 4 illustrates the finalization of the processing of a request that could be a classified as a very complex type. Figure 4 presents the engineering of the busi-

*Table 3. Use case: Process request*

| Use Case: | Process request. |
|---|---|
| **Actors:** | Client, *CWBS*, directory level1 and directory level 2. |
| **Description:** | Client requests a service or product (an inquiry) from the *CWBS*. |
| **Pre-condition:** | Client has to be using Web Services. |
| **Post-condition:** | 1. The system looks for Next Industry/Organization if the request is uncompleted.<br>2. Client receives a report on the request. |
| **Type:** | Very complex. |
| **Normal Course of Events:** | 1. *CWBS* accepts the request and identify the member area (A1)(A2)<br>2. Directory level 1 checks directory level 2 to identify the party capable of handling the requests.<br>3. *CWBS* eliminates the options that do not meet the environmental boundaries (geographical, budget, member optional preferences).<br>4. *CWBS* follows eliminations of the capable parties that have received recent prior requests.<br>5. *CWBS* processes the client request and collaborates with selected members regarding the request.<br>6. *CWBS* flags the members involved in the process not to receive the next query.<br>7. Processes request (A3).<br>8. *CWBS* prompts a message to client informing him/her about the outcome of the requested application.<br>9. Client logs out. |
| **Alternate Course of Events:** | A1: If the client is not a member, the *CWBS* prompts an optional form requesting details for registration.<br>A2: If the industry is not available, the *CWBS* prompts a message denying the request.<br>A3: If other industries should be involved in the request, the *CWBS* goes through the process of locating them. |
| **References** | |

ness process enabling the collaboration across multiple organizations. Figure 4 also clearly demonstrates how they collaborate without even knowing each other. The Web Services technology creates an opportunity for their application to process and progress, regardless of the original platform used for their ordinary process.

Collaborations, facilitated electronically, are feasible only when they are supported by certain infrastructures. These infrastructures span across various aspects of a business as well as their collaborations. The existing structure of the organization is bound to have an impact on the way in which it participates in electronic collaborations. Not only is the organization required to be structured to handle collaborations, but given the complexities associated with work in a collaborative environment, all the activities and tasks dealing with communications, information and transactions should also be well structured and well balanced. E-Collaboration is more complex and sophisticated, it is slowly changing the functionality and nature of the organization of the business as well as of the structures of the standard collaborating groups.

## ACTION POINTS

1.  Identify the important collaborative business processes of your organization and model them using the Business Process Management Notation (you may need a modelling tool to do this).
2.  Discuss how the Collaborative Web Based System can add value to the existing business processes by creating opportunities for these processes to collaborate.
3.  Identify how the *CWBS* can manage to offer the products or services that are offered by your organizations in a collaborative manner by making use of services available through partnering organizations to the customers
4.  Describe how each of the identified processes in the *CWBS* would handle calls for products or services that could enhance the performance of your organization.
5.  Create the outline of a Test plan that will help test CWBS specific to your organization (this testing will include interfacing with potential collaborators).

# REFERENCES

Aalst, W. M. P., Hofstede, A. H. M., & Weske, M. (2003). Business process management: A survey, in business process management. In *Proceedings of the First International Conference.* Springer Verlag.

Bragg, S. (2002). *10 symptoms of poor supply chain performance. ARC advisory group.* Retrieved July 21, 2003, from http://www.idii.com/wp/arc_sc_perf.pdf

Gledhill, J. (2002). Create values with IT investment: How to generate a healthy ROI across the enterprise. *Food Processing, 63*(9), 76–80.

Jacobson, I., Christerson, M., Jonsson, P., & Overgaard, G. (1992). *Object-oriented software engineering: A use case driven approach.* Reading, MA: Addison-Wesley.

Notation Working Group Membership. (2001, November 1). Business process modeling notation working group chapter (BPMI Document No. NWG-2001-09-01R4). Retrieved from http://www.bpmn.org/Documents/NWG-2001-09-01R4%20Charter.pdf

Shaw, M., & Garlan, D. (1996). *Software architecture: Perspective on an emerging discipline.* New York: Prentice Hall.

Tyndall, G., et al. (2002). *Making it happen: The value producing supply chain. Centre for business innovation—Ernst & Young.* Retrieved July 21, 2003, from http://www.cbi.cgey.com/journal/issue3/features/makin/makin.pdf

White, S. A. (2005). BPMN fundamentals. *Object Management Group.*

Yildiz, U., Marjanovic, O., & Godart, C. (2006). Contract-driven cross-organizational business processes. In *Proceedings of the ACIS Conference, ACIS 2006,* Adelaide, Australia.

Zieger, A. (2001). *Preparing for supply chain architectures. PeerToPeerCentral. com.* Retrieved July 21, 2003, from http://www-106.ibm.com/developerworks/web/library/ wa-supch.html?dwzone=web

# Chapter 7

# Organizational Structure and Technology Adaptation

*I haven't failed; I've found 10,000 ways that don't work.*

Thomas Edison (1847-1931)

## CHAPTER KEY POINTS

- Discusses the effect of collaborative business approach on the organizational structure.
- Discusses the various technology acceptance models in the context of collaborative business.
- Highlights the importance and relevance of mobile technologies including mobile devices, mobile networks and mobile contents to collaborative business
- Discusses and analyses a detailed survey that is used to understand the effect of the various technical factors of web services and mobile technologies that influence the organization;
- Discusses the results from the survey related to adoption of collaborative technologies.

DOI: 10.4018/978-1-60566-689-1.ch007

- Discusses the global management issues and challenges that organizations need to face resulting from global collaboration.

## INTRODUCTION

This chapter discusses the effect of the technologies of Web Services (WS) and Mobile Technologies (MT) on the organizational structure of an enterprise. Subsequently, this chapter also discusses the various technology acceptance models in the context of collaborative business. The survey described in this chapter highlights the importance of the various emerging technologies (as outlined earlier in Chapter 2 and discussed in greater detail in Chapter 5) in terms of their adoptability and their impact on the collaborative business. Thus, in a way, this chapter further extends the *Collaborative Business Process Engineering (CBPE)* model, but from a technology adoption viewpoint.

The organizational structure for a business that is collaborating electronically with other businesses is different from a non-collaborative business. This is because the organizational motivation for collaborative business is open and interactive, as opposed to the closed (and usually hierarchical) organizational structures. Web Services (WS) and Mobile Technologies (MT) influence various dimensions of a business – such as its technology usage, its business processes and its socio-cultural facets. The changes to the organizational structure are an interesting and important part of the social dimension of a business. The survey-based industrial feedback derived from an earlier study, and discussed here from a technology adoption viewpoint does quiz the organizations in terms of their readiness to adapt WS and MT in undertaking business collaboration.

## ORGANIZATIONAL STRUCTURE IN COLLABORATIVE MANAGEMENT

The effect on business process re-engineering, as discussed by Hammer and Champy, and later by numerous authors, led to the creation of a flattened organizational hierarchy. This was so because, by using information technologies, it was possible for an individual to carry out the function that required two or three layers of management above her. For example, an account officer in a bank is able to open an account easily through the information and knowledge available to her by use of information technology.

The information *and* communications technology – especially Web Services – have a similar significant impact on the organizational structure. Cabrera and Kurt

(2005) highlight this impact of WS by discussing the interoperation of organizations that is enabled by the interaction and exchange of data and information of the business applications' through the Extensible Markup Language (XML). Alag (2006) further states that the adoption of mobile technologies (MT), and the subsequent modeling and use of mobile business processes, render the user (worker) of the organization independent of location. This freedom from the need to be present at a particular location in order to carry out business activities is a crucial factor that brings about change to the organizational structure. For example, through MT, the need to supervise a worker, face-to-face, is simply not there, rendering that particular management activity and, eventually even that hierarchy redundant. Gan (2006) again highlights that the adoption of MT, besides improving the user's experience, also has an effect on the work environment. These changes to the work environment, as discussed here, also change the organizational structures and the type of the organization itself. To discuss the impact of WS and MT on collaborative business, we consider the four different structures of the organizations (Bartlett and Ghoshal 1998). These structures are classified as multinational, international, global and transnational. Lan and Unhelkar (2005) have done a detailed study of these organizational structures in the context of globalization. However, here, these organizational types and their corresponding structures are discussed as they undergo changes when they are subject to collaborative business approaches.

## Collaborative Structure of Multinational Organization

The structure of a multinational organization consists of the headquarters, as the top level of corporate management in the country of the enterprise's origin and a number of national and foreign independent subsidiaries. These subsidiaries are always required to report to the top level of corporate management. When these multinational organizations utilize collaborative technologies, particularly WS and MT, their structures undergo changes. Table 1 shows the advantages and disadvantages of the multinational organization structure.

## Collaborative Structure of International Organization

An enterprise with the international organization structure contains a large national headquarters and a corresponding international department. These two departments report to the CEO directly. This kind of organizational structure increases the control of non-national companies and provides frequent knowledge sharing and communications between subsidiaries. This kind of organizational structure is good at transferring knowledge and expertise to foreign markets, which may be less advanced in the development of technology and business operations. On the

*Table 1. Advantages and disadvantages of the multinational organization structure and effect of WS and MT on these organizational structures*

| Factors | Changes Due to Collaborative Technologies |
|---|---|
| Transportation of goods. | Reduced movement of goods as some of the products can be utilized from a partner's warehouse etc. |
| Access to the raw materials. | Enhanced communication between subsidiaries. |
| Tax and tariffs. | Lower taxes depending upon the agreement with nations. |
| Market demand. | Enhanced strategic vision in global market demand. |
| Product design adjustment. | Reduction time on production design<br>Subsidiaries use collaborative technologies in order to have enhanced communications. |
| Information sharing-controlling. | Enhanced cooperation and information exchange between the headquarters and the subsidiaries. |

other hand, the local subsidiaries are free to adopt the new product, technology and strategy. Table 2 shows the advantages and disadvantages of the international organization structure.

## Collaborative Structure of Global Organization

Global organization structure usually utilizes a highly centralized structure with a centrally located global world headquarter. Most of the strategic decisions in such organization are made by the world headquarters and it usually does not request any suggestions from any national or international subsidiaries. The structural configuration is based on the central assets of the organization. Resources, responsibilities and

*Table 2. Factors influencing the structure and operation of an international organisation due to adoption of collaborative technologies*

| Factors | Changes Due to Collaborative Technologies |
|---|---|
| Strategy for foreign business operation. | Causes potential collaboration between the domestic headquarters and the international department. |
| Business integration. | Collaboration has a crucial influence on the entire enterprise's organization structure. |
| Central control and coordination. | Increase control and coordination while the foreign subsidiaries still have quite flexible autonomous power. |
| Management of international departments. | Develop environment for managers of international departments. International departments can focus on developing new subsidiaries and support subsidiaries with uniform assistance for better strategic decision. |

the business operations of foreign subsidiaries are limited to only sales and services; thus, the configuration can be described as a centralized hub. All subsidiaries are treated equally no matter whether they are regional, national or international. In the global organization structure, the enterprise pursues maximum scope of economy efficiency and the fastest decision-making, and becomes a corporation without a nationality.

The global strategic vision in a global organization structure is developed and decided by the headquarters. The consideration of the strategic vision decision is focused on the benefit of the entire enterprise; the individual subsidiary's benefit is expelled. In other words, all the strategic decisions must be made based on the advantageousness of the entire business operation and implementation. A global organization structure can be further classified into three types: global area structure, global product structure and global functional structure. There are many factors that should be considered before the enterprise decides to adopt one of these types. The factors are maturity of the production line, level of coordination required across borders, scope economic importance, specific technologies required, level of product flexibility in satisfying various local market demands, and level of expected centralization. Table 3 shows the advantages and disadvantages of the global organization structure.

## Collaborative Structure of Transnational Organization

A transnational model by Bartlett and Ghoshal (1998) contains a combination of the advantages of the traditional models (multinational, international and global). The transnational company defines the problem in very different terms. It seeks efficiency- not for its own sake- but as a means to achieve global competitiveness. It acknowledges the importance of local responsiveness, but as a tool for achiev-

*Table 3. Factors influencing the structure and operation of global international organization due to adoption of collaborative technologies factors influencing*

| Factors | Changes Due to Collaborative Technologies |
|---|---|
| Scope of economy and domestic demand. | Provides better correlation between the economy and the domestic demand and at the same time widens the scope for satisfying demand through collaboration. |
| Strategic vision. | Provides an integrated, centralized and focused global strategic vision that enables the organization to collaborate with other partnering organizations to satisfy customer demands. |
| Subsidiaries in the region. | Increases the communications between subsidiaries and partnering organizations in the geographical region. |

ing flexibility in international operations. Innovations are regarded as an outcome of a larger process of organizational learning that encompasses every member of the company. This redefinition of the issues allows managers of the transnational company to develop a broader perspective and leads to very different criteria for making choices.

Furthermore, the role of subsidiaries in the transnational structure varies in the business operations. In some markets, national subsidiaries adopt standard global products from headquarters and the role of the subsidiaries is limited to implementing the central decisions effectively. Some other subsidiaries are encouraged to differentiate or to develop products that other subsidiaries adopt. In this case, headquarters will give up its leadership power and hand it over to the subsidiary. In addition to the global products, there are a number of factors that are considered in determining the role of subsidiaries in the transnational model. These factors are government regulations, the availability of technologies and the position of global competitors.

Flows of knowledge and information are in both directions: between headquarters and the subsidiary and from subsidiary to subsidiary in the transnational enterprise. Some knowledge or business solutions may be created by the joint effort of subsidiaries for the dispersed units. The competence of knowledge creation in subsidiaries balances the central solution dependency and provides the worldwide learning opportunity.

## ORGANIZATION STRUCTURE IN A COLLABORATIVE ENVIRONMENT

The organizational structure of a business also undergoes change when the CBPE processes are implemented. This is so because each organization needs to modify their products and/or services to not only cater to the global collaborative processes but, in addition, they also need to comply with their local and national conditions. Any ordinary organization that enters the *CBPE* is automatically classified as a global organization as such organization will have to be fully equipped to handle the requirements of cross-border transactions. They therefore should restructure their capabilities to be able to satisfy the international demand. As discussed earlier, these restructures help the organization to match their skills to the requirements of the global factors such as supply chain, government regulations (such as tariffs) and variation in the local currency in the global market.

# TECHNOLOGY ACCEPTANCE BY ORGANIZATION

Acceptance of Web Services (WS) and Mobile Technology (MT) by organizations requires a good understanding of the technologies (as discussed in Chapter 5) and a solid approach to their adoption within the organization. While organizations are investing heavily in information and communications technologies, the effect of these technologies in bringing about collaborative business is still not fully realized. One of the reasons for this lack of exploitation of collaborative technologies could be corresponding lack of a well-defined approach to its adaptation. In order for WS and MT technologies to improve collaboration, these technologies must be simultaneously accepted and used by many organizations. Furthermore, the individual employees and customers need to be sufficiently interested in order to make these technologies work as well.

## Extending the Technology Acceptance Theories to Collaborative Business

There have been many research studies in the area of technological acceptance by individuals and organizations, such as the *Unified Theory of Acceptance and Use of Technology (UTAUT) model* by Venkatesh et al. (2003).

Figure 1 presents the UTAUT model where there are links between gender, age, experience, voluntariness of use and performance expectancy, effort expectancy, social influences and facilitating conditions. All the mentioned issues will impact on each other to generate behavioral intention and use behavior.

The UTAUT model is constructed based on eight models (see Venkatesh et al., 2003). We develop these models further from the point of view of utilizing them for adoption of collaborative technologies (they are summarized in Table 4.).

The Theory of Acceptance Model (TAM) is designed to predict IT acceptance and usage in the workplace. The TAM is that the perceived usefulness of a system and its perceived ease of use determine an individual's intention to use the system, which leads to the actual use of the system. Figure 2 depicts the theory of the acceptance model and its use in *CWBS*. TAM can be made relevant through the success stories of other previously successful implementations of the WS and MT in collaborative businesses

TAM is tailored to Information System contexts, and was designed to predict information technology acceptance and usage on the job. In *CWBS*, TAM facilitates the measuring of the perceived usefulness, as well as ease of use. This enables the organizations to measure the behavior of the users of the *CWBS*. TAM measures the degree to which a person believes that using a particular system would be free of effort (Davis, 1989).

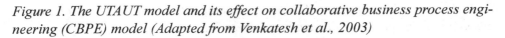

*Figure 1. The UTAUT model and its effect on collaborative business process engineering (CBPE) model (Adapted from Venkatesh et al., 2003)*

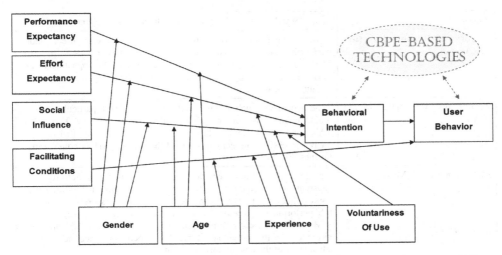

The theory of *Diffusion of Innovation (DoI)* has been designed to explain adoption of innovations (including those within IT) by dividing the population into categories (innovators, early adopters, early majority, late majority and laggards). This model can help the organizations to understand the user's behavior from the collaborative system perspective. The diffusion process follows an S-curve, and the rate of adoption is affected by four main factors described below. These factors are explained in terms of the proposed collaborative environment:

1. Perceived attributes of the innovation (relative advantage, compatibility, trialability, observability and complexity) of the proposed collaborative system. This factor provides information for the further enhancement of the proposed collaborative system.
2. Type of innovation decision (optional, collective, authority). This factor facilitates the decision makers to measure the novelty of the collaborative system.
3. Communication channels (mass media, interpersonal). This factor identifies the channels of the interoperation in the collaboration. The technology further can enhance these channels of collaboration.
4. Nature of the social system (norms, degree of network interconnectedness (Rogers 1995). This factor enables collaborative system to become familiar with the political nature of the social system. The system could be further improved to match the socio-cultural importance. Figure 3 depicts the S curve

*Table 4. The various theories of technology adoption and the way they are made relevant in practice for collaborative business*

| Theory | Relevance to Collaborative Business Environment |
|---|---|
| Theory of Reasoned Action (TRA) | "An individual's positive or negative feeling (evaluate affect) about performing the target behaviour" (Fishbein and Ajzen 1975, p. 216). This theory can be used in collaborative business by appealing to the positive advantages of WS and MT by individual employees and users within the business. |
| Technology Acceptance Model (TAM) | "The degree to which a person believes that using a particular system would enhance his or her job performance" (Davis, 1989, p. 320). TAM can be made relevant through the success stories of other – previously successful – implementations of the WS and MT in collaborative businesses |
| Motivation Model (MM) | "the perception that users will want to perform an activity "because it is perceived to be instrumental in achieving valued outcomes that are distinct from the activity itself, such as improved job performance, pay or promotions" (Davis et al., 1992, p. 112). MM model can clearly demonstrate the benefit of the collaborative environment for the individual adopters since people can see the achieved advantages of the collaborative environment. |
| Theory of Planned Behaviour (TPB) | "TPB has been successfully applied to the understanding of individual acceptance and usage of many different technologies" (Harrison et al., 1997). TPE pattern the understanding of the adopters of collaborative technologies. This pattern provides people with better understanding of the collaborative environment. |
| Model of PC Utilisation (MPCU) | "The extent to which an individual believes that using a technology can enhance the performance of his or her job" (Thompson et al., 1991. p. 129). MPCU model shows the individual achievements of the participants from the collaborative environment. MPCU provides similar result of the MM model with almost different representation. |
| Innovation Diffusion Theory (IDT) | "The degrees to which an innovation is perceived as being better than its precursor"(Moore and Benbasat, 1996. p. 195). IDT demonstrate the benefit of the collaborative environment for the early as well as the late adopters. |
| Social Cognitive Theory (SCT) | The performance-related consequences of the behaviour, specifically expectations deal with job-related outcomes (Compeau and Higgins, 1995). SCT demonstrate the job related benefits of the collaborative environment for an individual user of the collaborative technologies. |
| Technology Acceptance Model (TAM2) | Experience was not explicitly included in the original TAM (Davis et al., 1998). TAM2 provides all the benefits of TAM for the collaborative environment as well as including the experiences of the users of the new collaborative system. |

of early and late adopters of the diffusion process and shows the impact of the diffusion process on collaborative business system.

DoI theory is concerned with the manner in which a new technological idea, artifact or technique, or the new use of an old one, migrates from creation to use.

*Figure 2. Theory of Acceptance model and its effect on collaborative Web based system (Source: Adapted from Davis et al., 1989; & Venkatesh et al., 2003)*

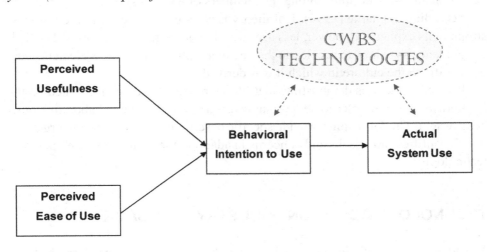

*Figure 3. The diffusion process when applied to collaborative Web based system (Adapted from Rogers, 1995)*

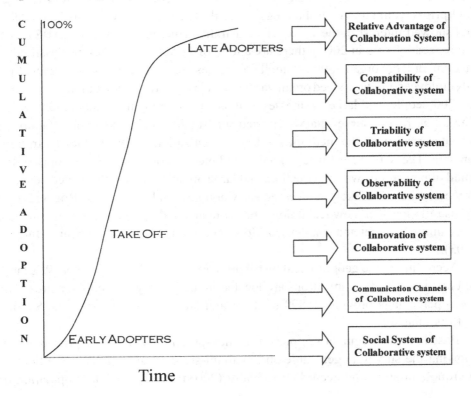

According to DoI theory, technological innovation is communicated through particular channels, over time, among the members of a social system.

According to Clarke (1999), DoI theory is at its best as a descriptive tool, less strong in its explanatory power, less useful still in predicting outcomes and providing guidance as to how to accelerate the rate of adoption. Many of its elements may be specific to the culture in which it was derived.

The above theories demonstrate that literature has already concentrated on the theoretical issues in order to adapt to new technologies for the collaborative business system. The followings provide specific descriptions identifying the organizations' identified drawbacks and concerns in adapting the mobile and Web Services technologies.

## TECHNOLOGY ADOPTION: INDUSTRY FEEDBACK

The adoption and diffusion models discussed thus far in this chapter form the basis of a detailed exercise undertaken by the authors to glean feedback from the industry in terms of the relevance, advantages and challenges of the factors that affect this technology adoption. This study was primarily focused on the medium to large enterprises within the Australian region – as these enterprises were easily available and showed interest in the work. The Australian Bureau of Statistics (ABS) (also referenced by Trewin 2004), there are a total of 11,500 organizations classified as medium or large organizations (small businesses are organizations having less than 20 employees, medium sized organizations are classified as organizations employing 20–200 people, and large businesses as those that employ more than 200 people). The targets for this survey that was carried out to understand the technology adoption by enterprises were the medium and large organizations in the Sydney metropolitan area. The reason for surveying large and medium organizations, as opposed to small organizations was that medium and large organizations with defined business processes are more likely to become early adopters and innovators (Rogers 2003) in assimilating such new technology, rather than smaller organizations that have a more limited budget and smaller workforce (Lawson, Alcock, Cooper and Burgess 2003).

According to the geographical distribution report by ABS, 86% of NSW's large and medium-sized organizations are located in the Sydney metropolitan area. The given percentage provides 9,890 medium and large organizations in the Sydney metropolitan area.

Based on the judgment samples of the non-probability sampling procedure, by knowing the survey target (large and medium-sized organizations in the Sydney metropolitan area) and according to Nardi (2003), 5% of the total population of medium-sized to large organizations, amounting to 495 were targeted for the survey. As a result, in practice, a total of 600 questionnaires were sent out and approximately 12% responses (amounting to 60 responses) were received. As stated by Falcnor and Hodgett (1999), response rates in the information systems management area are likely to be within the range of 10% to 36%.

## UNDERSTANDING AND DISCUSSING THE RESULTS FROM THE INDUSTRIAL SURVEY/FEEDBACK

### The Organization

### Question: The Organizations' Size

This section of the chapter depicts the general demographic of those 12% organizations that have responded to the surveys. As mentioned earlier, the medium and large organizations are the early adaptors of the technology. Therefore, the surveys have only been distributed to these large and medium organizations. Hence, different size organizations are likely to undertake collaborative business in different ways due to the various factors such as affiliated cost, complexity of the business process and so on.

*Figure 4. The percentage and size of the participating organizations*

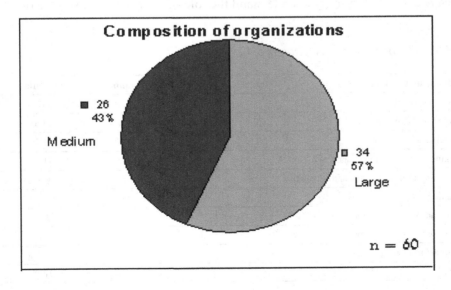

Forty-three per cent of the organizations (amounting to 26) are medium-sized and 57%, (amounting to 34) have been classified as large-sized organizations. Figure 4 illustrates the demographics of the organizations, based on their organizational size.

The organizations span across different industries, as listed in Table 5.

## Question: The Organizations' Category

This question is related to the category of the participating organization hence different categories of organizations are likely to undertake collaborative business in different ways. The study identifies the importance of this section, as it is very important to reach different industries to be able to evaluate the general technological adaptation in different organizations. Table 5 demonstrates the organizational categories that responded to the distributed survey.

The majority of the participants are from the information technology sector of the industry. The government departments, education and banking sectors follow in order. The study was able to proceed, as the distribution of the questionnaire had been correctly allocated and the study could evaluate the results achieved based on the different categories of the organizations.

## Question: The Position of the Participant in the Organization

This question is related to the position of the individuals in the organizations who actually responded to the questions. This question is also very important, since its answers can help the study to understand the role of the respondents in the organi-

*Table 5. The organizations' categories*

| Organizations' Categories | Number | Percentage |
|---|---|---|
| Information technology | 20 | 33.3% |
| Government departments | 14 | 23.3% |
| Education and training | 7 | 11.7% |
| Banking, finance and insurance | 7 | 11.7% |
| Professional services (legal and accounting) | 5 | 8.3% |
| Retailing | 3 | 5% |
| Health and community services | 2 | 3.3% |
| Utility services and equipment | 1 | 1.7% |
| Manufacturing and processing | 1 | 1.7% |
| **Total** | **60** | **100%** |

*Table 6. The position of the respondent in the organization*

| Position | Number | Percentage |
|---|---|---|
| General management | 13 | 21.7% |
| Marketing manager | 8 | 13.3% |
| Senior management | 8 | 13.3% |
| Systems analyst/programmer | 8 | 13.3% |
| IT/MIS manager | 6 | 10% |
| Technical support | 6 | 10% |
| Executive manager | 5 | 8.3% |
| Sales officer | 4 | 6.7% |
| Customer care | 2 | 3.3% |
| **Total** | **60** | **100%** |

zation and also be aware of their control over the organization. People in different roles influence CBPE differently. The decision makers take the risk and enforce the business policies in the services; the technical people implement the CBPE in CWBS, then maintain it. The database managers source and update the contents of the collaborative system. The positions held by the respondents are presented in Table 6.

The participants who held the general management positions in their organizations represent 21.7%, while marketing manager and senior management account for 13.3% of the respondents. The remaining 48.3% of the respondents hold key positions in their organizations. These people are the decision-makers in the organizations.

## Mobile Technology Information

This section of the chapter demonstrates the result of the survey with regard to the respondents' thoughts about mobility in collaborative business environment. The importance of the mobile technology has been defined in depth in Chapter 2 and the chapter 5 of this book. Mobile Technologies (MT) provides better facilitation for the collaboration since the user of this technology can collaborate disregard of the location and time boundaries. Possibilities are endless.

Mobility is vital to the collaborative business world. The commercial transactions are conducted on mobile devices, thereby; this commercial transaction can be enhanced further for the collaborative commercial transactions. These collaborative advantages and corresponding benefits emanate from the application of mobility to collaborative business world.

The interoperable nature of mobility in an enterprise in a *strategic manner* goes far beyond the simple act of providing mobile gadgets to customers, employees and business partners. Larger enterprises are keen to capitalize on the abundant availability of mobile technologies and devices in their customer base to reach those customers in innovative ways and provide them with greater collaborative value and wider ranger of services. The following sections demonstrate the industrial feedback for the adoption of mobile technology.

## Question: Importance of the Mobility in the Organization

The question relates to the use of mobile technology (use of mobile devices) in the daily activities of the business. The question further queried whether the organizations are already using mobile technology, or are planning to use it in the near future. The responses are detailed in Figure 5.

A substantial 87% (63% already using, and 23% that plan to use in the near future) of the organizations responded in the affirmative to this question. These answers indicate that the key personnel in the selected sample are very much aware of the value of mobility and mobile technology for their organizations. 13% of the respondents said that they do not have a plan to use mobile technology in the near future.

*Figure 5. The use of mobile technology in organizations in terms of helping them with location-independent collaboration*

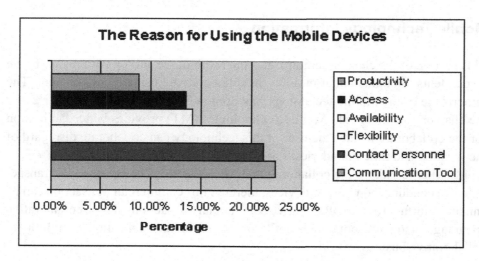

## Question: Used Mobile Devices in the Organization

The question is meant to identify the kind of the devices that are in use by the organizations. The answers provide an insight into the current use of mobile technology in the organizations. The responses for this question are listed in Figure 6.

The main issue to consider in this section is whether the organizations can use different devices in order to proceed with their daily collaborative business activities. The survey identified that 40% of the organizations are currently using mobile devices such as mobile phone, laptop, Personal Digital Assistants (PDA) or tablet Personal Computer (PC), while 30% of the respondent use mobile-enabled laptops. Figure 5 clearly demonstrates that organizations have realized that they need to take advantage of the location independence provided by the mentioned devices.

## Question: Current Application of Mobile Technology

The question asked whether there are any new applications and areas in which mobile technology could be included in the daily business activities of the organization, under four *propositions*, as listed in Table 7.

**P1:** Mobile technology as a special technology improves efficiency in customer meetings. The survey shows that the majority (78.7%) of the respondents either agreed or strongly agreed with this proposition. The response identifies the impact of technology on improving the efficiency of the business processes.

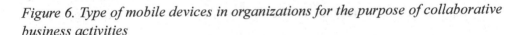

*Figure 6. Type of mobile devices in organizations for the purpose of collaborative business activities*

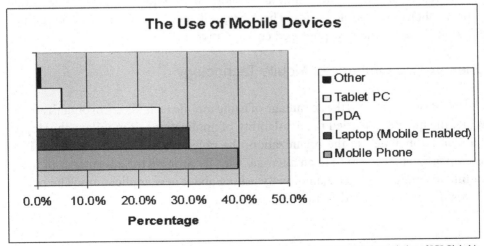

*Table 7. New applications/areas for use of mobile technology*

| New Applications | TOTAL | VSA | SA | AG | DA | SD | VSD |
|---|---|---|---|---|---|---|---|
| P1 – Special Technology – Improve Efficiencies | 47 | 6 | 15 | 16 | 8 | 1 | 1 |
| PERCENTAGE | 100 | 13 | 32 | 34 | 17 | 2 | 2 |
| P2 – Advertise in Captured Markets | 44 | 2 | 9 | 20 | 8 | 2 | 3 |
| PERCENTAGE | 100 | 5 | 20 | 45 | 18 | 5 | 7 |
| P3 – Contacting Office (Any where/ any time) | 47 | 13 | 15 | 12 | 3 | 1 | 3 |
| PERCENTAGE | 100 | 28 | 32 | 26 | 6 | 2 | 6 |
| P4 – Track Goods in Transit | 51 | 8 | 12 | 16 | 8 | 3 | 4 |
| PERCENTAGE | 100 | 16 | 24 | 31 | 16 | 6 | 8 |

**P2:** Mobile technology has been used as a special tool to advertise in a captured market. The survey shows that 70.4% of the respondents agreed with this proposition. The response identifies that mobile technology enables organizations to capture the market by using the mobile devices.

**P3:** Mobile technology as a tool has enabled people to contact the office for employees engaged in official travel. The survey shows that 63.8% agreed to this proposition. The response reveals that more than half of the organizations currently use mobility to connect for business purposes while the personnel are not physically in the office.

**P4:** Mobile technology has enabled the business to track goods in transit. The survey shows that 70.5% of the responses agreed with this proposition. The response demonstrates that mobile devices are used to track goods globally.

The results indicate that mobile technology is a major technology that could improve their business activities. Therefore, this technology could also facilitate this study to enter the new proposed collaborative environment.

## Question: Advantages of Mobile Technology

The question establishes the advantage of using mobile technology in organizations. While the question queried the availability of applications of mobile technologies that can be included in the organization; the objective of the next question is to re-emphasize this question in an alternate way, by probing the advantages of using mobile technology, rather than directly asking about new applications. The results of this question are listed in Table 8.

**P1:** Mobile technology as a special technology is very cost-efficient. The survey shows that 72.7% of the respondents either agreed or strongly agreed with this proposition. The response reveals that mobility enables the organizations to save money.

**P2:** Mobile technology has been connecting people while out of the office. The survey shows that 93.8% of the respondents agreed with this proposition. The response identifies that connection with the personnel while out of the office is also crucial for increasing the efficiency of the business processes.

**P3:** Mobile technology has been improving the business productivity. The survey shows that 71% of the respondents agreed with this proposition. The response reveals that the use of mobile technology has increased the productivity of the businesses.

**P4:** Mobile technology has enabled employees to be more flexible, hence they can work regardless of their location and time. The survey shows that 72.3% agreed to this proposition. The response demonstrates that the location independency enables the personnel to be more flexible and increases productivity.

**P5:** Mobile technology has created better access methods for the customers to contact the organization. The survey shows that 85.4% of the responses agreed with this proposition. The response identifies that mobility cause the customers to have better access to the organizations.

*Table 8. Main advantages of mobile technology for organizations*

| Mobile Advantages | TOTAL | VSA | SA | AG | DA | SD | VSD |
|---|---|---|---|---|---|---|---|
| P1 – Cost Savings | 44 | 8 | 8 | 16 | 10 | 1 | 1 |
| PERCENTAGE | 100 | 18 | 18 | 36 | 23 | 2 | 2 |
| P2 – Connect Employees | 48 | 21 | 15 | 9 | 3 | 0 | 0 |
| PERCENTAGE | 100 | 44 | 31 | 19 | 6 | 0 | 0 |
| P3 – Improve Productivity | 55 | 13 | 26 | 10 | 6 | 0 | 0 |
| PERCENTAGE | 100 | 24 | 47 | 18 | 11 | 0 | 0 |
| P4 – Flexibility of Employees | 47 | 7 | 10 | 17 | 12 | 1 | 0 |
| PERCENTAGE | 100 | 15 | 21 | 36 | 26 | 2 | 0 |
| P5 – Better Access for Customers | 48 | 10 | 13 | 18 | 6 | 0 | 1 |
| PERCENTAGE | 100 | 21 | 27 | 38 | 13 | 0 | 2 |

*Table 9. Factors influencing the use of mobile technology in an organization*

| Factors Influencing Mobility | TOTAL | VSA | SA | AG | DA | SD | VSD |
|---|---|---|---|---|---|---|---|
| P1 – Mobility Demand by Employees | 52 | 7 | 12 | 20 | 13 | 0 | 0 |
| PERCENTAGE | 100 | 13 | 23 | 38 | 25 | 0 | 0 |
| P2 – Mobility Demand by Customers | 50 | 4 | 12 | 21 | 12 | 0 | 1 |
| PERCENTAGE | 100 | 8 | 24 | 42 | 24 | 0 | 2 |
| P3 – Mobility Demand by Supply Chain | 48 | 3 | 12 | 17 | 12 | 3 | 1 |
| PERCENTAGE | 100 | 6 | 25 | 35 | 25 | 6 | 2 |
| P4 – Mobility Demand by Social–Psych Factor | 47 | 4 | 8 | 19 | 14 | 1 | 1 |
| PERCENTAGE | 100 | 9 | 17 | 40 | 30 | 2 | 2 |

## Question: Advantage of Mobile Technology for the Business

The question has asked about other factors that would enhance the demand in introducing or using mobile technology in the organization. Four *propositions* from which to choose were presented to the respondents. Table 9 lists the results for the question.

**P1:** Employees demand and show interest in using the mobile technology. The survey shows that 75% of the respondents either agreed or strongly agreed with this proposition. The response reveals that personnel of the organizations prefer to be flexible and perform their daily tasks while they are not necessarily in the office.

**P2:** Customers demand and show interest in using the mobile technology. The survey shows that 74% of the respondents either agreed or strongly agreed with this proposition. The response reveals that even customers show interest in using mobility to increase personal productivity.

**P3:** The supply chain sector is more interested and shows interest in using the mobile technology. The survey shows that 66.7% of the respondents either agreed or strongly agreed with this proposition. The response demonstrates the importance of the mobile technology in the supply chain sector.

**P4:** Social–psychological factors are influencing people to use mobile technology. The survey shows that 66% of the respondents either agreed or strongly agreed with this proposition. The response identifies that social–psychological factors are also important factors in using mobility, as people can perform their tasks anywhere and at any time.

*Figure 7. Mobile technology benefits to collaborative business activities*

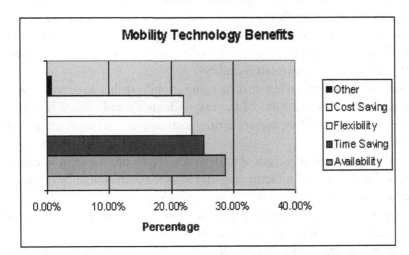

## Question: Improvements Caused by Mobile Technology

This question investigates the perceived value of mobile technology in the daily activities of the organization. This section allows the respondents to select more than one choice. The survey results are listed in Figure 7.

The most important benefit of using the mobile devices, as predicted, has been classified as the availability to be contactable at any time, and anywhere. A fact revealed by this question is that cost savings are not the main driver for organizations to use mobile technology.

## Question: Problem/Difficulties of Mobile Technology

The question has investigated the anticipated problems, difficulties and complaints the respondents may have when using the existing mobile gadgets. The results are listed in Figure 8.

The results state that the most important difficulty is the small screen, while the limited applications, battery life span and complexity of mobile devices are classified as the remaining problems of mobile devices.

## Question: Disadvantages of Mobile Technology

The question has investigated the disadvantages of using mobile technologies, as perceived by the respondents. The results are listed in Table 10.

**P1:** When asked whether the cost of establishment of mobile applications is a concern for the organization, the survey shows that 74% of the respondents either agreed or strongly agreed with this proposition. The response identifies that the establishing costs of the mobile applications are the major concern, rather than the utilization of mobility.

**P2:** When asked the recurring cost of using mobile technology as a major tool, the survey shows that 83% of the respondents agreed with this proposition. The response identifies that recurring costs are also a major concern for the organizations.

**P3:** When asked whether technical drawbacks, which are inherent in current mobile technologies, are a factor considered as a disadvantage by organizations, the survey shows that 93% of the respondents agreed with this view. The response reveals that technical drawbacks are the major disadvantages of mobile technology's utilization by the organizations.

**P4:** When asked legal and privacy concerns using mobile technology, around 80% of the respondents showed concern about the legal and privacy issues with regard to mobile technology.

**P5:** When asked about adoption and training issues in an organization with regard to mobile technology, the survey shows that 78% of respondents in the selected sample agreed that such issues are a concern for their organizations. The response identifies that the adoption and training issues are also a major concern in the utilization of mobile technology by the organizations.

## Web Services Technology

The following questions help the authors to evaluate the participants' opinion in terms of adapting Web Services (WS) technology in their business. The questions

*Figure 8. Problems faced by organizations using the mobile gadgets*

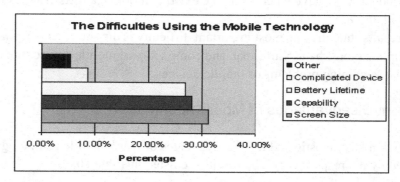

*Table 10. The recognized disadvantages of mobile technology*

| Disadvantages of Mobile Technology | TOTAL | VSA | SA | AG | DA | SD | VSD |
|---|---|---|---|---|---|---|---|
| P1 – Establishment Cost of Applications | 56 | 6 | 15 | 20 | 11 | 2 | 2 |
| PERCENTAGE | 100 | 11 | 27 | 36 | 20 | 4 | 4 |
| P2 –Recruitment Cost of Mobility | 54 | 5 | 16 | 24 | 6 | 2 | 1 |
| PERCENTAGE | 100 | 9 | 30 | 44 | 11 | 4 | 2 |
| P3 – Technical Drawback | 57 | 12 | 16 | 25 | 2 | 2 | 0 |
| PERCENTAGE | 100 | 21 | 28 | 44 | 4 | 4 | 0 |
| P4 – Legal and Privacy Issues | 56 | 9 | 12 | 24 | 9 | 1 | 1 |
| PERCENTAGE | 100 | 16 | 21 | 43 | 16 | 2 | 2 |
| P5 – Training and Adaptation Issues | 55 | 5 | 24 | 14 | 9 | 1 | 2 |
| PERCENTAGE | 100 | 9 | 44 | 25 | 16 | 2 | 4 |

below deal with the three significant dimensions of adoption of WS technologies – namely, the technical, methodological and social dimensions.

## Question: Technical Drawbacks of Adaptation of Web Services

The question has investigated the adaptation to WS technology from the technical perspective presented in Figure 9.

**P1:** When asked whether the unfamiliar concept of the Web Services technology is a great concern for the organizations in order to adapt Web Services, the survey shows that 70% of the respondents either agreed or strongly agreed with this proposition. The response demonstrates that unfamiliarity with the concept of WS technology is a major concern in adapting the WS technology.

**P2:** When asked whether the limitation of the Web Services is important, the survey shows that 65% of the respondents agreed with this proposition. The response reveals that limitation of the WS technology is also a concern for the organizations in adapting the WS technology.

**P3:** When asked whether the ambiguity of the Web Services is a major concern (what it is and what it does), the survey shows that 70% of the respondents agreed with this view. The response indicates that the importance of the WS technology for interoperation is also not recognized by the organizations.

*Figure 9. Technical issues involved in adapting the Web services*

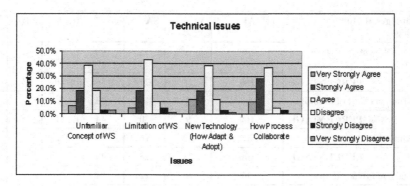

**P4:** When asked whether the participants understand how WS could facilitate collaboration, the survey shows that 80% of the participants agreed with this proposition. The response also reveals that the unfamiliarity with the concept of WS technology is a great importance for the adaptation rate of the technology by the organizations.

## Question: Methodological Drawbacks of Adaptation of Web Services

The question has investigated the adaptation to WS technology from the methodological perspective. Results are presented in Figure 10.

**P1:** When asked whether the impact on WS on existing business process is a major concern while adapting the WS, the survey shows that 64.9% of the

*Figure 10. Methodological issues in adapting the Web services*

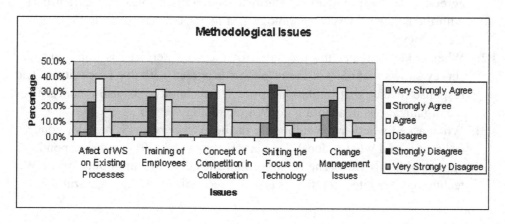

respondents either agreed or strongly agreed with this proposition. The response demonstrates that the organizations are concerned about the impact of the WS on existing business processes.

**P2:** When asked whether the training of the employees is a major concern, the survey shows that 61.5% of the respondents agreed with this proposition. The response reveals that training costs and change management are also a concern for the organizations.

**P3:** The concept of the competition while collaborating (how can you collaborate with your competitor?). The survey shows that 86.6% of the respondents agreed with this view. The response demonstrates that organizations are not willing to collaborate with their competitors.

**P4:** The focus will shift to technology rather than process. The survey shows that almost 80% of the participants agreed with this proposition. The response reveals that the adaptation of the WS technology shifts the concentration of the organization to technology rather than the actual business process.

**P5:** How to manage the change when adapting the WS technology. The survey shows that almost 75% agreed with the proposition. The response reveals that organizations need to introduce a change management plan before the introduction of the WS technology.

## Question: Social Drawbacks of Adaptation Web Services

The question has investigated the adaptation to WS technology from the social perspective. Results are presented in Figure 11.

**P1:** Evaluate the adaptation rate by customer and the employees. The survey shows that about 60% of the respondents either agreed or strongly agreed with this proposition. The response demonstrates that the users (employees) and the end-users (customers) are also concerned when the organization introduces the new technology.

**P2:** How the competitors react to change. The survey shows that 75% of the respondents agreed with this proposition. The response reveals that it is important to identify the competitors' reaction to the introduction of new technology.

**P3:** How the technology provides support in order to trust the competitor. The survey shows that almost 75% of the respondents agreed with this view. The response demonstrates that it is important to trust your competition before collaborating with it.

**P4:** How the introduction of the WS technology impacts on the relationship with the organizations already in the line of collaboration. The survey shows that

*Figure 11. Social issues in adapting the Web services*

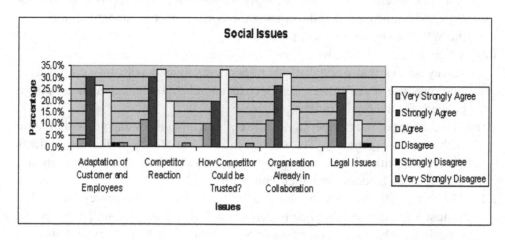

almost 65% of the participants agreed with this proposition. The response reveals that the introduction of the WS technology impacts on the relationship with the organization that is already collaborating.

**P5:** The legal issues involved in collaboration (government and internal policies). The survey shows that almost 65% of the participants agreed with the proposition. The response reveals that legal issues are also a major concern for collaboration, especially when collaborating with global organizations.

The organization category (refer to Table 4) indicates that the highest response was from IT, which represents 33% of the total responses. The second highest was the government departments, including more than 23% of the participants. It has been mentioned previously that the survey was targeting large and medium-sized enterprises.

The positions of the individuals who filled in the survey have also been evaluated. The result has clearly identified that the surveys were filled in by participants who holds management (decision-maker) positions. In fact, 66% of the participants have held managerial (senior to executive) positions.

The organizations and the key role positions of the respondents have improved the quality of the sample selected from the actual population.

## Mobile Technology Information (Evaluation)

Mobility appears to be an important technology for the businesses to use in proceeding with their daily activities. Figure 4 demonstrates that 63% of the organizations are already using their mobile devices to run their ordinary activities, while 23% stated that they are planning to adapt them in the near future. A total of 87% of the organizations recognizes the importance of the mobile technology, while currently the majority of these people mainly use their mobile phones and mobile-enabled laptops.

The respondents have defined that mobility is a great communication tool, making it easier to find and locate personnel, creating more flexibility and increasing the general productivity. The major advantage of mobile technology is providing availability to people, regardless of their location and time. The study revealed that accessibility is one of the greatest advantages of the *CBPE* model, therefore the advantage of mobility (anywhere – any time) could provide benefits to the proposed *CBPE* model.

An example is the action research undertaken in Protect B, presented in Chapter 12. Without the aid of mobile devices, the proposed *CBPE* model would have been a failure, because the businesses that Protect 2 requires are always out of the office. The most important concept in here is that with the aid of a Global Positioning System (GPS), Protect B locates the closest tradesperson to the work location. The proposed model increases productivity as well as providing better customer relationship management (CRM).

The survey has also investigated the current and potential application of mobility, the advantages and disadvantages of mobility and the improvements caused by mobility to provide a better understanding of this technology.

Interestingly, the survey has identified that the cost of mobility is not classified as a big disadvantage in comparison to the benefits it provides. All these disadvantages and drawbacks seem to be due to the fact that the technology is new and still evolving. When there is more commercialization of the technology, applications will become cheaper and recurring costs will be lower. The decreasing cost of technology while the capabilities are improving rapidly is highlighted by Roth (1998).

## Web Services Technology (Evaluation)

The interoperation among multiple organizations needs a technology to support the collaboration across their business processes, especially when the participating organizations are not necessarily known to each other, and have never collaborated previously.

According to Barry (2003), the main driving forces for adopting Web Services are classified as interoperable network applications, emerging industry-wide standards, easier exchange of data, reduced developing time, reduced maintenance costs, availability of external services and availability of training and tools.

The main restraining forces are also classified as different semantics in data source, the semantic translation effect on operation systems for up-to-the-moment data request, evolving standards not being fixed, and mergers and acquisition.

Based on our survey, all the issues identified by the study, such as unfamiliar concepts of Web Services, limitation of Web Services, how to adapt the new technology and how the processes collaborate, are classified as the major concerns of the organizations in relation to adopting Web Services. Only a minority, 10% of the participants, agreed very strongly to understanding how Web Services could help the collaboration, while close to 30% of the participants had the same concern, ticking the strongly agree box. The study has concluded that the organization knowledge with regard to the technical issues of WS is very limited. This lack of knowledge could be classified as the major drawback to the adaptation of Web Services. More work is required to educate enterprises with regard to the capability and functionality of Web Services from the technical point of view.

Based on the result of the survey, all the issues identified by the study, such as the impact of Web Services on existing processes, training of the employees, concept of competition in collaboration, shifting the focus of technology and the concept of change management, have been classified as important concepts. Almost 40% of the participants agree with these issues while close to 30% strongly agree. Close to 20% of the respondents classify the concepts of change management as their greatest concern in adopting WS technology for their organizations. However, about 20% and 30% of these organizations disagree that the effect of WS on existing business processes and training the employees are of great importance. There is no doubt that methodological issues play an important role in adopting Web Services technology.

Based on the survey, the customer/competitor reaction and the impact of the proposed *CBPE* model on the organizations that are already in collaboration have been classified by the participants as a strongly agree point. Almost a similar number attracted the very strongly agree comments, however, up to 35% of all participants classified all the issues identified by the study as the major drawback for adaptation of WS by organizations.

This study has concluded that technical, methodological and social factors influence the adaptation and adoption of new technology by organizations. The business opportunities resulting from WS have seen these technologies being rapidly adopted across the world. For example, an IDC Report in 2003 revealed that 30% of Australian organizations are already using Web Services – although a large number of these organizations' applications are behind the corporate firewall. Another survey conducted by CSC found 105 of Australia's largest organizations are already using Web Services or are planning to do so (Mackenzie, 2003).

In general, the issues of incompatible technology, competition, licensing agreement (legal issues) and mistrust have also been classified as additional major concerns when adopting the new technology. This are discussed later in this book.

## ACTION POINTS

1. Identify the type of organization that is undertaking CBPE (e.g. whether it is a multi-national, transnational, global or local organization?)
2. Identify the size of the organization – as this becomes relevant in terms of its organizational structure and the changes to that structure
3. List the most used and popular mobile devices by that are part of your organization including those used by your customers.
4. List the typical reasons for the usage of the mobile devices by your organization and your customers.
5. List the potential problems that would be faced by your organizations when it attempts to collaborate with other organizations as well as customers using mobile devices.
6. Discuss the technical, methodological and social issues in order to adopt the Web Services technology.

## REFERENCES

Alag, H. (2006). Business process mobility. In B. Unhelkar (Ed.), *Mobile business: Technological, methodological and social perspectives.* Hershey, PA: Idea Group Publishing.

Barry, D. K. (2003). *Web Services and Service-Oriented Architecture. The savvy Manager's Guide.* USA. Morgan Kaufmann Publishers. ISBN: 1-55860-906-7.

Bartlett, C. A., & Ghoshal, S. (1998). *Managing across borders: The transnational solution* (2nd ed.). Cambridge, MA: Harvard Business School Press.

Cabrera, L. F., & Kurt, C. (2005). *Web services architecture and its specifications: Essential for understanding WS.* Redmond, CA: Microsoft Press Corporation.

Clarke, R. (1999). *A primer in diffusion of innovations theory.* Retrieved March 4, 2007, from http://www.anu.edu.au/people/Roger.Clarke/SOS/InnDiff.html

Compeau, D. R., & Higgins, C. A. (1995). Computer self-efficacy: Development of a measure and initial test. *MIS Quarterly, 19*(2), 189–211. doi:10.2307/249688

Falcnor, D. J., & Hodgett, R. A. (1999, December). *Why executives don't respond to your survey.* Paper presented at the 10th Australian Conference on Information Systems, Wellington, New Zealand.

Fishbein, M., & Ajzen, I. (1975). *Belief, attitude, intention and behavior: An introduction to theory and research.* Reading, MA: Addison-Wesley.

Gan, J. (2006). Developing smart clients to mobile applications. In B. Unhelkar (Ed.), *Mobile business: Technological, methodological and social perspectives.* Hershey, PA: Idea Group Publishing.

Harrison, D. A., Mykytyn, P. P., & Riemenschneider, C. K. (1997). Executive decisions about adoption of information technology in small business: Theory and empirical tests. *Information Systems Research, 8*(2), 171–195. doi:10.1287/isre.8.2.171

Lan, Y., & Unhelkar, B. (2005). *Global enterprise transition: Managing a process.* Hershey, PA: Idea Group Publishing.

Lawson, R., Alcock, C., Cooper, J., & Burgess, L. (2003). Factors affecting adoption of electronic commerce technologies by SMEs. *Journal of Small Business and Enterprise Development, 10*(3), 265–276. doi:10.1108/14626000310489727

Mackenzie, K. (2003). Web services put to work for food safety. *The Australian.*

Moore, G. C., & Benbasat, I. (1996). Integrating diffusion of innovations and theory of reasoned action models to predict utilization of information technology by end-users. In K. Kautz & J. Pries-Hege (Eds.), *Diffusion and adoption of information technology* (pp. 132-146). London: Chapman and Hall.

Nardi, P. M. (2003). *Doing survey research: A guide to quantitative methods.* Boston, MA: Pearson Education, Inc.

Rogers, E. M. (2003). *Diffusion of innovations* (5th ed.). New York: Free Press.

Rolstadas, A., & Andersen, B. (2000). *Enterprise modeling – improving global industrial competitiveness.* Amsterdam: Kluwer Academic Publishers.

Roth, J. (1998). The network is the business. In D. Tapscott, A. Lowy, & D. Ticoll (Eds.), *Blueprint to the digital economy: Creating wealth in the era of e-business* (p. 410). New York: McGraw-Hill.

Thompson, R. L., Higgins, C. A., & Howell, J. M. (1991). Personal computing: Toward a conceptual model of utilization. *MIS Quarterly*, *15*(1), 125–143. doi:10.2307/249443

Trewin, D. (2004). *Small business in Australia (2001)* (ABS Catalogue No. 1321.0). Canberra, Australia: Australian Bureau of Statistics.

Venkatesh, V., Morris, M., Davis, G., & Davis, F. (2003). User acceptance of information technology: Towards a unified view. *MIS Quarterly*, *27*(3), 425–478.

# Chapter 8
# Quality Assurance of the Collaborative Web Based System

*Knowledge must come through action; you can have no test which is not fanciful, save by trial.*

Sophocles (496 BC - 406 BC)

## CHAPTER KEY POINTS

- Presents the importance of quality management and quality assurance in the context of collaborative business.
- Argues for applying the principles of quality assurance to the information architecture (especially service oriented architecture) for collaborative business.
- Discusses the importance of quality assurance and quality control (testing) for the *collaborative web based system (CWBS)*
- Discusses the testing strategy and processes in solution space of *CWBS*.
- Outlines the details of test data that should be prepared and used in the testing of *CWBS*.
- Discusses the execution of tests and collation of results.

DOI: 10.4018/978-1-60566-689-1.ch008

# INTRODUCTION

This chapter discusses the important issues related to quality management, quality assurance and testing of information systems that are used by collaborative business. The discussion thus far in this book has been in the area of collaborative business models, technologies for collaboration and their effect on business organization. Each of these areas of collaborative business can be, and should be, subjected to quality assurance and testing. This chapter discusses how these important aspects of quality can be applied to a collaborative business. The overall strategic approach to quality, which starts with quality management, is also explained. This chapter further discusses the testing strategy, testing processes and the test data required in the solution space of *CWBS*. The practical checklists approach to enhance the quality of software model created in Chapter 6 using the Business Process Modeling Notation (BPMN) goes a long way in ensuring a smooth transition of the business to a collaborative business.

# QUALITY DIMENSIONS IN COLLABORATIVE SYSTEMS

The entire quality domain, as applicable to collaborative systems, can be made up of three significant dimensions: the management, the assurance and the control aspect of quality. These quality dimensions, as shown in Figure 1, range from being strategic (more abstract) to tactical (more concrete).

Quality Management (QM) provides the strategic basis for quality for the transition of the business to collaborative business. Quality management starts during the planning stages of the overall transition project and it can bring in both technical and management aspects of quality in the project. For example, from a management perspective, the concepts in Lean systems (Littlefield, 2008) and Six-sigma (Pyzdek, 2003) provide important value in ensuring that the collaborative business processes are modeled and executed with minimum or no wastages. From a technical perspective, there are opportunities to bring in capability maturity models (www.sei.cmu.edu) and related process issues in improving the technical quality of the services and applications used in the project. Documenting and studying the validity of organization-wide policies and procedures that can be implemented internally, and policies from external organization are all a part of this strategic approach to quality.

Quality assurance (QA) is more specifically focused on the collaborative processes, their modeling, the quality of the models themselves and ensuring the prevention of errors from a technical angle. The capability maturity model, mentioned above, can be implemented in assuring the quality of the collaborative system. QA

*Figure 1. Strategic versus tactical aspects of quality*

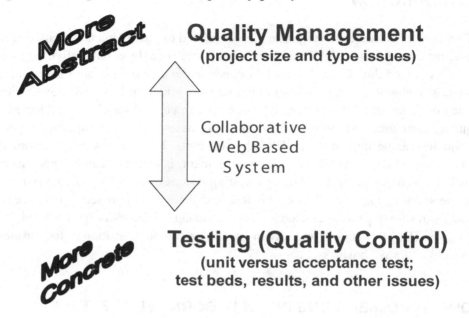

deals with configuration and deployment of process that would reduce errors and increase the chances of a more satisfactory acceptance test. Quality assurance also provides all necessary techniques to verify and validate the models. These techniques include syntax, semantics and aesthetic checks as have been discussed by Unhelkar (2005) when the requirements as well as solutions are being modeled. A good quality assurance approach also provides the templates for deliverables that need to be produced in the transition and verifies the compliance of the deliverables to the standards within the project. This results in an overall quality of models and processes, which is reassuring to the stakeholders in terms of the expected and accepted level of quality of the system.

Quality control (QC), the third important dimension of quality, deals with the actual testing of the collaborative system. This testing is tactical in nature and requires specialist testing skills that can be applied to the applications and services that comprise *Collaborative Web Based System (CWBS)*. This testing leads to identification of errors ("bugs"), their recording, analysis and, later, their re-testing after they are fixed. Testing involves executing a suite of varied test data through the services (or software components) to test them individually – followed by testing of multiple services before the suite of collaborative services that make up the system are released into production.

# QUALITY MANAGEMENT AND COLLABORATIVE SYSTEMS

Quality management is a strategic approach to quality. This strategic approach to quality has been studied and applied in information systems for more than a decade. Quality management includes organizing the entire quality function – including people, processes and technologies that deal with quality. Therefore, quality management includes defining quality roles, placing right people in those roles, identifying and formalizing the processes that will be used within the organization (including both business and software processes) and procuring and managing the tools that will be used to carry out the quality function.

These quality management functions get extended and expanded when it comes to applying them to collaborative business. The organization of a collaborative business, as discussed in the previous chapter, is different to the traditional business. There are people and processes within a collaborative business that are intertwined with many other businesses that participate in the collaboration – albeit on a shorter time scale. Collaborative business processes need support from software applications – which are themselves made up of smaller sized and self-contained services. Therefore, when it comes to organizing the people for the quality function, there is a need to consider who will be responsible for these numerous services that can be offered and consumed globally by collaborating businesses.

*Figure 2. Factors influencing quality of a collaborative system*

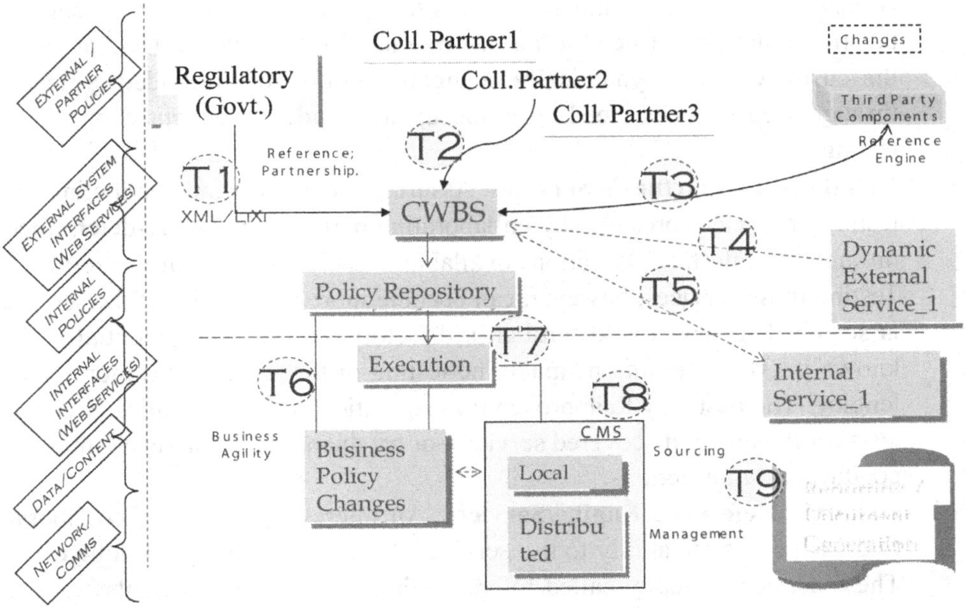

The quality management function changes from being responsible only for production of good quality services by the organization to *also* ensuring that the interactions amongst collaborating organizations and the resultant service offered are also of highest quality. Thus, the quality management in a collaborative environment goes beyond an organization and extends to multiple organizations. While the services can be offered and consumed electronically on a portal, that which is being offered and consumed may not necessarily be of the desired quality. For example, a banking organization that makes use of "foreign exchange" rate calculation services offered by, say, a semi-government organization needs to be assured of the quality of those rate calculations. Thus, quality management in collaboration needs to extend its vision and its reach beyond the organizational boundaries in order to enable offering of high quality services to the customers. The need to keep track of the history of the services being offered from a particular organization, the level and accuracy of documentation (modeling) of the services, and the ease of use (consumption) of those services are all vital quality management functions.

Figure 2 demonstrate the emphasis on the focused area labeled T1 through T9 (for Test areas). These focused areas provide interest of quality management when it comes to collaborative business.

T1  **Government Services**: Testing of the interfaces that deal with regulatory bodies is crucial to the success of a collaborative system. For example, collaborative systems have a continuous need to update their business logic with services provided by the regulatory authorities such as government bodies. A bank may need government services that provide information on current taxation policies that need to be incorporated by the bank in its charges to the customer. This dynamically changing information, provided typically through web services, need on going updates and, subsequently, on going testing.

T2  **Collaborating partner's Services**: Assuring the quality and conducting the testing of services provided by collaborating partners can be pre-determined through the interface definitions available to the consumers of the services. Testing these services, however, can become more challenging if the service is searched for and found through a directory service. The potentially unknown interface definitions make the testing of those interfaces more challenging. The best way to approach these situations is the dynamically create tests for the newly discovered services, or try them out, before using them to conduct real transactions.

T3  **Dynamic Reference Engine/Services**: An interesting aspect of collaborative business is the ability to use services that provide business intelligence. These services, usually called reference engines, are *super* calculators that provide indicative information on risks associated with, say, an insurance transaction. The testing and quality assurance of these services also has to be dynamically conducted by creating test scenarios with varying test data, and 'test harnesses' that use these services and match the results with the expected results.

**T4    Dynamic / Mobile External Services**: The testing of these external and mobile services within a collaborative business requires creating of the test environment and test designs that handle not only variation in data, but also variation in the location and timing for the same type of data. For example, an external service that provides information on traffic condition for an ambulance bringing a critically ill patient to the hospital would require ongoing updates to those traffic conditions as it moves through the traffic. The test cases for such external traffic update service need to test the results against the location of the moving consumer of the service (the ambulance).

**T5    Internal Services (within the organization's application suite)**: The testing of internal services of an organization in a collaborative environment is relatively easier than the testing of external services. This is so because internal services are the 'known' component in the mix of collaborative services. However, if the external services are going to have an impact on the way in which an internal service is carried out, then that impact needs to be also thoroughly tested. For example, if there is a change in the supplier's delivery strategy, then its impact on the internal inventory services needs to be tested specifically.

**T6    Business Policy updates:** Testing of these policy updates can be a combination of testing the way in which the workflow operates and the way in which the changes to the workflow is reflected in the changes to the web services that have implemented those policies. For example, changes to the way in which mortgage serviceability is calculated can change on almost daily basis – requiring changes to the business policies and corresponding web services. While every policy change cannot be anticipated, still there is a need to test the way in which policy changes are reflected in the services.

**T7    Execution / Orchestration**: Testing of execution of collaborative web services implies testing the execution of all relevant services together. This testing will almost always involve a practical tool that provides for the orchestration mechanism.

**T8    Content Management System:** These are the databases that contain varying types of contents. The need to create correspondingly varying types of data inputs is crucial in testing the content management systems. In addition to testing with different types of data, there is also a need to conduct tests using different sizes of data. For example, loading and indexing a voice output from a service would be only one aspect of the testing of contents; the other aspect would be the volume and the speed with which such data can be loaded on to a database servicing the collaborative business processes.

**T9 Reporting**: Testing of reporting features usually tends to be left behind, in comparison with testing of other modules and features of a collaborative system. However, it is important that the reporting features that will be used by users in different regions, using varying standards for printing and report, is tested upfront.

## QUALITY ASSURANCE AND QUALITY CONTROL

The quality management function that covers the wide areas of focus for a collaborative web based system translates into a quality process. This quality process is a suite of activities, tasks, roles and deliverables that is used to ensure high quality *CWBS*. A typical quality process, based on Unhelkar (2003) is shown in Figure 3. This quality process shows the roles, deliverables and activities involved in carrying out the process.

### Roles in the Testing Process for CWBS

The developer, the tester and the quality manager get together to carry out the testing of a *CWBS*. The developer, as shown in Figure 3, represents the group of people who are not only involved in the creation of the *CWBS*, but also all technical roles (such as a database administrator and a technical writer) that are involved with the developer. The tester represents the test analysts, the test designers and the actual

*Figure 3. The testing process for CWBS (extended from Unhelkar, 2003)*

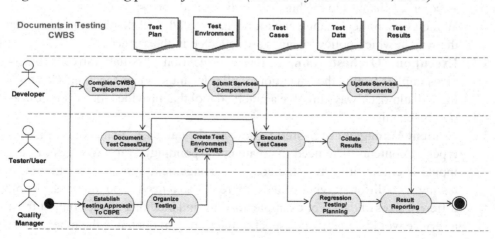

testers executing test cases. The quality manager remains responsible for the strategic approach to planning, organizing and executing the testing.

## Deliverables in the Testing Process for CWBS

The deliverables related to quality assurance and testing of CWBS include the following:

*Test plan*: Documents the overall organization of testing

*Test environment*: Deals with creation of a technical environment that represents the real-life collaborative environment as closely as possible in order to carry out the testing.

*Test cases:* Are the smallest units of tests that deal with CWBS testing. These test cases can be based on a unit of functionality (as represented by a use case) or a unit of code (as represented by a class).

*Test data*: Needs to be for both valid and invalid inputs. Each test case needs a suite of test data, and so does the entire subsystem and system.

*Test results*: Need to be recorded, analyzed, used for feedback and re-recorded after regression testing.

## Activities in the Testing Process for CWBS

The activities, shown in Figure 3, depict the sequential flow of work undertaken by the roles within the quality assurance space. These activities include establishment of the testing approach and organization of testing by the quality manager. The developer, in the mean time completes the development of services and components iteratively and submits them for testing. The tester creates the test cases and implements the test environment before executing the test cases. The results from the testing are then collated, the bugs and errors fixed, and the regression testing is undertaken. The reports from the testing effort are regularly reported by the quality manager to the stake holders of *CWBS*.

## TESTING OF CWBS IN A COLLABORATIVE ENVIRONMENT

One of the crucial aspects of quality assurance is testing or quality control. Software testing has always been a challenge because the product being tested is not a physical product built on an assembly line. In the engineering domain, quality control results in 'accepting or rejecting' a manufactured product—in software it's more often the case of 'correcting' than 'rejecting' (see Figure 4).

*Figure 4. Combining testing options (based on Unhelkar, 2005)*

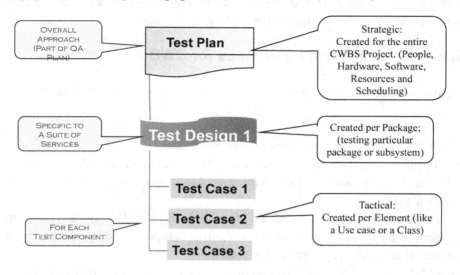

     Going for Class-based Testing as against Use-case based Testing
- Creating Test Data for unit and system tests
- Use Case Testing
- Executing Tests and Collating Results
- Advances in Testing Services
- Verify and validate the design and code for their correctness and completeness.
- Identification of bugs and errors and prevention of their occurrence.

Testing can be planned and executed in number of different ways. For example, the entire *CWBS* can be tested through a combination of automated test tools as well as manual testing carried out by testers. The approach to testing can also change – depending on how the system is *sliced* to carry out the testing. A vertically sliced system would imply that the use cases developed for the *CWBS* (as described earlier in chapter 6) would for the basic unit for testing. A horizontally sliced system for testing would result in a technical component (such as an interface or a database class) being the unit for testing.

The test cases for the *Collaborative Web Based System (CWBS)* consist of the following headings:

- **Identification:** Based on name and number to identify a test case.
- **Purpose:** Based on the reason for the test (e.g. verifying business logic or checking the validity of the date field on a screen).
- **Prerequisites:** Prerequisites are necessary before the test can be carried out. These prerequisites relate to a particular test case. The prerequisite for the entire test design for the module will be documented separately.
- **Input:** In order to examine both valid and invalid data is also a crucial factor for quality assurance in the *Collaborative Web Based System (CWBS)*.
- **Actions:** The actions or steps required on part of the tester in order to carry out the test
- **Expected output:** This will determine whether the test was a success or a failure
- **Actual output:** Or a placeholder for recording the actual output as the test case gets executed
- **Administrative details:** Of the tester carrying out the tests etc.

Figure 5 demonstrates, through an example, how the testing function would be carried out on the current collaborative environment. The collaboration by the group of hospitals in this instance is pre-determined and it does not allow for dynamic formulation of services to the CMO shown on the left of Figure 6. The testing of such system would only be restricted to registration of the hospitals on a web portal to provide pre-determined services.

We recognize four major areas in the collaborative environment to assure the quality and good performance of the system. The collaborative environment shown in Chapter 1, Figure 8 of this book, demonstrate the processes that needs the testing for the quality assurance of the proposed systems. These four areas consists of the registration of the hospitals in the portal, registration of the chief medical officer in the system, checking of the remaining registered hospital when the required number of personnel is not completed and inform when process is completed. The system must also inform if all numbers of the required personnel are selected or the system has not been able to complete and satisfy the requirements.

Based on the following discussion the following test cases are classified to verify and validate the proposed *CWBS*.

The Chief medical offices submit an application requesting 50 doctors, 300 nurses, 100 surgeons in an emergency situation. *CWBS* receives the request and check the validity of the request before processing and checking the hospitals. The system validates the request when there is suitable demand. However, as demonstrated in Table 1, when the request includes less than one doctor the system rejects the request.

As demonstrated in Table 2, the system should also check to make sure that chief medical officer is registered in the system. The system should allow the registration

*Figure 5. System testing in current collaborative environment*

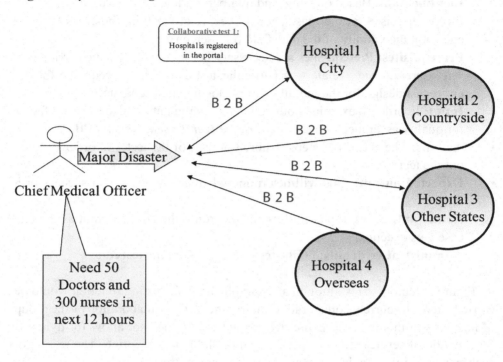

*Figure 6. System testing in proposed collaborative environment*

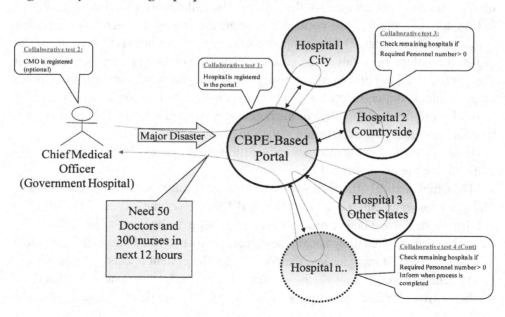

*Table 1. Valid and invalid inputs for test case*

| Input | Expected Outputs |
|---|---|
| Book 50 Doctors | Typical valid standard input. Access; Pass. |
| Book 300 Nurses | Typical valid standard input. Access; Pass. |
| Book 100 surgeons | Typical valid standard input. Access; Pass. |
| Book < 1 Doctor, Nurse and Heart Surgeon | An invalid input. System should reject this input for the test to pass; |

*Table 2. Testing for checking the user registration*

| Input | Expected Outputs | Actual Outputs |
|---|---|---|
| Send Request: • Is CMO registered? | Provide option for the user to register if the user is not already registered in the collaborative system. | • CMO is Register: Continue • CMO is not registered: Offer Registration Box If Yes: Submit Form          Register member and continue Else Continue |

*Table 3. Testing for sending request*

| Input | Expected Outputs | Actual Outputs |
|---|---|---|
| Send Request 1 (H1) • 50 Doctors, 300 Nurses and 10 Heart Surgeons are required Send Request 2 (H2) • Remaining Doctors, Nurses and Heart Surgeons calculated manually. | Availability of H1 (only) Availability of H2 (only) | • Forward the list of booked doctors, nurses and hear surgeons (H1) • Forward the list of booked doctors, nurses and hear surgeons (H2) |
| Send Request: • 50 Doctors, 300 Nurses and 10 Heart Surgeons are required. | The request should be checked in order to identify that the organization capable of handling the request are registered in the collaborative system. | Check Industry: • Hospital exists in the Collaborative System • Send message if hospital does not exist |

*Table 4. Testing to check the locating hospitals*

| Input | Expected Outputs | Actual Outputs |
|---|---|---|
| Initial forwarded Request<br>• Book 50 Doctors, 3000 Nurse and 10 Heart Surgeons | • Locate the hospitals capable of providing the desired personnel.<br>• Provide a message with the details of the booked personnel. Inform the user if required personnel are booked otherwise inform when checking for hospital 2 booking the remaining desired personnel. | • Provide the list (name, Specialty, Hospital)<br>• Provide the number of remaining required personnel<br>• If required<br>personnel number: 0<br>Finish Process<br>Else<br>    Message check hospital 2 |

if the user is not registered before processing the request.

After the initial validation of the request (see Table 3), the request is forwarded to *CWBS* which is an interoperable system. The system should check for the availability of the hospital 1 and book the available personnel and forward the list to chief medical office before going to hospital 2 if the required personnel are not rostered to work in the emergency.

Table 4, shows the required check points for checking the personnel availability, confirmation of the registration and making sure that the system checks the next hospital when the process is not completed and indeed more doctors and nurses are required. The testing also demonstrates that the current collaboration model is not supporting the proposed business process. This is beyond the boundary of known B2B model.

## ACTION POINTS

1. Create the test plans based on the requirements, architecture, and design of your *CWBS* implementation.
2. Describe how you will undertake testing in the solution space
3. Create test cases based on requirements (through use cases) and test harnesses (through classes).
4. The system tester needs to identify Valid and Invalid set of test data and update it on to the test cases.
5. Identify the process models created in earlier chapters as a part of *CBPE* that require testing in the current collaborative environment.
6. Discuss the processes that require testing in the proposed collaborative environment in order to assure the quality of the proposed *CWBS*.

# REFERENCES

Littlefield, R. (2008). *Institute for lean systems' response to the Australian federal government's 2008 review of the national innovation system*. Retrieved October 25, 2008, from http://www.innovation.gov.au/innovationreview/Documents/238-Institute_for_Lean_Systems.pdf

Pyzdek, T. (2003). *The six SIGMA handbook: A complete guide for green belts, black belts, and managers at all levels*. New York: McGraw-Hill Professional.

Software Engineering Institute. (n.d.). Retrieved October 25, 2008, from http://www.sei.cmu.edu

Unhelkar, B. (2003). Understanding collaborations and clusters in the e-business world. In *Proceedings of the We-B Conference,* Perth, Australia.

Unhelkar, B. (2005). *Practical object oriented analysis.* Australia: Thomson Social Science Press.

# Chapter 9
# Socio–Cultural Factors and Collaboration

*The deepest problems of modern life derive from the claim of the individual to preserve the autonomy and individuality of his existence in the face of overwhelming social forces, of historical heritage, of external culture, and of the technique of life.*

George Simmel (1858–1918)

## CHAPTER KEY POINTS

- Discusses the social aspects of information and communication technology in general and how they affect businesses.
- Discusses the ever important social issues of trust, law and security in the context of collaborative business.
- Discusses the impact of the collaborative environment on the customers of the business.
- Discusses the impact of the environmental factors on the collaborative businesses.
- Discusses the unique cultural features of the collaborative environment.
- Discusses the social challenges resulting from the collaborative environment.

DOI: 10.4018/978-1-60566-689-1.ch009

# INTRODUCTION

This chapter discusses the importance of the socio-cultural factors of collaboration. This social influence is experienced not only in the society where the customers exist, but also within the internal organization, employees, business partners and senior management. The transition to a collaborative business will affect all these involved parties and it is important to understand that effect and prepare the parties for the transition. This chapter starts by providing some definitions of the social aspects in information technology. The correlations between the IT changes and corresponding changes to the society are demonstrated. The discussion, in this chapter, is aimed to handle some of the risks associated with transitioning to collaborative business that are non-technical in nature.

# SOCIAL ASPECTS OF INFORMATION & COMMUNICATION TECHNOLOGY

The social aspect of information and communication technology is one significant dimension of collaboration that tends to be left on the backburner as the business transitions to a collaborative one. The reason the social dimension gets ignored is because it is very difficult to put this dimension of collaborative business in a well-defined formula. The technologies of web services are promising communication and transaction between two or more parties that may not even know each other. However, in order to translate these technologies of communication into worthwhile business strategies, it is important to understand the underlying human element in collaborative business. Whenever collaboration becomes substantial and large, with ongoing service exchanges and business transactions that need support from people – the social issues start coming into play.

Information and communication technology has already moved from being used exclusively in the large computer centers of businesses to almost every aspect of our homes, schools, organizations and society in general. People need to gather and keep records and exchange information in order to remain active and be part of the ever-changing society. Based on Ranjbar (2002), no other technology has had such profound impact on our daily lives as information and communications technologies since it enables us to gather, store and exchange various records.

The computer applications in today's society are very broad and include online banking, online shopping, working at home (telecommuting), leisure, artificial intelligence and robotics to name but a few. Powerful search engines and the capability of sharing information are among the great advantages of the Internet. Some advocates such as Katz and Rice (2002) claim that the Internet is the greatest technology invented, as it provides an overwhelming potential for the development of liberating communities, for exponential increase in human and social capital, and for the achievement of each individual's full democratic participation in every policy decision. Web 2.0 (has particularly revolutionized the computer-mediated society. Web 2.0 allows easier collaboration of people by facilitating functionalities that enable sharing web-based information such as video, audio, wikis and blogs in a easy way. Web 2.0 includes social aspects of the utilization of the web, wherein users generate and distribute contents. This generation and distribution of the contents through the facilitation of Web 2.0 transforms websites into easily accessible portals – paving way for greater human collaboration.

The social dimension of Information and Communication Technology (ICT) focuses on "who" are the players and how they influence, and are influenced by, the impact of ICT on society. These people include the clients, employees and other users of the business. The issues that face these users when they interface with an ICT-enabled business include usability and privacy, and the way their relationships change with the organization. The changes to work formats, including telecommuting and changing organizational and social structures, are all part of this social dimension. Furthermore, this social dimension also incorporates the nature of electronic connectivity that indicate the highly individual nature of electronic gadgets and the subsequent challenges to the security and privacy of individuals.

Businesses undertaking electronic collaborations need to consider how the collaborative software applications and services are going to be used by people. What are the advantages and risks associated with their use? What should a collaborative business do, from a socio-cultural aspect, to ensure that electronic collaborations are accepted by the users?

## The Connected Society

Computer technologies, especially network environments, have enabled people from different socio-geographical background to connect within a free framework. This technology has enabled ordinary people to corporations and government agencies to locate, meet and communicate their social life, as well as solving problems.

This computer-mediated network of people can work in formal and informal atmospheres which demonstrate the transformation of an ordinary society to interactive society.. This transformation, as presented in Figure 1, has evolved from the technological capabilities in a way that match our needs and wants. In the connected society, people learn to interact with the systems. This interaction has already revolutionized our society; making us seek further advancements through the incorporation more computer systems.

*Figure 1. Relationship of collaborative computing and society*

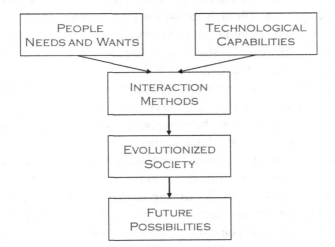

The technological advancement in our society demonstrated in Figure 1 shows how the technology allows people to justify, explain and expand their requirements. Research and development conceptualizes our society by providing a powerful means of understanding to the abstract, as well as the complex desires in the new collaborative business order. This chapter continues the investigation in the impact of collaboration on structure of the society and organizations in order to provide a useful socio-cultural framework.

The need for such discussion within electronic collaborations is justified owing to the fact that, despite their potential benefits, many electronic alliances manage only initial or cursory service exchanges. These electronic alliances do not flourish into extensive collaborative businesses. Many electronic alliances fall apart very quickly and, if there has been any financial investment, these breakdowns leave the investors empty handed. One of the major reasons for this failure appears to be the inability of the organizations to accommodate different cultures (Grambs and Zerbib 2000). These cultural differences are not merely socio-cultural but also related to corporate and political cultures (Laudon and Laudon, 2002).

## SOCIAL IMPACTS OF COLLABORATION ON ORGANIZATIONS

The learning of organization seems to become one of the prominent aspects of the enterprises business strategies. As the enterprise evolves, there have been many changes and require resolution. These changes are often associated with leadership and management styles, the implication of technology, and the business environment.

As a result of swift technological development, enterprises are capable of applying knowledge management. Through the online learning environment, also, organizational learning can be promoted. Laudon and Laudon (2002) define knowledge management as "the process of systematically and actively managing and leveraging the stores of knowledge in the organization".

The strategy of business operations focuses are to ensure the existing and potential customers only purchasing the goods or services. When the customers are already in the collaboration process or in the situation of global searching for sources, the domestic enterprises would probably lose them.

In multinational corporations, business units and subsidiaries are often spread across nations and have quite distinct cultural attitudes and characteristics. This requires employees in such global companies to be prepared for cross-cultural interactions. In order to achieve better communication and information flows between employees and customers from different cultural backgrounds, corporations should consider the introduction of multi-cultural skills development programs. These programs may consist of language and communication learning, recognizing and understanding of cultural differences and focusing on delivering value to the customer. Thus, teams take non-traditional non-hierarchical formats in a collaborative environment. This is because members of the team with different responsibilities may be physically sitting in different working environments and offices. Therefore, collaboration and coordination are the two imperative ingredients of successful teamwork in the organization. Coordination refers to the extra tasks required for amalgamating tasks performed to accomplish the final goal, while collaboration deals with multiple teams working jointly toward the same objective. These two ingredients make a good virtual team, and in collaborative organizations, more often than not, the teams are going to be virtual rather than physical. As a result, even well-known team building exercises take on a different meaning and format, requiring coordination and collaboration across time, space and cultural boundaries. In order to succeed in global coordination and collaboration, there is a need to establish common standards in terms of communication method, language, management rules, and information technologies (as well as hardware platforms and software applications).

Collaborative organizations must regularly invest in research and development (R&D), engineering, manufacturing, marketing, sales, distribution, accounting, and finance. The team members must have clear objectives in mind for better performance in order to collaborate toward the enterprise objectives.

This collaboration facilitates the team members in sharing a common vision with the leader. The level of alignment with the common value and vision is the key to eliminate tight control of any kind and increase the efforts made by each individual. Hence the leader of this team model has less workload in supervising and guiding the team members to carry out their responsibilities.

When customers grasp more information and face more and more diversified markets, the demand for product consistency and standardization is also increased. This kind of demand for consistency will bring down the enterprises' inventory, purchasing and production costs, and advance their competitive advantages.

Controlling the end user computing equipment and facilities is a complex assignment, especially in the proposed environment where business units are dispersed across nations. Managing supply chain in the global collaborative environment should be taken into account when planning and design of the *CBPE*. Tasks involved in the end-user facilities management may include the identification of facilities in each of the business units and subsidiaries, verification of facilities availability, development of standard maintenance procedures, and the development of standard facility purchasing, logistic and distribution procedures.

## SPECIFIC ISSUES RELATED TO ROLES

This section concentrates on the use of communication and information technology from the customer, employee, organisation and environmental point of view in the proposed *CBPE* collaborative environment discussed in Chapter 1 of this book.

### Customers in Collaboration

Information systems provide customers with better access to products and services, especially when organizations collaborate in a global environment. This access to products and services is achieved when users are able to use the proposed CBPE software. Users must also understand the value this software provides to them when they search and submit their request. They must have sufficient control over the design and development of global information systems to ensure that business functions and operations are accurately incorporated. Moreover, the design of global information systems should be based on all stakeholders. In other words, the lack of users' involvement in the design of global information systems is the major cause of systems failure.

The users of the collaborative system are from different socio-cultural and physical background meaning that people with different languages, color preferences, and different requirements will be accessing the global collaborative system. Understanding this diversity is crucial to success of the proposed collaborative environment. As per Kincaide (1999) performing business requires a deep respect of the language, country's culture, religions and institutions. Considering these variables will provide organizations with a certain level of competitive edge in the global collaborative business environment.

Language barriers require multiple interfaces, unless the system uses an agreed common language. Culture can be divided in high and low context culture in which high-context cultures assign meaning to many of the incentives surrounding an unambiguous message. There are several aspects pertaining to culture that need to be heeded by an organization planning to globalize its information systems management. These include education levels, geographical and time zones, religion, demographics, individual significance and objectives, communication, and leadership style. There are no perfect or standard solutions to overcome the various cultural differences however the organizations need to comprehend the various socio-cultural aspects in each culture and fine-tune the appropriateness to their working environment. Communication is also a major concern in most collaborative environment. Enterprises should ensure a standard communication typology is embedded in the policy and implemented in daily operations.

There are always benefits associated with involving users as part of any information system development teams. However, it is even more important to engage users in the collaborative information systems development. As mentioned above, users are people who understand the business functions and operations. Involving various types of users through the entire information system analysis and design phases is crucial. It helps in making sure the collaborative information system would appropriately implement business processes and bring extra value to the business. It is also believed that users who have been involved in the design and development phases would become agents of change for the new systems. The agents of change play the role of disseminating the concept of the new systems to members in their local business unit and they may also be involved in developing training programs.

## Employees in Collaboration

People are major players in designing, implementing and utilizing information systems. Disregarding the location of the employee, people have their own objectives and outlook on life. These objectives can be identified in three aspects: personal, social, and professional. These aspects are also variable since, from time to time, the emphasis of these aspects conflicts with others. For instance, an individual's personal objective is to spend more time with family, but a promotion opportunity is given to the individual with the condition of working several months overseas. Hence, the individual has to decide whether to take the promotion opportunity and sacrifice the family commitment. Similarly each organization has it own objectives. These objectives may conflict with employees' personal objectives. To overcome this conflict, the organizations must realize their employees' objectives, and negotiate with a realignment strategy to achieve a win-win situation.

Hiring employees for a collaborative global organization is not as easy as for domestic companies. The recruitment process requires careful planning to provide the best strategy for the organization in obtaining suitable employees for appropriate positions and locations. For example, Unhelkar (2002) has suggested the importance of a best-fit approach to recruitment. In preparation of the global recruitment plan, the organization's human resources department firstly needs to transform itself into a global operation. Traditionally, human resources are an independent and unique system for each subsidiary in multinational corporations (MNCs). For example, the human resources department in the Sydney subsidiary may have no relationships or connections with the human resources department in Tokyo of the same MNC. In addition, each subsidiary's human resources department may maintain its own operations. This may be enough to fulfill the local requirements, but certainly would not have the flexibility to facilitate the management of employees in the global scale. This uniqueness of the human resources function in the traditional organization leaves the organization with no centralized control and standardized operations in regard to people management.

Furthermore, training is a critical agenda to continuously improve the quality perspective in products, services, management aspects. It also strengthens organizations in the proposed collaborative environment. In designing and developing the training programs, a number of factors are identified to ensure appropriateness and effectiveness. These factors can be classified as various stages in collaboration process: target employee situation, considering various methods of training, such as computer based training programs to develop and deliver the training programs which allow the employees to participate in learning anywhere and anytime. However, the standardized training programs may require some variations, for example in languages and cultural aspects, to suit the foreign subsidiary contexts.

The management of the portal in the proposed *CBPE* environment also plays an important role in keeping the users satisfied when performing business tasks through the global information systems. The employee needs to have a clear understanding of what are the services and products the users anticipate, and accurately and timelessly responding to problems reported by users. Figure 2 illustrates a proposed help desk structure for the *CBPE* portal to accommodate the information systems help services.

The end users are the last group of people using the collaborative information systems on a regular basis. The task of managing and supporting end user groups is not only in maintaining business information operations, but is the key to evaluating and improving the *CBPE* environment. The fundamental concerns of the end user management category in the collaboration context include managing end user computing facilities, end user computing education, introducing and learning new global information systems, help desk support, and end user involvement in collaboration.

*Figure 2. Organization of a help desk in collaborative business*

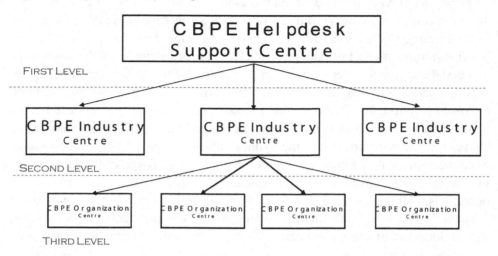

In the modern business environment, employees' capabilities of using computers to perform business tasks seem to be part of the job requirements. The basic computing skills such as producing documents, sending emails, and browsing the Internet are required in most office environments. However, the level of employees' computing education in the global organization varies from subsidiary to subsidiary. Thus, there is a need to incorporate an end user computing education plan in the global transition process. The main objective of the plan is to ensure that the employees have obtained the required computing skills in all business units. It may consist of the identification of the employees' current computing skills and levels, identification of essential computing skills development of training programs, and implementation of training programs.

## BUSINESS AND ENVIRONMENTAL FACTORS IN COLLABORATION

The organizations are proactive in determining the factors, which will influence the transformation to collaboration. These factors are continuous development of new markets, scale of the economy, trends in product-service consistency, costs in global transportation, government regulations, telecommunications and equipment costs, and trends in technology standards.

Continuously developing new markets provide opportunities to enterprise collaboration. Customers search for their required products and services from anywhere and everywhere in the world. This access to international collaborative market benefit the customer by finding the better quality with the lowest possible costs, better transportation facilities including the demand satisfaction.

Government's support of the domestic industries by tariff regulations can be classified as one of the crucial factors for the proposed collaborative environment, in which an additional tax is charged on the product when it has arrived at or departed from a country's borders.

The variation of market exchange rates would seriously affect the enterprise's profit. When the enterprise deals with foreign suppliers, the payment method and terms should be discussed before the order is completed, because the longer the term of payment, the higher risk the exchange rate variation. Purchasing staff in the enterprise should also have enough skills and understanding of the variation of exchange rates when they decide to deal with foreign suppliers.

Since the early 1980s, the rapid progress of new technology has had an influence on enterprise profit and operations. Improvement of production procedures have caused the restructuring of the enterprise's market share. More and more enterprises have invested in the research and development field and have employed these latest technologies to develop better ideas and products that will make a fortune for the enterprise.

The influence and degree of transformation of the above environmental factors enforce the acceleration of the processes of enterprise globalization. The enterprises with the majority of business activity in the domestic market are facing competitive pressure form overseas; however, global enterprises are also struggling in the extreme competitive environment for their survival.

In order to survive in the global business environment, the enterprises must carefully evaluate these environment factors and analyze current and future foreseeable influences and trends. This procedure also leads the enterprises in the development of global strategic vision.

## Changes in Economic and Social Environment

The most obvious and overwhelming trend in the collaborative environment is the rapid and ongoing industrialization of the organizations. As organizations improve their business processes, they have a huge impact on each other. These impacts will be all the larger when they consider developing new methodologies where necessary, and remaining true to their own cultures in the process. While there are undeniable benefits to this paradigm, there are also undeniable weaknesses, such as the tendency to only worry about the next quarter and to let the long term take care of itself. Some organizations are trying to moderate the worst excesses of this wide-open, chaotic environment with various types of built-in controls. Admittedly, some of the economic experiments have shown more promise than others, but with so many cultures trying so many different methodologies, new and different conditions are bound to develop.

On a micro level, there is little effect, as individual local operations will continue to only worry about their niche; but on a macro level, the effect is huge. As economies grow and change, the world becomes a smaller place. As such many companies no longer only market their product locally or source their materials locally; rather, they extend these requirements globally. As companies grow and network, they need to be cognizant of how local conditions in areas other than their home ground affect their business. They need to build products that appeal to their customers in different locations, usually through some form of niche marketing that requires some form of niche forecasting. They need to firmly understand how different economic conditions will affect the marketability of their products.

Just as many of the economic changes are driving sociological changes, so many sociological changes are driving economic changes. The change will always maintain a sort of dynamic tension between where changes in one will invariably create offsetting changes in the other. This means that alert and successful organizations not only must be aware of changes in their environments, but they also must be able to accurately extrapolate what sort of further changes will be caused by this tension and plan for how they will affect their organizations and markets.

As companies begin, merge, diverge, and die in response to changes in the environment, they create their own effects on that environment. This affects how a company forecasts on both a micro and a macro level. Changes in the local environment must be tracked, anticipated, and corrected at a local level. Globally, organizations must maintain enough control to drive the organization, yet they need to leave enough autonomy at the local level to deal with local differences. Different countries or regions often have different legal requirements; therefore, forecasting, manufacturing, and distribution processes must take this into consideration, as a labelled product may not be interchangeable, even if the product is identical.

Considering the fact at an even more micro level, we need to consider individual people and their effect on an organization's forecast. Historically, the consumer was thought of and acted like big blocks of interchangeable components of the market, with them all buying the same thing. Think about the mindset of Henry Ford's alleged statement, "The customer can have any color they want, so long as they want black." Under the new system, individual consumers are becoming more discriminating and more demanding, which causes much more variability. People are very specific about what they want and are not willing to be dictated to by the supplier.

This reality changes the forecast paradigm as much or perhaps even more than any technological changes. As manufacturing adopts lean methodology and moves to a "lot size of one," so demand planning must move to ever finer levels of distinction in forecasting. In the new net-enhanced environment, there always will be a balance of dynamic tensions between actual demand from consumers, based on the changes in their buying patterns, and the need and ability to accurately forecast this demand. The shift is away from maintaining large stocks of finished goods at various locations and toward lean manufacturing and distribution practices. This means that, as stocks are driven down and consumer expectations rise, it becomes ever more important not only to accurately forecast requirements, but also to monitor proactively those forecasts against real sales to quickly spot divergences before they can impact customer service. This means taking advantage of new technologies, such as Radio Frequency Identification (RFID), to monitor movement within the system, using early warning triggers to spot trends away from the official plan and a willingness of the new companies to take risks in responding to these potential issues before they can impact the customer. These technological changes mean that customers can be anywhere and can have their needs addressed the moment they think about them. The organization that can fulfil the needs of these customers in the easiest, fastest, and most cost-effective way will win their business. Such organizations will win over their competition and, in the process, reap profits.

## CULTURAL FEATURES OF COLLABORATION

Awareness of different cultures, value systems and ethos can be of immense help in ensuring the growth of a collaborative global business. Learning to overcome cultural differences in a positive way can help collaborative businesses to flourish rapidly. At a fundamental level, culture is the ethos exuded by a group of people. Practically, it is the way members of an entire society live their lives. These members of the society are our consumers, managers, employees and governors. On a more formal level, according to an anthropological definition by Hall and Hall (1990): "Culture is 'a system for creating, sending, storing and processing information.'" These definitions themselves seem to indicate that whenever different cultures try and intersect, there are bound to be differences. Culture refers to the total way of life – the underlying patterns of thinking, feeling and acting – of particular groups of people. It is learned, not inherited, and transmitted from generation to generation primarily through conditioned learning. Therefore, it does not come as a surprise, that collaborative global alliances face cultural disparities as one of their major challenges.

## Cultural Issues in Electronic Collaboration

A successful collaboration should not imply an imposition of one organizational culture over another. Rather, it should create a new culture that brings together the best elements of each one (Brooks 1998). This is what is known as "synergy" and is something we sorely need in order to successfully handle the cultural differences in global collaborations (Unhelkar 2002). However, synergy is usually lacking in global collaborations because they are often viewed solely from a financial perspective, leaving the human resource issue as something to be dealt with later and hopefully without a great deal of effort. And whenever change is imminent as a result of collaborations, it is usually assumed that the smaller, weaker company is the one that has the obligation to change. Errors like these are commonplace, resulting in failure to achieve even the basic aim of financial success. While creation of synergy between global partners with different contextual background is expensive and time consuming, it is still vital that this issue is addressed right from the beginning. The end result is far more valuable in terms not only of financial rewards but also employee satisfaction, broadening of cultural viewpoints, and a deeper and perhaps longer time sustainable collaboration. To achieve this aim, let us consider some of the major reasons for cultural disparities in global collaborations, and what can be done to ameliorate them.

## Communications Gap

While the electronic communication continues to ease the challenge of connecting organizations and the services they have to offer, still basic cultural hurdles can occur in social communication. Communication between collaborating companies that may be in different parts of the globe – or even a parent company and its foreign subsidiaries can be hampered by diverse language, culture heritage and physical distance. A popular example is a service collaboration being setup between an Australian company and Chinese company. Although few Australians would be able to converse in a Chinese language, there are increasing numbers of Chinese who have taken courses in English in high school. Moreover, many Chinese people with advanced technical degrees have attended graduate school in Australia. So the default language between Chinese and Australian business professionals is English. While this situation is certainly fortunate for communication for this collaboration for those that speak and write English; the "Western" partners of this alliance should be extremely sensitive and understanding as their counterparts attempt conversation in a foreign language. There are obvious major differences in the nuances of expressions from these two different cultures. The Australian culture is predominantly "low context", wherein what "you do" is important. This requires people from these cultures to express themselves as well, and occasionally as hard, as they can. The Chinese culture is context-based, and depends on the pedigree of the person, to a certain extent. Therefore, a person with Chinese cultural background, despite conversing in English, is bound to show the restraint expected of him or her in similar conversations within the Chinese context. It is recommended that special efforts be made before and after formal meetings to search for thoughts that might otherwise not have been expressed and meanings should be clarified by spelling them out rather than taking them for granted. Furthermore, written communications between alliance partners must receive special attention; it is easy to unintentionally offend by virtue of subtle language inflections that are misunderstood. Emails are most notorious in this regards, and more so when they come from a different cultural background.

## Social Incompatibility

Socio-cultural incompatibility results when two companies with different social environment, as well as disparate financial backing, try to get together into cross-border collaboration as a means of expanding and competing overseas. While "going global" seems to be a strategic move, this incompatible collaboration fails because partnering companies fail to give culture the credence it deserves. For example, the American socio-cultural context can be quite different to the German work culture and ethos. An collaboration casually put together to capitalize on the German engineering skills and American markets can degenerate into an ugly fracas if the differences in social and cultural contexts are not spelled out and studied prior to the collaboration formation. While the American focus may be on the financial aspect of the collaboration, it is possible that the German focus is on building a strong foundation for the collaboration or perhaps creating a knowledge base.

In yet another common example, a collaborative alliance almost collapsed because the two organizations had disparate staff policies. One organization gave half-day Fridays in the summer; the other didn't. One gave staff a day off on Election Day; the other didn't. At first, there was grumbling, but both organizations came together frequently, giving everyone a chance to air their feelings. These meetings let people come to terms with their differences and remain productive.

Failure to address differences and disparate values or operations can quickly lead to the demise of an otherwise strong strategic alliance. The key to beating the odds is to assess and monitor partner compatibility up front and at every step of the way-constantly highlighting differences and creating solutions (Gupta 2000).

## Dissimilar Management

Dissimilar management styles can cause culture conflict too. One leader may be forward thinking, while the other is of the old school of management thinking, relying on hierarchical management style. A common result of these management styles is often seen in Scott Adams cartoon character Dilbert: For example, Dilbert is often shown as a staff member who is left with no private space at all, working in a cubicle. However, if one organization has a flattened hierarchy and an open seating plan and another one doesn't, and if people and managers from these organizations have to work together, they are bound to have different perceptions of the entire alliance exercise. If handles properly, exposure to different approaches can be liberating and enlightening. The important thing is to be sure staff members have a chance to discuss their feelings and work through solutions together.

## SOCIAL CHALLENGES OF COLLABORATION

Socio-cultural incompatibility results when two companies with different social environments, as well as disparate financial backing, collaborate in a cross-border alliance. This alliance is made possible by the technical ability of WS-based applications to interact with each other. Social impacts of collaborations have led to challenges in terms of privacy, trust, legal as well as cross-cultural issues between the organizations. Based on this brief outline of the challenges, a more specific framework for these challenges has been identified by Ghanbary and Unhelkar (2007a and 2007b). This framework is helpful in handling the socio-cultural aspects of otherwise technical alliances. The failure to address differences and disparate value systems and operations between collaborating global organizations can lead quickly to the demise of an otherwise strong strategic alliance. This is more likely to happen in electronic collaborations, as the participating businesses may focus only on the electronic aspect of the collaborative transaction, not paying sufficient attention to the supporting physical communication required among businesses. Communication between participating companies within collaboration, or even a parent company and its foreign subsidiaries, can be hampered by diverse language, culture heritage and physical distance (Siegel, 1999). Overcoming the potential cultural hurdles, in terms of verbal or physical face-to-face communications, is an important challenge in collaborative business. Thus, collaborations between businesses that operate in separate domains, geographical regions and cultures, need to understand, accept and resolve the unique socio-cultural challenges. Management needs to come up with innovative ideas and approaches to create and "gel" such organizations and their corresponding virtual teams. While the collaborative team management tools mentioned in the technical challenges earlier can play an important role in achieving coordination amongst separate organizations and their people, there still need to be innovative approaches in order to manage geographically widespread collaborations. Traditional hierarchical management is unlikely to satisfy the needs of such teams and there is likely to be an impact on the organizational structures of these businesses. Organizational structure required to support human interactions is central to efficient e-collaboration (Rutkowski et al. 2002); however, electronic collaborations change the functionality and nature of the organization, as well as those of the structures of the standard collaborating groups. Successful collaborations require a supportive organizational structure that is based on trust-building and restructuring of group-based processes. The core need for employees and managers of participating organizations in collaboration to interact directly with their counterparts in other organizations further disturbs the well-known hierarchical organizational structure. The need to provide a unified view of a collaborative business process to the client also results in a "flattened" organizational structure – as the client is simply not interested in the internal hierarchy of the organization and, as such, the internal hierarchy of the organization loses significance. Such flattened hierarchies of organizations result in a loss of middle-management organizational structures that simply become redundant.

Corporate mistrust is an important management challenge when it comes to globally collaborative businesses. While it is accepted that each collaborating party would attempt to protect its own interests, including assets, intellectual property, reputation and customer base, the very opportunity to collaboratively take up business opportunities requires the development of a win–win relationship. This development of a win–win relationship requires each collaborative party to enter in an electronic relationship with a certain amount of trust in its partner, and as discussed by Brooks (1998), with an attitude that the partner's success is just as important as its own. In fact, the very nature of collaborative businesses requires them to open themselves up to their customers and business partners and, without trust; collaborations are not likely to succeed. Mutual trust between collaborative businesses and their customers and business partners is an integral part of building the e-economy. Indeed, building trust is seen as a subtle but key issue during e-collaboration activities (Rutkowski et al. 2002).

Collaborations also occasionally need mediators and facilitator, despite the fact that electronic collaborations enable businesses to directly deal with each other and its clients. The reasons for such mediators and facilitators arise from the numerous social, legal, and business requirements that can be easily resolved only with the involvement of a third party. A common example is the popular auctioning site eBay; although the vendors and the buyers are transacting directly, they need the facilitation of eBay, as well as its protocols, rules and regulations to abide by, in order to conduct business successfully. This scenario becomes more complex when numerous large organizations are involved in collaborating electronically – eventually giving rise to the roles played by standards bodies like W3C, OASIS (www.oasis.org) and OMG (www.omg.org). Furthermore, these collaborative business processes across wide geographical regions require a corresponding legal framework that is also binding on the ensuing collaborative business transactions that are also on different software application domains (Neely and Unhelkar 2005).

Finally, privacy (as against security, which has been earlier discussed in the technical challenges) is another significant social factor that needs to be considered in collaborative business processes. Privacy is the need and capacity of individuals to negotiate social relationships by controlling access to personal information. As laws, policies, and technological design increasingly structure people's relationships with social institutions, individual privacy faces new threats and new opportunities (Agre and Rotenberg 1997). While a legal framework usually exists for privacy, the challenge to enforce that legal framework for collaborative transactions is enormous (as discussed, and also mentioned earlier in this book (Neely and Unhelkar 2005). The response to this privacy challenge from management requires the creation of policies and procedures, both internal and external to the organization, that are acceptable to the stakeholders. Examples of such policies from an institution are provided by (Abood 2006).

## Trust in Collaboration

Since the primary purpose of alliances is to make money, it does not come as a surprise that alliance partners tend to eye each other sceptically in the beginning. Given the communication gaps that exist between people in similar cultures, let along varied ones, this scepticism can quickly build up to paranoia, resulting in a break of alliance. Thus, corporate mistrust is a serious problem that is unfortunately further exacerbated by managers from both countries who have achieved their success by nurturing a tough, critical business image. Of course, it is important that each party to an alliance protect its own assets, intellectual property, reputation, customer base, etc. But it is equally important to appreciate that only a mutual win-win relationship can succeed and endure. Hence, each party should enter a relationship with a certain amount of trust in its partner, and with an attitude that the partner's success is just as important as its own (Brooks 1998). Cross checking of references and getting third-party commends on business alliances, as well as checking each others corporate history, is one good way of trying to reduce corporate mistrust.

Further work is required to evaluate the implications of trust in the collaborative environment. Trust is a very important issue in society and, in the case of *CBPE* that challenge of trust translates into the challenge of implementing collaborative business.

Trust is also directly related to ethical issues in both society and business. Ethics are the principles used to determine the purpose of our decisions. Ethics are very important, especially in a society that is constantly influenced by the change of the technology. Further investigation is also required to identify the theoretical foundation of the ethical issues, specifically in the rapidly changing technological society.

The preferred relationship between the *company* and *consumers* takes place while the most influencing factor of *trust* is respected. According to Greenspan (2004), the factors are classified as positive customer service experience, length of the relationship with company, company or product reputation, brand familiarity and privacy policies. Therefore, the factors most likely to damage the trust could be classified as online security fears, telemarketing, the company's reputation through past incident(s), general suspicions of the company and disapproval of the company's business practice.

The new technological change requires new ethical issues that arise with the use and abuse of the technology.

## Legal Issues in Collaboration

Legal issues have been classified as the greatest concern of the organizations that have legal liabilities in order to operate. The study in Perpetual Resources Group (defined in Chapter 11) identified that there are many legal issues involved in collaboration. The personnel (especially security guards) at Perpetual Resources Group must have current approval. The *CBPE* enables Perpetual Resources Group to hire staff from other organizations without any mechanism in place to check their license validity.

Further investigation is required to identify how the *CBPE* model can solve the legal issues. The study by Neely and Unhelkar identified that the Web Services technology has revolutionized the concept of e-commerce, leading to "collaborative commerce," wherein a large number of business applications can publish, locate, and consume services by transacting with each other in 24/7 mode and across geopolitical boundaries. We are thus entering an era where a large number of Web services-based applications could be dealing with each other, resulting in collaborative commerce transactions that need of a more robust legal framework.

## Security Issues Arising from the Collaborative Environment

Security is an area that has not been considered in this book, since it is outside the scope of the main focus of methodological considerations. The security, privacy and the integrity of the data are very important concepts for the success of the *CBPE* model. Further work is required in order to establish secure channels for the collaboration in place. Secure channels increase the availability of the channels and provide a robust and secure collaborative environment in which organizations can participate. The other potential areas of this work are in the areas of the risk involved in participation, the full support of the future technologies in *CBPE* and the relative consequences of those impacts.

## ACTION POINTS

1.  List the important socio-cultural factors that are likely to impact your organization when it undertakes CBPE.
2.  Identify the impact of the electronically interconnected society on the collaborative business processes of your organization.
3.  Demonstrate the impact of the electronically interconnected society on the customers of your organization and their own ability to collaborate.
4.  What are the environmental factors in the collaborative environment of your organization?
5.  Evaluate the impact of "services-based" approach to collaboration on the organizational structure and reporting hierarchies of your organization.
6.  Identify and document an approach to overcoming the socio-cultural changes that you expect to face when you transition to a global collaborative organization.
7.  Identify and document the issues of trust and legality in collaborative environment.

## REFERENCES

Abood, C. (2006). Mobile camera phones – dealing with privacy, harassment and spying/surveillance concerns. In B. Unhelkar (Ed.), *Handbook of research in mobile business*. Hershey, PA: Idea Group Publishing.

Agre, P. E., & Rotenberg, M. (Eds.). (1997). *Technology and privacy: The new landscape*. Cambridge, MA: MIT Press. Retrieved June 6, 2007, from http://polaris.gseis.ucla.edu/pagre/landscape.html

Brooks, A. (1998). Organisational strategy. *Supply Management, 3*(12), 49.

Ghanbary, A., & Unhelkar, B. (2007a). Collaborative business process engineering (CBPE) across multiple organisations in a cluster. In *Proceedings of the IRMA Conference, IRMA 2007*, Vancouver, Canada.

Ghanbary, A., & Unhelkar, B. (2007b). Technical & logical issues arising from collaboration across multiple organisations. In *Proceedings of the IRMA Conference, IRMA 2007*, Vancouver, Canada.

Greenspan, R. (2004). *Perceptions of trust. Clickz navigation.* Retrieved February 5, 2007, from http://www.clickz.com/stats/markets/professional/article.php/3312681#table2

Gupta, A. K. (2000, March). Managing global expansion: A conceptual framework. *Business Horizons.* Retrieved from http://www.zdnet.com

Hall, E. T., & Hall, M. R. (1990). *Understanding cultural differences: Germans, French, and Americans.* Yarmouth, ME: International Cultural Press.

Katz, E. J., & Rice, E. R. (2002). *Social consequences of Internet use.* Cambridge, MA: The MIT Press.

Kincaide, J. (1999, February). A CT passage to India. *Computer Telephony*, 100-114.

Laudon, C., & Laudon, J. (2002). Business information systems: A problem solving approach. Fort Worth, TX: Dryden Press.

Miller, J., & Mukerji, J. (2003). *Model driven architecture (MDA) guide version 1.0.1.* Retrieved October 5, 2006, from http://www.omg.org/docs/omg/03-06-01.pdf

Neely, M., & Unhelkar, B. (2005). The role of a collaborative commerce legal framework in IT-related litigation. *Cutter IT Journal*, *18*(11), 11–17.

Oasis, Inc. (2007). *Oasis gift shows.* Retrieved February 20, 2007, from http://www.oasis.org

Ranjbar, M. (2002). *Social aspects of information technology.* Australia: University of Western Sydney.

Rutkowski, A. F., Vogel, D. R., Genuchten, M. V., Bemelmans, T. M. A., & Favier, M. (2002). E-collaboration: The reality of virtuality. *IEEE Transactions on Professional Communication*, *45*(4), 219–230. doi:10.1109/TPC.2002.805147

Unhelkar, B. (2002). *Process quality assurance for UML-based projects.* Reading, MA: Addison-Wesley.

White, S. A. (2005). *BPMN fundamentals*. Retrieved February 20, 2007, from http://www.omg.org/docs/pm/05-12-06.ppt

# Chapter 10
# Change Management in Collaboration

*If you want to make enemies, try to change something.*

Woodrow Wilson (1856-1924)

## CHAPTER KEY POINTS

- Discusses the general concept of the Change Management in business.
- Presents the concept of change management within the context of *CBPE*.
- Discusses the various types of changes and how they affect an organization.
- Highlights the need to manage the people aspect of change for organization undertaking *CBPE*.
- Discusses the types of changes caused to the organizations as a result of the implementation of the *CBPE*.
- Discusses the strategies for managing the change in *CBPE*.

DOI: 10.4018/978-1-60566-689-1.ch010

## INTRODUCTION

This chapter discusses the importance, relevance and the activities related to managing change in a business as it undergoes transformation to a collaborative business. One of the most significant changes that needs to take place when collaborative business is undertaken is the redefinition of traditional organizational boundaries. Senior management of the organization must understand the upcoming change process and totally support the change that follows the effort to collaborate through electronic channels. Collaborative business, especially through the use of a collaborative web-based system, will find that other participating businesses are able to come 'inside' the organization in order to offer as well as consume services. While this initially happens in the electronic domain, large, service-based organizations that depend on their far-flung collaborative partners will also discover that the management of change is not just at a technological level but also at a socio-cultural level.

The needs of formal change management and their application to an organization are vital for the success of collaborative business. While organizations understand the need to initiate, rather than respond, to change, the process of undertaking that change plays a crucial role in its success. In this book, we have discussed how an organization can become collaborative by using the concept of well-defined and well-encapsulated services to offer and consume. Transitioning to this service-based approach deals with issues of cultural differences, trust and understanding, and the desire of the companies to share their resources in order to satisfy customer needs. Change management, in this context, requires the organization to determine the scope, pace and the depth of adjustments that are required to the systems, people and processes. Thus, managing the change within collaboration requires undertaking changes to the way the systems are implemented, the way in which people behave and the modeling, understanding and use of re-engineered business processes. This chapter discusses these change management issues for the *CBPE* exercise using the *CWBS*.

## CHANGE MANAGEMENT IN COLLABORATIVE CONTEXT

Business Process Reengineering (BPR), as discussed in earlier chapters of this book (and elsewhere in the business literature (e.g., Hammer and Champy, 2001), involves a fundamental rethinking and redesigning of business processes to achieve dramatic improvements in cost, quality, timeliness and services. Thus, re-engineering of even a single business process is bound to involve change that requires the organization to toss aside old processes and systems and to invent newer and better processes.

Re-engineering of processes for collaborative businesses requires further dramatic changes to the entire setup of the business. The dramatic nature of changes to the processes (rather than merely 'making progress' in a step-by-step or incremental manner) encompasses lateral thinking that goes beyond management of small and piece-meal change. The shifting of focus from the organization and its hierarchy to a customer-centric approach that is mandated by collaborative business is, in itself, a significant change to the known business practices of an organization. This is so because the organization is not merely focusing on servicing the customer as a single business entity. Rather, the organization looks around for business partners whose services can be used together with its own, in order to better serve the customer. This brings about a fundamental change in the way the business operates. Undertaking collaborative business includes changes to the organizational structure, shifting of processes from paper-based to electronic, changes to the viewpoint of the business from competition to support and partnership, and elimination of numerous steps within the existing manual processes.

Thus, one of the major challenges in managing organizational change in collaborative businesses is the *re-engineering* of these business processes. By their very nature, collaborative processes require consideration to multiple organizational policies, procedures, and applications – all of which undergo change in order to provide organizational synergy. This organizational synergy is the output of the modeling and development of a single collaborative process that provides a unified view of the service to the client. Modeling of such collaborative business processes needs to be undertaken in earnest (Ghanbary and Unhelkar, 2007a) and the change as a result of these collaborative processes to be understood and implemented. Changes to business processes require modeling standards (such as the Business Process Modeling Notation - BPMN) and the use of those standards in creating actual processes that go beyond modeling interfaces between organizational boundaries and delve deeper into databases and applications, and the use of tools and techniques to undertake these changes.

Changes within a business due to collaborative approach may be embraced, tolerated or even resisted. The result of the change depends on how the management approaches this change. For example, a certain amount of planning, anticipation and execution on the part of senior management can immediately help an organization embrace change. However, if the management itself is unsure of what the change entails, as it moves towards collaboration, then the employees will not be able to undertake that change successfully. The management of successful change can draw on disciplines from psychology, sociology, business administration, economics system engineering and the study of human and organizational behavior.

*Figure 1. Categories of change affecting a business transitioning to a collaborative business*

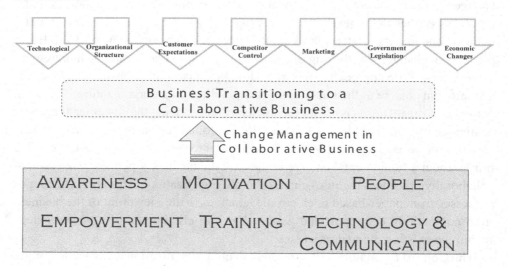

## TYPES OF CHANGES DUE TO CBPE

Change management involves understanding the level of change that a project will cause to an organization and its people, and proactively developing strategies and action plans to manage the impact of that change. Change management is often one of the most significant components of a project and can be a larger and more complex task than the project's development and implementation phases.

We have mentioned that there are many changes that an organization faces when it starts electronic collaboration. We have also highlighted the acute need for managing those changes. These various categories of change, as a business undergoes as it transitions to collaborative business, are shown in Figure 1 and discussed next.

**Technological changes:** These are changes to the software applications and databases resulting from collaboration. The technologies of web services, discussed earlier in the book, bring about a change to the way in which data is stored and the way in which software applications are executed. This collaborative, service-based approach brings about a change to not only the software aspects, but also the hardware, the network and the hosting of the servers – to name but a few. Thus, there are all-round technological changes that are brought about by collaboration and that require careful planning

**Organizational structure changes**: Collaborative business radically changes the business processes of the organization. These collaborative business processes do not require the same rigid hierarchies that a non-process based organization requires.

Thus, with **CBPE** the changes to the organizational structure are imminent. The new structure of the organization will be much flatter than the hierarchical structure. This new structure will not be rigid and will continue to evolve as the collaborative processes evolve. More interestingly, though, the changes to the structure include the way in which personnel from different collaborating organizations interact and deal with each other. Clear definitions of roles and responsibilities *across* the organizations are required in order to bring about successful change to the organizational structures of collaborating businesses.

**Changes in customer expectations**: The best way to change the expectations of the customers is to serve those expectations in the best possible way. Collaborative business enables the provision of that service through the partnering organizations. Customers would start expecting services from collaborating organizations whereas earlier they would themselves seek out the services from corresponding competing organizations. Thus, changes to customer expectations are significant in **CBPE** and need to be managed by updating the customer on the options that are now made available to them through collaborations.

**Changes from competitors to collaborators:** This is a major philosophical change that needs to be brought about by businesses as they undertake **CBPE**. Through collaborative business processes, an organization is now able to offer variety as well as quantity to its customers which it could not, in an earlier, non-collaborative era. An airline that was earlier competing with another airline is now able to quickly satisfy the needs of a customer that is organizing a large conference (for example) by providing the number of airline seats that it could not have before . The change in the way a collaborating business handles its partner businesses is crucial, and it involves a certain amount of trust and acceptance of the competitor as a collaborator.

**Marketing changes:** Collaborative businesses can be the most difficult and challenging to market – as the organizational boundaries are not clearly defined. As mentioned above, the erstwhile competitor is now a collaborator! How to market a service, such as airline seats or hotel rooms, when that service is likely to be provided by a group of collaborating companies that may have competed (and may still compete). Electronic marketing, promotions, usage of mobile devices as well as privacy of customers – all comes into play when marketing changes to collaborative marketing.

**Changes resulting from multiple government legislations**: Collaboration across geographical boundaries brings about the challenge of handling legislations from multiple governments and regulatory authorities. A service-based approach also opens up opportunities for businesses not only to collaborate with each other, but also with government services. There is a need to change the organizational systems and applications to incorporate regulations, legislations and policies that may be made available as services.

**Economic Changes**: There is a major global economic crisis as this book is being written. The risks associated with collaboration and the need to manage economic impact of changes on one organization by all other collaborating organizations could not have been highlighted better than by the current economic turmoil. The heavy dependencies of organizations – such as banks and insurance companies – on one another is going to be further exacerbated by collaborative business processes that are supported by software services. Economic models that incorporate far flung businesses are important in bringing about successful changes that do not threaten the business during rapid external economic changes.

The people aspects of change will be more challenging than the technological aspect – and this is especially true in *CBPE* where people from multiple organizations are involved. Therefore, it is vital to communicate with all people involved by setting up informative electronic channels, forums for discussions and feedback and providing sufficient training to people to equip them to carry out their changing tasks.

## STRATEGIES FOR MANAGING CHANGE IN CBPE

Strategic approach to managing change requires an understanding of what is the exact change, who the stake holders that will be affected by the change, and how could the anxiety of the change be reduced. This understanding also highlights, to the person in charge of bringing about the change, the area of resistance to the change. The primary area to work in terms of change management, when it comes to collaborative business, is the crucial people element even more than the technology element. However, the overall change management initiative in collaborative business encompasses the changes to the organizational structure, changes related to strategic planning, vision and values as well as socio-cultural issues related to multiple collaborating organizations. There will also be changes related to number of people required to carry out a task, the way in which these people need to managed and lead, the collaborative style needed in decision making, the communication strategy and of course, the way in which information technology is used by the organization.

Following are some specific points that can be considered as vital in strategically implementing change (these are also shown in Figure 1):

- Being fully aware of what exactly the change is. In case of collaborative business, this change is in the way in which the business operates and the manner in which it satisfies customer demands. Rather than competing continuously, collaborative business requires a certain amount of collaborative effort from organizations with which it has been competing in the past. This is a significant change to the business philosophy. There are also changes associated with the way in which a customer is dealt with – for example, if a product or service is not available where the customer wants it, collaborative business offers it from its partners that may be locally present where the customer is. This brings about changes to the manner of serving the customer.

- Motivation on the part of senior management to participate in and support the change. For a collaborative business transformation, the senior management and the decision makers will be themselves changing. However, at the same time, they will have to motivate their staff to change. Thus, there will be more pressure on the management to motivate both themselves and their staff to undertake the change that collaborative business entails.
- People in charge of the change need to know about the change process and understand how to go about changing the organization. The knowledge related to the change includes the process of change, availability and ability to use reference frameworks and enterprise architectures, and having access to relevant tools and techniques for change.
- Empowerment of change managers is vital to carry out successful changes on a day-by-day basis. Therefore, a person who has both the capability and the authority to carry out change plays a crucial role in *CBPE* and should be able to carry out and manage changes in professional manner.
- Training plays a vital role in equipping the people involved in a change to carry out their newly defined activities. Constructive and positive behavior involving and motivating people in the project is produced by professional training, clear directions and help in carrying out new tasks.
- Use of technology in changing the organization as well as communicating the change. The level of ambiguity and uncertainty can be reduced, both for individuals and groups, by clear and ongoing communications through various means – particularly electronic means including websites, emails, and mobile messages, etc. The success of change depends on the perception of individuals as to how the change will affect them. Therefore, a clear image of the future state must be developed and communicated to the parties involved.

Change management plan aids to provide a framework for managing and coordinating collaboration. Communication is a critical aspect of the change management plan ensures that the project is consistent within internal and external parties involved in the collaboration.

Two-way communication facilitates the participating organizations to solicit actively and, where possible, respond to feedback from the stakeholder groups. In this way, the change-planning document is both dynamic and ongoing.

It is envisaged that through effective change management and communication planning, the *CBPE* implementation will be able to successfully accomplish objectives with the cooperation of the relevant stakeholder groups.

## Stakeholder Analysis

The organizations should identify the various stakeholders involved in the implementation of the *CBPE*. The identification these stakeholders is a crucial factor for the success of the change management, as the change plan must be communicated, and the expectations of these stakeholders should be analysed. These expectations in the collaborative environment could be classified as cost of the project, experience with the technology, implementation of the *CBPE* and the social implications of the collaborative environment on the culture of their relative organization. Effective communication needs the support of the organizational community at large, as well as the specific subsets involved in the collaboration.

## Approach and Principles

Successful change management in collaborative context has a lot more to do with people than the other elements influencing the organization. This is so because people need to understand, model, and use these new collaborative processes which are continuously opening up the organizational boundaries. Change strategies need to be aimed particularly at supporting those who will be most affected by this redefinition of the organizational boundaries. Communications strategies, as a part of change management approach deal with providing this support on an almost one-to-one basis for people influenced by changes. Interactive, two-way communications and undertaking a people-centred approach produce broad levels of participation and engagement with the change. This is combined with strategic visioning and strategies that assist to align and integrate critical support and services for the proposed collaborative environment.

## Plan and Schedule of Collaborative Events

Change management in *CBPE* occurs in phases. However, these phases are not necessarily linear. Following are some elements of the planning and scheduling of collaborative events that are incorporated in the change management plan of the organization. Figure 2 demonstrate the various phases in the progress of the change management caused by the *CBPE*.

*Figure 2. Various phases for the change management for a business undertaking CBPE*

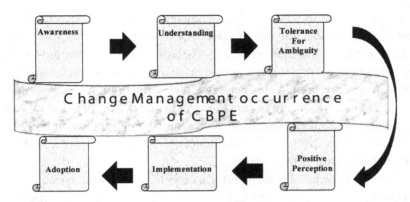

A Clearly Defined Business Objective: The objective of the change caused by *CBPE* must be clearly documented and communicated to all individuals who will be impacted by the change. In particular, it is essential that the business objective is clearly understood by the sponsors and stakeholders.

**Awareness**: Stakeholders develop knowledge of the change from the initial stages of the implementation of the *CBPE*. This awareness is created by the initiation of meeting, evaluating the potential business processes for collaboration, proposal for re-engineering or engineering new fully *CBPE* enabled processes.

**Understanding**: Stakeholders comprehend the nature and intent of the change caused by *CBPE* and starts to develop an understanding of what the new collaborative environment will mean for them.

**Tolerance for Ambiguity**: While the objective of the change caused by *CBPE* must be clear at the start of the project, the exact nature and extent of the changes will become progressively clearer during the progress of the project.

**Positive Perception**: Strategies are implemented to try and engage stakeholders in developing a positive perception of the change caused by *CBPE*.

**Pilot Implementation:** The change caused by *CBPE* becomes operational for a selective group of stakeholders in order to test strategies, support and systems. This will in turn inform full implementation of the *CBPE* model in the organization.

**Implementation**: The *CBPE* is fully implemented and is operational across the multiple organizations.

**Adoption**: The *CBPE* has been operational for long enough to evaluate its benefits and impact on the participated organizations as well as those organizations that did not wish to enter the proposed collaborative environment.

**Institutionalization:** The change caused by *CBPE* becomes embedded into routine operating procedures of the participated organizations.

## Applying Change Management Theories

There are number of theories related to change management that can be used in handling the change ensuing from *CBPE*. For example, one theory of change proposes that people are rational in their decision making and that they will follow their self-interest once that interest becomes clear to them. However, another theory states that people are social beings and that they will continue to adhere to cultural norms and values. According to this theory, change is best handled by redefining and reinterpreting existing norms and values, and developing commitments to new ones. Other theories discuss the compliance mentality of people and the need to exercise authority and impose sanctions.

While these theories have some relevance in bringing about successful change, what is most important is the application of some or all of the above theories when an organization adopts *CBPE*. The change brought about by *CBPE* requires the organization to understand the new circumstances and gradually transfer the line of thinking of their people from the old single-organization approach to the new collaborative approach.

*CBPE* demands constant focus on the customers whom might be regularly collaborating and dealing with the organization electronically. These collaborations create an organizational synergy that requires change in the business processes in both internal and external. Successful change must be supported by at least one senior executive who has been a key player in developing the business case for *CBPE*. Such a person will be highly motivated for the change as she or he will have clear idea of the goals and visions for the company to be achieved through *CBPE*. Furthermore, such person will also have the authority and the capability the carry out those changes.

In conclusion, change management is a continuous process, not a single event. During this process people may experience high levels of confusion and uncertainty as they move through a transition stage before achieving full implementation of the change.

Changes to the culture of an organization are the most difficult to manage and implement.

Culture is normally the most powerful force opposing change and the implementation of cultural change is a long-term process which needs to be managed carefully and requires large amounts of sponsorship at all levels.

## ACTION POINTS

1. Identify the areas of the organization that will be changing due to **CBPE**. These areas of change including organizational structure, people, processes and related technologies. All areas that will change need to be listed.

2. Nominate a 'resident' change management expert – a person who has played a role in putting together the business case for **CBPE** in the first place. A person who knows the vision of the organization and who has sufficient authority to carry out that vision.

3. Implement the change in a dynamic manner – that is, apply change management and then continue to monitor it on a day by day basis. Fine tune the process of applying change depending on the feedback received from earlier stages of change.

4. List the people involved in the daily collaborative activities of your organization. Evaluate their importance in the change management process.

5. Identify how the change management process could fail if the change is not communicated to the involved people.

6. List the change events of your business processes that are caused by re-engineering of your business processes. Investigate the application of the change management theories on the collaborative business processes of your organizations.

## REFERENCES

Ghanbary, A., & Unhelkar, B. (2007a). Collaborative business process engineering (CBPE) across multiple organisations in a cluster. In *Proceedings of the IRMA Conference, IRMA 2007*, Vancouver, Canada.

Ghanbary, A., & Unhelkar, B. (2007b). Technical & logical issues arising from collaboration across multiple organisations. In *Proceedings of the IRMA Conference, IRMA 2007*, Vancouver, Canada.

Hammer, M., & Champy, J. (1993). *Reengineering the corporation, a manifesto for business revolution*. UK: Nicholas Brealey Publishing.

Hammer, M., & Champy, J. (2001). *Reengineering the corporation, a manifesto for business revolution*. UK: Nicholas Brealey Publishing.

# Chapter 11
# Case Study 1:
## A Security Organization
## (Medium Size Organization)

*"We all agree that your theory is crazy, but is it crazy enough?"*

Niels Bohr (1885-1962)

## CHAPTER KEY POINTS

- Introduces a security organization that forms basis of the case study
- Discusses how to plan the transformation to a *CBPE*-based organization
- Discusses how to undertakes the transformation to a collaborative business
- Shows how the feedback is obtained from the transitioning organization to improve the functioning of the organization
- Discusses the utilization of the *CBPE* model in the organization.
- Discusses the global factors of the collaboration for the organization under study.
- Discusses the restructure of the organizational hierarchy based on the implementation of the proposed collaborative environment.

DOI: 10.4018/978-1-60566-689-1.ch011

# INTRODUCTION

This chapter describes a case study that is carried out in an organization that provides physical security services in Australia. The case study has been carried out with the aim of applying the *CBPE* model to some parts of this medium-sized organization that is called upon by event organizers such as those managing large public meetings, conventions and exhibitions, and so on. The primary focus of this chapter is to present how the *CBPE* framework helps in introducing newly-engineered processes for the organization. These new processes, mainly internal in this case, are able to make practical utilization of the concept of collaboration in order to reduce their time and cost. Similarly, there are some external processes that benefit external people who collaborate with the organization on regular basis.

The interface between collaboration as a business process and information communications technology as the implementer of that business process is an important factor in achieving the advantages from *CBPE*. Information and communications technology provides the tool for the efficient coordination of the different process links throughout the collaboration. While the company discussed in this case study will acquire the advantage in terms of collaborative customer service, the advantage is also derived internally by use of collaboration. The technology discussed here serves as a new channel of interactions as well as an efficient tool of communicating with each other within and outside the organization.

# ORGANIZATION DETAILS

Perpetual Resources Group specializes in the provision of fully licensed and professional security operatives to the hospitality industry. Perpetual Resources Group focuses its business on hospitality - providing event, site, and asset protection. According to the organization's business portfolio and the organization's training documentation, Perpetual Resources Group is an organization that has been trading since 1989 in Sydney, New South Wales, Australia. Perpetual Resources Group believes that its ability to adapt to the changing needs of the industry is its main reason for success. Perpetual Resources Group holds a regular client base in the Sydney metropolitan area, with a number of licensed venues. Apart from being a service provider for the industry, Perpetual Resources Group is also a Registered Training Organization (RTO for the Vocational Education and Training Accreditation Board (VETAB in New South Wales. Perpetual Resources Group is also fully licensed to carry out training activities in Victoria and Queensland.

New licensing requirements came into effect in February 2005, requiring a Certificate 1 in Security Operations (Pre-License) to be the entry point of work in the security industry. The current licensing arrangements create a more hands-on approach to the training and assessing of candidates. The training arm of Perpetual Resources Group provides training to new and existing security personnel. Perpetual Resources Group offers training in various levels of Security Operations.

Perpetual Resources Group has over 230 regular employees in its security and training operations. The security operation of Perpetual Resources Group is two-fold:

1.  Operations with regular on-going services
2.  Ad-hoc operations with sports/entertainment venues

Operations with regular on-going services provide security services to organizations in various industries such as hospitality, business and education industries. Perpetual Resources Group provides security personnel to cover regular shifts in these locations. Ad-hoc operations are services provided to events such as sports events and concerts. These ad-hoc services differ from one another and always have to be organized at the very end as the actual requirements are received only towards the end. Needless to say, the ad-hoc services offer tremendous opportunities for Perpetual Resources Group to collaborate with other service providers, although the normal planned services are also set to benefit by *CBPE*.

Perpetual Resources Group uses a workforce management tool named "Powerforce", which provides functionality such as storing and billing clients, logging employee details, scheduling employees, paying employees, and interfacing with the accounting system. Powerforce also records employees' biographical details, including their certifications with the expiry dates and on-the-job incidents. Subsequent to the requirements of the client being keyed in, Powerforce can choose a suitable list of people for a given job. Powerforce uses a modular approach and has the ability to analyze schedules using an award interpreter. The Operations Manager at Perpetual Resources Group sought the study to concentrate on the futuristic collaborative environment of their business processes.

## ANALYSIS OF THE PERPETUAL RESOURCES GROUP BUSINESS PROCESSES

### The Value of Long Term Collaborative Relationship for PRG

Perpetual Resources Group needs collaborative relationship with other businesses. The first relationship involves the establishment of a long-term relationship with other security companies, while the second relationship involves to the building of a relationship with various business firms seeking the security and expertise of the company's offered services. These relationships are important to the company because the success of its operations depends upon the efficiency of its information communications system throughout the different process links of the entire collaboration.

The collaborative relationship developed through the information communications technology that the company will utilize is important because the existence of the company depends upon the strength of its collaboration that involves a solid relationship with key business partners. A collaborative relationship is important because the company is assured of reliable partnership in its current and future projects. Long-term collaborative relationship also enables the company to procure supplies according to its unique or specific requirements and arrangements and to provide services that considers the particular needs of its industrial partner and customers.

The provided services by Perpetual Resources Group contribute to its efficiency and its collaborative nature translates to cost minimization and output maximization. The proposed collaborative environment will allow the collaborative parties to work with Perpetual Resources Group and also find the suitable prices and services form the *CWBS* database. Perpetual Resources Group only has to post its offered services and requirement advertisements in the *CWBS* that invites interested parties to apply for a job or provide Perpetual Resources Group with new contract.

## Identifying Potential Collaborative Business Processes

The problem has been formulated on the basis of how the business processes of Perpetual Resources Group could collaborate with the business processes of other organizations. The first task is to identify the business processes that could be classified as having potential for collaboration. Once the existing business processes are studied, the authors are able to engineer business processes to be added into the main streamline of existing business processes. The functionality of the engineered processes has to be further observed in order to achieve a smooth flow of business. The case study was initiated by performing the following tasks:

- Meetings with the Operations Manager and Managing Director
- Visits to the sites regularly serviced by the organization, and getting first-hand information from on-site supervisors
- Reading the organizations manuals for their daily performances as well as their software system

The specific area was classified in three categories, as demonstrated in Table 1.

*Table 1. Core area of investigation at perpetual resources group*

| Technical | Methodological | Social |
|---|---|---|
| Collaboration of Perpetual Resources Group system with other parties (incompatible technology). | How the existing business processes will change after placing the engineered process in to the streamline. | Organizational structure. |
| The channels of collaboration | | PRG business partners' attitudes toward the change. |
| Enterprise Application (EA) and Service-oriented Architecture (SOA) use in the existing system. | | Legal. |
| | | Trust. |

Three processes are identified as having the potential for validating the *CBPE* model through case study. This identification of the processes takes place in conjunction with the information gathered from the Operation Manager (OM). The three processes are carefully studied and modeled in order to analyze the potential for incorporation of *CBPE* in them. This study is assisted ably through inputs from the OM of the Perpetual Resources Group, who is able to assist in verification of the existing processes and work flows, as well as commenting on the strategic value of collaborative environment in the engineered processes. This results in a correct picture of the entire modeling exercise.

## Difficulties Faced by MAC in Managing Collaboration

Perpetual Resources Group experienced several interconnected problems in managing the collaboration due to the difficulties of coordinating different process links simultaneously. Perpetual Resources Group has to find security officers and new venues for new contracts on regular basis. Looking for new contracts on the national and international levels is difficult and time consuming. Negotiations, bidding and contracts consume too much time and effort when done manually or through personal meetings. The company realized that it has to upgrade and improve its collaborative environment. Apart from the process link, the company also realized the need to establish a system of communicating with customers in the international market that is convenient for customers. This will give them information about the company's capabilities and policies, as well as the option for the customer to pose further inquiries into the company.

Security is a protracted endeavor requiring the people in charge of coordinating process links to develop a system for tracking the progress of the different processes in collaboration. Networking the communication between headquarters and the field site is also necessary. Perpetual Resources Group has experienced difficulties in updating headquarters on the progress of providing services manually, and there are problems requiring the decision of headquarters without technological communications tools.

## IMPLEMENTATION OF CWBS

The investigation has been conducted through interviews with Perpetual Resources Group management and staff in order to study the current confidential documents. This case study could be classified as the provision of Perpetual Resources Group expertise to a client, organization and other related mentioned entities.

### Requesting Staff (From Other Venues)

Perpetual Resources Group needed to improve the staff list on a regular basis since these people are employed on a casual basis; therefore they only work at desired events.

The majority of the staff (70%) on the active list and 10% of the staff on the inactive list accepts their allocated roster on a busy day. The remaining 20% are currently being filled by two other selected venues as sub-contractor. The most important concern for the organization is how to fill the staff shortage on busy occasions, especially if the other venue requires more staff.

The investigation is initiated to identify how the technology could aid and rectify the mentioned problem. Figure 1 presents the recommended solution in a BPMN diagram.

Figure 1 demonstrates that Perpetual Resources Group submits a request on the proposed *Collaborative Web Based System (CWBS)*. The request will go the UDDI directory level 1 to identify the desired industry. The level 1 directory submits the request to the relevant level 2 directory. The system will search all the venues registered in the level 2 directory to detect which of them has additional staff to offer. This benefits both parties, as the organizations will fill the staff shortage and the other part gains a sub-contract, which generates profit.

The *CBPE* model enables Perpetual Resources Group to hire staff from the other security-guard provider when Perpetual Resources Group is unable to supply staff. Currently, Perpetual Resources Group has to prioritize the venues and provides a limited number of staff to the less important job. The reduction of the staff is due to causing them to generate less profit, while increasing risk.

*Figure 1.Borrowing staff for specific roster*

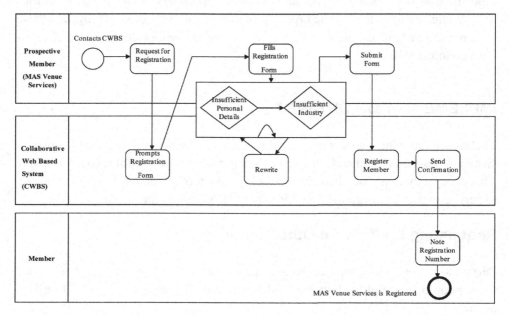

## Advertising the Performed Services

Currently, the organization advertises in the Yellow Pages directory, on the organization's website and by word of mouth. The proposed *CWBS* would help the organization to register its offered service on the system for people who need its services. The proposed system is an electronic Yellow Pages directory that directs the request to a relevant industry and party for further processing. In this case study, the organization under study already has its own website, and the system could submit the request to it directly. Figure 2 presents the process of registering the organization's services on the proposed system of *CWBS*.

Figure 2 illustrates that the organization can submit a request by offering its services on the proposed system. When the request is submitted by parties in need of the services that are offered by the organization, the request would go to it. Alternatively, if other venues need staff and the organization has additional staff on the mentioned date, it could sub-contract its staff to the other venues if desired.

## Recruiting Staff

The organization has to advertise for recruitment on a monthly basis. The security guards are employed on a casual basis. The security guards have to work in a full

*Figure 2. Registering the PERPETUAL RESOURCES GROUP performed services on CWBS*

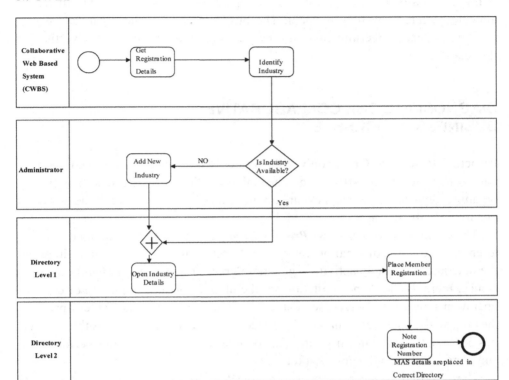

financial year; otherwise the Operations Manager of the organization will place the guards with fewer worked rosters on the inactive list at the end of the financial year. This is based on operational work, such as disciplinary action, work availability and the guards' general performance. The information on these people is registered in the Powerforce system; however the system will never allocate them for roster work.

The existing system requires the Operations Manager to place advertisements in newspapers and on the organization's website. Interested people must contact the organization to submit their résumé by fax and post. The Operations Manager reads the résumé and, after approval, will call them for an interview time for the final phase of recruitment. The Operations Manager needs to advertise on a monthly basis, however, due to the busy schedule, the Operation Managers fail to do so.

During this case study, it has also been identified that the organization could place its recruitment advertisement on the *CWBS*. Figure 2 shows how the recruitment advertisement could be posted on the proposed collaborative system.

In the proposed model, after submitting the request, people submit their résumés online and, based on the approval of the Operations Manager, the system would allocate an interview time to them. The busy schedule of the organization will have no impact on recruitment, since by clicking on a button it can advertise for the recruitment.

## DIAGNOSIS TO THE COLLABORATIVE BUSINESS PROCESSES

Perpetual Resources Group only collaborates with two other selected security venues to roster their staff for the venues that require large numbers of staff. The organization loses money and eventually the contracts if it cannot fill the positions due to the staff shortage.

The *Collaborative Business Process Engineering* (*CBPE*) is applied in order to engineer three additional processes for Perpetual Resources Group to improve the outcome of its daily activities, generating more revenue and reducing the risk. Hence, there would be no limitation for the number of staff, purchase of cheaper operation supplies and advertisement of its products and services. Table .2 presents the proposed engineered collaborative processes and demonstrates how these activities occur in the existing daily activities to increase the organization's performance and compatibility in the new market.

The proposed engineered processes enable Perpetual Resources Group to provide faster and more accurate operations that provide more satisfaction to the customer and staff.

*Table 2. The proposed and existing electronic collaborative processes at Perpetual Resources Group*

| Proposed CBPE-based Processes | Existing Processes that will be affected (upgraded) due to CBPE |
|---|---|
| Requesting Staff (from other venues) | • Collaborating with two selected venues (not online) |
| Offering performed services | • Yellow Pages directory which may not be a manual process but will be using services • Advertised on Perpetual Resources Group website • Word of mouth – may deal with personal collaboration but not the electronic collaboration; hence this will change |
| Job Advertising and Recruiting | • Newspapers may still play some role – but the demands can be directly plugged into the CWBS. • Advertised on Perpetual Resources Group webpage • Send résumé (fax or post) • Calling them back for appointment |

## ACHIEVED RESULTS

The discussion with the Chief Executive Officer (CEO) and also the Operations Manager revealed that the *CBPE*-based engineered processes improve the existing processes of the Perpetual Resources Group. The following improvements are required.

- **Incompatible technology:** When different organizations are using very old technology or no IT technology at all.
- **Competition:** Different organizations prefer not to share, in order to drive the competition out of the market. For example, why would an organization allow its competitor to use its staff when it prefers the competitor to lose the contract? This will provide an opportunity to submit a new tender.
- **Legal issues:** How to collaborate when legal issues are involved, such as licensing agreements. Also includes the roles and regulations imposed by the government.
- **Mistrust:** How can an organization trust its competitor or its employee to provide the correct times?

Performing services and recruiting staff engineered processes are considered important for the future of the business. Perpetual Resources Group, being an established company, realizes the importance of retaining existing customers as well as recruiting on a regular basis. The proposed engineered processes would be much more cost-effective than advertising in the Yellow Pages and in newspapers. Therefore the engineered processes are believed to be a very important area for marketing.

The following section concludes the Perpetual Resources Group case study and outlines some future directions where technology could be further used to enhance the organizational engineered processes.

## EXPLORING GLOBAL COLLABORATIONS FOR PERPETUAL RESOURCES GROUP

The subsequent paragraphs discuss the global collaborative issues in the context of the transformation of the business processes of Perpetual Resources Group.

The services offered by the Perpetual Resources Group are classified into two categories. Category one is providing the security offices to venues. This is currently very strong in the domestic market and cannot go global, as the need hardly ever arises. Category two is offering security guards as well as the first-aid training courses.

The offered training courses can be offered in the global market specifically for the less developed countries. However, it is very important that these offered services are also accessible from those overseas companies. Such maturity of the Perpetual Resources Group must be acquired through gradual development of the organization ability to collaborate, first within the local business and with domestic customers, followed by international customers. The governments of those nations could also benefit from the offered services by Perpetual Resources Group to train their police and SWOT team.

A comprehensive analysis of the overseas opportunity by the management of the Perpetual Resources Group concluded that there are some opportunities available in the world, especially with global threat of the terrorism activities. These opportunities help Perpetual Resources Group to demonstrate its strengths to domestic customers, as well as acquiring a clear view of the overseas market.

In the global electronic environment, the Perpetual Resources Group has the opportunity to explore the foreign market and offer their services. In the proposed collaborative environment, the customer can easily reach Perpetual Resources Group.

Perpetual Resources Group can also greatly benefit from the global market by collecting the required training information in order to expand and provide more comprehensive training courses. Collaborations of the Perpetual Resources Group with that overseas organization enables them to renovate the course information through knowledge-sharing, leading to enhanced employee and customer satisfaction.

The additional advantage for the Perpetual Resources Group is to take advantage of the local rules and regulations of the governments of the environments where they operate. For example, if they provide their services to a country in Asia, they are entitled to pay less tax in comparison to the country of origin.

## CHANGE MANAGEMENT IN PERPETUAL RESOURCES GROUP

Change management needs to come into play in order to provide a successful transition for Perpetual Resources Group to a collaborative business. One of the major changes to Perpetual Resources Group is its organizational structure. This organizational structure changes in CBPE, as there is modification of the reporting structures that were used earlier to reach and serve the customer. Figure 4 demonstrate the current structure of the Perpetual Resources Group.

Two divisions of the organization (training and operation) are directly controlled by the CEO of the organization. The operation manager is involved in finding new contracts and rostering the security guards for the venues. Each venue can have multiple supervisors depending on the required number of the security guards. The

*Figure 4. The Perpetual Resources Group structure prior to CBPE*

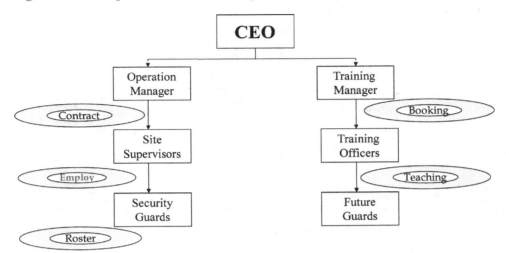

security guards are also on casual or permanent basis depending upon their contract with the management. The operation manager also needs to make sure that the minimum number of the guards is always available. Otherwise, he needs to advertise and employ new security guards.

The training manager should run the various courses for updating existing security guards, training new security guards and first-aid courses. The training should contract a new teacher for every course and make sure the desired minimum number of students is registered in each course. The current structure of the organization demonstrated in Figure 4 fully supports the current operation of the organization. However, Figure 5 demonstrates how the **CBPE** restructure the organization and ease the pressure on training and operation manager of the Perpetual Resources Group.

The implementation of the theoretical concept of the **CBPE** through the **CWBS** restructures the organization. As demonstrated in Chapter 1, Figure 5, the proposed system enables the operation manager to find new contracts, roster and employ through the collaborative environment. The operation manager also benefits by booking the course, new teachers and register guards for the available courses. The comparison of Figure 4 and Figure 5 demonstrate the restructure of the Perpetual Resources Group through the facilitation of the proposed collaborative environment.

*Figure 5. The PERPETUAL RESOURCES GROUP structure after implementation of CBPE*

## Managing the Change

Application of **CBPE** in Perpetual Resources Group will change its organizational management and the given structure such as Payroll and Human Resource Management (HRM). These changes provide the organization with effective collaboration to serve its customer better. However, managing this change is very important to the success of the Perpetual Resources Group's implementation of the proposed collaborative environment. In order to manage the change, the management of Perpetual Resources Group has to undertake a capability evaluation, including the financial capability, as well as being able to remain in the competitive market.

As the Perpetual Resources Group is classified as a medium-sized organization, management can easily monitor the change. However, the recruitment of a team to monitor and evaluate the impact of this change on the customer can be classified as the crucial factor for the success of the new collaborative system. Formation of this team helps the implementation of Customer Relationship Management (CRM) applications on the new collaborative system. The team can measure the acceptance of the change and educate the customer on how to use the new collaborative system. This team enhances the relationship with the Perpetual Resources Group customers as well as providing better service quality by more understanding of their needs.

The changes caused to the structure of the Perpetual Resources Group business processes provide them with a significant shift from the ordinary transaction to a collaborative orientation. However, the rapid changes might cause Perpetual Resources Group to react differently, depending on how it will affect its management structure and organization's set of standards and policies.

## Managing Innovation

Innovations in the information communication technology have an overwhelming effect on the developments of collaboration. Because of these innovations, organizations in different levels can efficiently coordinate their relationship to maximize collaboration, in order to improve productivity. The key role of collaboration is its ability to provide a convenient venue for information-sharing through the various modes of communication. Thus, information communication technology is important to collaboration because it is the tool that enables the coordination of the different process links, by providing a venue for communications.

Implementation of the proposed collaborative environment for the Perpetual Resources Group entirely depends upon the use of the standard technologies in which the implementation of innovation is effective. The management of technologies also facilitate the success of the induced innovation. Companies with high growth and high technology are more open to the collaborative innovation by the advancement of the technologies. The need for continuous innovation in order to be in front of advances and not periphery to them should be considered and observed wisely by the Perpetual Resources Group management.

The Perpetual Resources Group management should be motivated in creating the cultural change for the innovation and identify the challenges involved in the introduction of the proposed collaborative environment. These factors affect much of the process of influencing the collaborative entities and their system or structure in dealing with the proposed innovation.

The cultural change in Perpetual Resources Group should be in both the individual and collective level. The understanding of the cultural change contributes to the collective consciousness of individuals which produces autonomy and innovative behavior. This sociological and organizational development perspective leads Perpetual Resources Group to understand the underlying significance of change within their organization.

These important factors contribute to the implementation of innovation in the Perpetual Resources Group's new organizational structures and systems. The support of the all members means a successful endeavour and will hopefully make Perpetual Resources Group more productive, as well as fairly competitive with more advanced organizations. Perpetual Resources Group Management should observe the constant changes and be conscious about the significant factors that may be detrimental to the implementation of these innovations.

## APPLYING THE CBPE MODEL TO PRG

Figures 1, 2 and 3 map the *CBPE* model to the processes in Perpetual Resources Group through the case study performed about Perpetual Resources Group. The mapping of the *CBPE* model with the activities of Perpetual Resources Group resulted in improvement of the organization's performance. This was confirmed though an interview with the CEO and OM of the organization.

Collaborative business processes of Perpetual Resources Group were investigated in order to understand the collaborative nature of the security industry. The collaboration occurs for employing staff, advertising the performed services and recruiting staff online. Perpetual Resources Group is interested in implementing the outcomes.

However, Perpetual Resources Group has become an early adopter in using the existing technologies in the venue services industry. The full implementation of the system is not yet complete at the time of writing this book; however, positive feedback has been gathered from the management of the Perpetual Resources Group.

The case study at the Perpetual Resources Group identified that the *CBPE* is functional. This is so because the model enables the organization to access other organizations that were not easily accessible prior to the introduction of the new collaborative environment.

The mapping of the discussed case study to the proposed *CBPE* model has demonstrated how it can be used as a generic model to connect the organizations together in new collaborative environment. Furthermore, this is also a demonstration of the dynamic nature of the collaboration. The study validated the introduced *CBPE* model in three organizations by engineering new processes to increase their performance in the market. There are, of course, numerous other business processes in the organizations that can be engineered and subjected to the *CBPE* model. The engineered processes are able to restructure the operation of the entire organization. Additional issues such as socio-cultural issues also need to be addressed in order to successfully transform an entire organization to a collaborative environment. This could be a base on the operation of the model in an area of future investigation.

*Figure 3. Recruitment request submitted on CWBS for PERPETUAL RESOURCES GROUP*

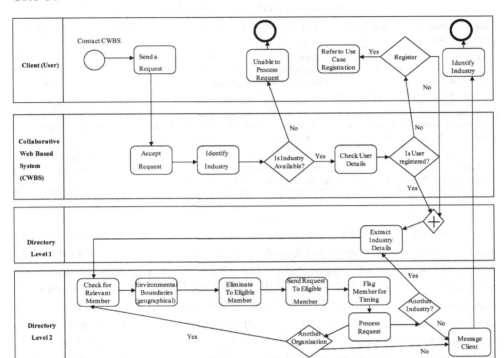

This study has been focused on the cross-organizational business processes. The case study involved in internal business processes can take place within one specific organization. Conversely, this study has been concentrated on the cross-organizational business processes while investigating the internal business processes.

The validation of the **CBPE** model can only take place when the business process of the organization (as per the case study) needs to collaborate with other entities. The introduced engineered process and the concept of the **CBPE** are very new, of course, and can be confusing to the organizations. The organizations are not familiar with the proposed environment that enables them to collaborate with other entities.

The case study (using the **CBPE** model) enables the organizations to identify those other organizations through their product/services offered. The discussion of the above case study has shown how the **CBPE** Model is applicable separately to

*Table 3. The summary of the case study (Perpetual Resources Group)*

| Updated Collaborative Processes for PRG |
|---|
| Identification of the business processes which could be classified as having potential for collaboration would be dynamically achieved. |
| As a result of dynamic collaboration, recruitment of security staff from other service providers (perhaps even erstwhile competitors in the security business) will be happening, especially when the demands are high Electronic Advertising the performed services will be moving towards SOA-based offerings that can be plugged in directly into the needs of the clients. |
| The Yellow Pages directory service will be most probably used as a UDDI engine in order to search for both customers as well as collaborators Advertisement on Perpetual Resources Group website will now be coupled with SOA-based software components that can send and receive XML messages to provide those services. |
| Issues to be handled include incompatible technology from the collaborator's side, which may not be technologically savvy. Also, the heightened security needs imply sensitivity in terms of legal issues that need to be considered perhaps by plugging into the government regulatory services. |

each organization. Therefore, the authors are able to *assume* that the proposed *CBPE* model provides a systematic methodology to enable organizations to collaborate with multiple unknown organizations. The *CBPE* model provides the necessary methodological consideration to mobile, WS, EAI, SOA and EBS technologies, enabling the collaboration among the multiple organizations. Therefore, the *CBPE* model aids the business processes of multiple organizations to collaborate in an entirely new collaborative environment. Tables 4, 5 and 6, in Chapter 5 provide a summary of the case study studies in the context of the four phases: plan, action, observe and reflect.

The evaluation of Perpetual Resources Group's collaborative business processes demonstrated that it has the capability of going beyond the ordinary B2B collaborative environment, validating the need for the proposed *CBPE* model (see Table 3).

The *CBPE* model enables the organization to advertise its services and products to people who are in need of those products and services. These people might not even be aware that such an organization exists.

In conclusion, the interface of collaboration and information communications technology is important to the achievement of the goals of Perpetual Resources Group. This is because information communications technology provides a tool for the efficient coordination of the different process links throughout the collaboration. The interface benefits the company internally and externally. External benefits include the efficiency in a collaborative links while internal benefits include the network communications between headquarters and the different field offices.

## ACTION POINTS

1. Compare the business processes of the business process of your organization
2. List the difference and similarity of the business processes of your organization versus the business processes of Perpetual Resources Group
3. List the collaborative business processes of the studied organization
4. Identify the potential need of the change in your organization
5. Identify how the **CBPE** can further change the current business processes of Perpetual Resources Group

## REFERENCES

Perpetual Resources Group. (2008a). Retrieved from http://www.prgp.com.au

Perpetual Resources Group. (2008b). *Protective services*. Retrieved from http://www.prgps.com.au

Perpetual Resources Group. (2008c). *Special operations*. Retrieved from http://www.prgso.com.au

Perpetual Resources Group. (2008d). *Training academy*. Retrieved from http://www.prgta.com.au

# Chapter 12
# Case Study 2:
## An Energy Provider Organization (Large Organization)

*I have never let my schooling interfere with my education.*

Mark Twain (1835-1910)

## CHAPTER KEY POINTS

- Introduces another organization in the energy sector that is used as a case study for modeling of collaborative business processes.
- Discusses how the *CBPE* model will be utilized in the organization.
- Discusses the introduction and implementation of the *CWBS* in the organization.
- Discusses the global factors that influence the collaboration for the organization under study.
- Discusses the restructure of the organizational hierarchy based on the implementation of the proposed collaborative environment.
- Provides recommendations and suggestions for strategic decision making with regards to the collaborative environment.

DOI: 10.4018/978-1-60566-689-1.ch012

# INTRODUCTION

This chapter describes a case study carried out in a large energy provider organization. The case study demonstrates the application of the *CBPE* model in practice. This chapter presents how the *CBPE* model introduces new engineered processes within the organization that facilitate collaborative activities of the organization.

# ORGANIZATION DETAILS

This case study was carried out in a real organization. However, in order to maintain the confidentiality of the organization, we shall call it '*Protect*'. *Protect* is a leading Australian energy-provider on the East coast that provides gas and electricity to over two million Australian homes and businesses. Protect is made up of number of business processes, both external and internal to the organization. For the sake of this case study, we decided to focus specifically on the fieldwork service contracts – as these contracts showed immense opportunity for collaboration. Currently, the service processes of the organization support the creation of Fieldwork Service contracts. The case study carried out here dealt with creation of new service contracts or cancel an existing service contract.

Providing a service to a new customer requires Protect to carry out certain identification processes. Apart from the identification of the customer, there is also a need to identify the model of the counter that is used in individual households to measure, monitor and charge the customer with the usage. The identification of the counters enables Protect to manage and provide the required service. It is worth noting here that Protect needs to collaborate with many other organizations such as gas, electricity, meter readers, electricians, plumbers and the people who will check the meter to identify what kind of services could be delivered to specific customers. The common Government body already exists for the communications across Protect and gas and electricity companies. Vancorp (for gas) and Nemco (for electricity) are the Australian Government bodies that unite the energy-provider companies.

Protect's deployment of a re-engineering process for the Fieldwork Service provides an opportunity for the business agility it needs to compete more effectively. The activities that need collaboration include the need to consult, design, build and manage enterprise solutions spanning all core businesses and IT management processes with regard to providing a better service to its customers.

Improving the process by delivering an extensive portfolio ensures successful outcomes through a combination of professional expertise, successful track records and capabilities, which lowers risk and ensures a return on investment.

In addition to better quality of service, there is also a need for collaboration in undertaking strategic marketing approach in terms of advertisement and promotion to make the market aware of the company's product. In addition, strategic market planning can also be attributed as a better solution to ensure that the product will be introduced effectively. The company must be able to use a more effective market planning and strategy which will enhance the market value of the product.

## ANALYSIS OF THE ORGANIZATION BUSINESS PROCESSES

The two specific business processes that are discussed here are: Arrange Fieldwork and Establish Billing Account. The initial effort is to investigate the processes under development to identify the potential of the applications of **CBPE**. Thereafter the processes have to be evaluated to assess their interfaces. The existing business processes are studied and the investigation is able to propose that an engineered section be added into the main stream line of existing business processes under development. The functionality of the engineered processes has to be further observed in order to achieve a smooth flow of business. The re-engineered collaborative process "Arrange Fieldwork" will support the following activities:

- 1: Single point of entry for information rather than re-keying
- 2: Support for handling multiple fuels and properties faster
- 3: New product model and tools to select the appropriate product
- 4: More information at sales point about the customer and its interactions with Protect.

- 1: Establish Billing Account
- 2: Terminate Billing Account
- 3: Reinstate Billing Account

The internal collaboration between the mentioned processes take place when setting up a billable account in the billing system for the purpose of recording financials such as billing charges and receipts as payments for the customer are required.

In order to provide better customer relationship management (CRM) the recent updated details are required for the specific period when any specific objective Billing Account is taking place. The Establish Billing Account process inters- collaborates with the Arrange Fieldwork process in order to locate a suitable external party to achieve the latest update to issue the bill.

## APPLYING OF CWBS IN PRACTICE

The investigation has been conducted through interviews with Protect's staff and also studying some of their current confidential documents. Protect's clients come from almost all sectors. A study could be classified as the provision of Protect's expertise to a client, organization and other related mentioned entities.

### Publishing the Service Required by Protect

Publishing the consumable product/services on the proposed *CWBS* directory makes them available to the people who are capable of performing the requirement of the application (electricians, plumbers or meter readers and checkers) but do not necessarily know Protect. Submitting a request to the directory allows the tradespeople to consume the request already published by Protect in the directory. Hence, these people are not necessarily in their office; the mobile applications could be included to the portal to deliver the request to the nearest tradesperson to the location by the aid of a Global Positioning System (GPS). The application of mobile technologies is very important, since this technology leads to the generation of more funds for Protect.

Protect requires the services of trades people such as electricians, plumbers and meter readers. These are mobile people and they are only accessible via their mobile devices.

Various technologies must be combined in order to provide collaboration amongst these multiple parties. Mobile technology, Web Services (combined Mobile Web Services) and GPSs are part of the technologies required to engineer the required external business process for the Protect. Understanding all these technologies and evaluating the application and limitation of them were classified as part of this study to distinguish how they can aid the proposed *CBPE* model specifically when these engineered processes are forming in the *CWBS.*

Figure 1 depicts how Protect could register in the *CWBS* in order to be part of the proposed collaborative environment of the *CBPE* model.

Figure 2 demonstrates how the *CWBS* would place Protect in the correct directory. Placing the organization's details in the correct directory would avoid pollution in the directory by providing enhanced future access.

Figure 3 shows the publishing of Protect's application when a tradesperson is required. At this point the application would forward the information to the tradesperson closest to the premises location that is in need of the service. The system checks the tradesperson's location on the GPS system and submits the application to that person. If the tradesperson does not accept the work, the system checks for the closest person.

*Figure 1. Registration of protect in CWBS*

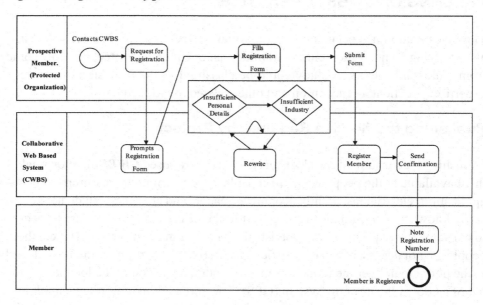

*Figure 2. Placing the registration in the directory*

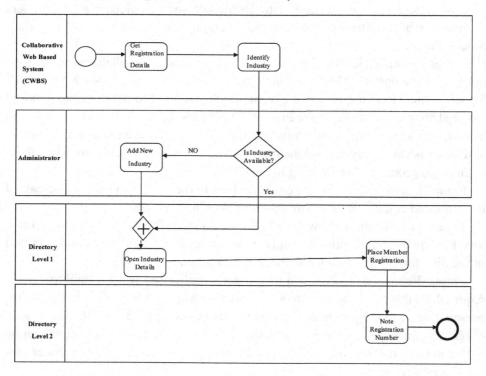

*Figure 3. Proposed CBPE-based for publishing request*

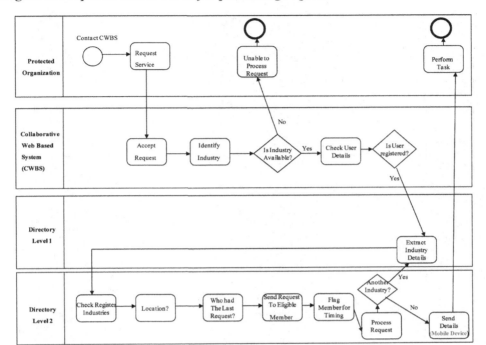

Figure 4 shows how the party that is unaware of Protect's services/products could access the services just by submitting an application.

## UNDERSTANDING PROTECT'S COLLABORATIVE BUSINESS PROCESSES

Figure 5 presents the integration of Protect's internal and external business processes. In the previous section the services that are offered by Protect were clearly identified. Figure 5 depicts those services that are available to internal as well as external parties. The core offering is also responsible for marketing, usability and the maintenance of the offered products and services.

The case study demonstrates that by re-engineering existing processes and additional engineered section, the other external parties such as electrician, plumbers, meter checkers and readers can also find the required services offered by Protect. Protect submits a request for a specific service and the proposed *CWBS* will use any technology such as the Internet or any mobile Internet devices to deliver the

*Figure 4. Consumption of the published request*

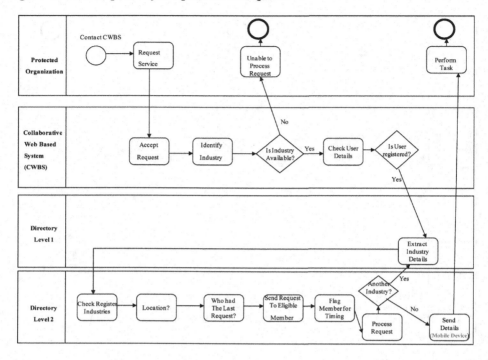

*Figure 5. The Integration of internal and external business processes*

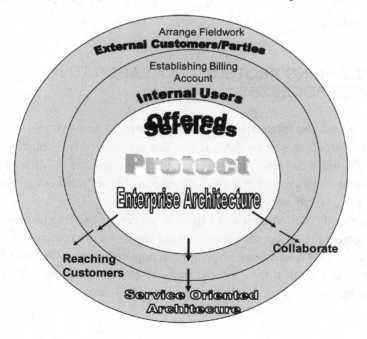

published application to the interested parties. The ticket will be logged, evaluated, allocated and the consultants will find the suitable package.

## Achieving Change

The case study aims at improving the business process called Arrange Fieldwork of Protect, and is only a preliminary one. There could be other processes and other technological advances, such as the m-transformation and Mobile Web Services which could demand a change in the future.

In the reflect phase, the case study has identified the need for the mobility in the proposed collaborative environment. In this phase, the study identified that more knowledge about the concepts of the mobile technology is required to propose the *CBPE* model for Protect's external business processes.

The study requires an understanding of the concepts of the mobile technology to propose new engineered processes for Protect's future collaborative environment. Chapter 2 of this book has already addressed the applications and limitations of the mobile technology.

## Managing Resources

There is a need to manage the people, information and infrastructure resources. Managing these three categories of resources are the essential and critical components in the company's collaborative transition and they are further expanded below.

- *People:* It is imperative that there are sufficient personnel available to initiate and manage the collaboration. Their timely availability and commitment will be vital for the successful collaboration. The identification and management of development teams for the software applications to be used is also an important part of managing this resource.
- *Information:* Related to Protect, as well as information needed by the transitioning personnel comes under this heading. Details related to the usage of the information by users, is a crucial part of this information gathering and dissemination.
- *Infrastructure:* This resource includes the hardware as well as the available development environment for Protect. Furthermore, changes to even the basic infrastructures, such as phones and faxes, computer servers and workstations, computer peripherals (printers, scanners), network components (hubs, routers and cables), and backup equipment would form part of this resource.

## Database Requirements

The availability of the data is an important issue for the success of protected organization. The proposed database system should be reliable, scalable, secure and cost effective. The data should be available 24/7. All chosen database components including hardware and software should be reliable in supporting the business processes of the protected organization and have the ability to serve high data enquiries. Data security is another important issue, as the database design must ensure that only authorized parties can access or modify the data. The last issue is about data storage since Protect are dealing with numerous files, an effective storage is required.

## Software Components

The software is needed for the protected organization to deal with the customer billing, financial information and energy usage purpose. The designed software is mainly for distribution-oriented businesses that require sophisticated functions and a powerful control system. It contains many advanced features such as three styles of invoicing (service, distribution and recurrent), and other advanced features. A typical system that can be upgraded to multiple users and that will include General Ledger, Accounts Receivable, Accounts Payable, Inventory, Distribution Invoicing, Purchase Orders, Sales Statistics and Purchasing Statistics is suggested here.

In addition, the final level is the electronic usage record. It is a more comprehensive collection of the individual's information. This level includes a network of provider and non-provider settings that requires an information infrastructure that involves homes, energy providers and other sites.

## Networking Architecture

Proper network infrastructures should be built to provide a robust and reliable system which enables access to the proposed portal from remote locations and provide high connectivity audio and video through adequate bandwidth. Virtual Private Network (VPN) is used for connection with other organizations. Wide Area Network (WAN) provides global communication and connectivity between users. Local Area Network (LAN) supports local communication within the internal departments of the protected organization. The design should be flexible for future expansion without affecting major impacts on the present system and allow easy updates to the infrastructure.

## Mobile Technology

The use of mobile technology provides the protected organization with major advantages. In fact, handheld devices like Personal Digital Assistants (PDAs), tablets and smart cellular phones can provide better decision support for the organization's decision makers and the tradesmen they deal with.

Correct application of mobile technologies into the business processes of the protect organization allows them to increase profits, satisfy their customers and speed the completion of the task required by their customer which creates greater customer loyalty. These customer-related advantages will accrue only when the organization investigates its customer behavior in the context of the mobile environment. It is very important to identify the sufficient information that is required to make the decisions while the protected organization is re-engineering their business processes. Ease of navigation and necessary links to other related web sites are crucial factors while the design of the new applications is progressing.

## EXPLORING GLOBAL COLLABORATIONS FOR PROTECT

The subsequent paragraphs, discusses the global collaborative issues in the context of the transformation of the business processes of Protect.

Energy as a resource is used to exploit all other resources. Nations are dependent on oil especially when economies will compete for hydrocarbons. The effects of global energy on the climate and the impact on change climate on future generations entirely depend upon how the energy provider organizations manage to collaborate and co-operate in the global market.

The scarcity of energy supplies and the energy imbalance between nations is a threat to prosperity and security of international community. Energy sources have long been a major strategic concern however there is a potential solution to the global energy crisis. This solution requires investment and few scientific breakthroughs.

One of these scientific breakthroughs could be implementation of a collaborative system that is capable to create a collaborative channel across energy provider organization. By collaboration, these collaborative energy provider organizations can communicate through the potential collaborative channels such as *CBPE* to evaluate how they can mature their company, evaluate overseas trade, evaluate foreign market potential, evaluate overseas demand for the product, capitalize their knowledge, sharing knowledge, expand their potential market and enhance their customer service.

Based on the previous explanation, the opportunities for protect to enter the global is unlimited. The product and services offered by the protect, as a energy provider organization could ease the pressure of the global energy crisis considering when other energy provider organizations around the global can manage to see the possible benefits.

## CHANGE MANAGEMENT IN PROTECT

*CBPE* restructure protect's organizational structure hence they need to modify their services in order to reach their global partners and customer. Figure 6 demonstrate the current structure of the Protect.

Restructure of the organization causes the change of existing strategies as well as organizational hierarchy. These restructure also change the performance of the existing business processes. The implied theory of the *CBPE*, behind possible proposals seems grounded largely on the assumption that new organizational structure will increase either the competencies or commitments of partner organizations and their customers.

This restructure of organizational hierarchy affect the factors such as business, human resources, end users, cultural, environmental and technology as illustrated in Figure 6. This affects aim toward particular competencies and commitments in order to define how the collaboration of multiple organizations and relative mentioned factors affect the business processes to be linked or coordinated to reach the desired competencies and commitments.

In general, the restructure of the organizations increase the quality and effectiveness of strategy and operation based on the following important issues such as

*Figure 6. Transition of the organization structure*

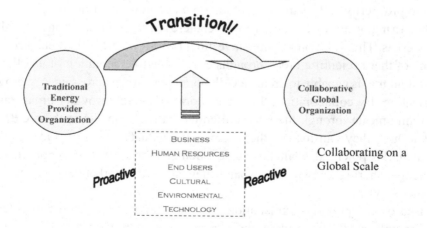

strategic planning, expansion of business, development of new business processes and development of collaborative network organizations.

## Communicating the Change Process

Good planning is the important factor for the success of the transforming the current business processes of Protect to a collaborative environment. Therefore, Protect management has to carefully plan the change within the transformation process. To achieve that, Protect will have to undertake a capability evaluation, which includes financial capability to enter a collaborative environment and also the capability of Protect to survive in the face of current market competition. Furthermore, it is extremely important that the planned changes are communicated to all stakeholders, which includes the trade's people who are associating with the organization.

Change management plays an important role in any organization considering that initially the reason for change should be recognized. Communication of the change helps the organization to embrace the change in order to improve the existing system and satisfy customer needs.

Successful change management involves the various stages such as identification of potential need for change, analyzes of the change report, evaluation of change, planning the change, implementing the change and final revision of the change.

Communication of the change in all stages is extremely important for the incorporation and implementation of the proposed collaborative environment. The effectiveness of the communication should also be measured while the people in the organization manage to share the knowledge. This share of the knowledge also encourages the employee among all departments to collaborate more effectively and efficiently.

The communication encourages the personnel to recognize the organization new strategy and reduce the risk to the collaborative organization. This internal communication should be extended to external communication with business partners and the customers.

Hence, the studied organization is classified as a large organization, the organization needs to place a change management team in order to setup training course and monitor the change. This team can also provide feedback from the collaborative system, help to use the software and manage the share of the information and knowledge.

This team also needs to facilitate the implementation of the new collaborative system and evaluate how the existing system could be linked to the new system. This control and management of the change could reduce the cost as the team is fully aware of the objective of the organization.

A team dealing with crucial change management aspects like training in changing business processes will be invaluable in managing the change. This team may also provide technical support such as how to use the software, how to share the information and knowledge, communicate effectively through the system, and so on and so forth. Furthermore, the team will assist employees in implementing the new service to customers such faster and efficient service. Without the formation of a change management team responsible for smoothing out the change process, it is likely that the costs of integration and training may increase.

## UTILIZATION OF CBPE MODEL

Figures 1, 2, 3, 4 and Figure 5 have initially mapped the *CBPE* model depicting the actual case study activities. The study has investigated the current systems in order to look at possible solutions to enhance the business processes of the company under study.

Selected business processes were studied in order to introduce the new collaborative environment to the organizations under investigation. The case study studies carried out resulted in introducing the engineered process to be added to those already under re-engineering. Currently, the organization is implementing this proposal systematically and carefully under the guidelines of the *CBPE* model. There have been many presentations, meetings and publications on this case study study. Eventually, when all the proposed business processes are fully operational, the actual impact of the *CBPE* model in *CWBS* can be recognized.

The *CBPE* model enables the protected organization to advertise its services and products to people who are in need of those products and services. These people might not even be aware that such an organization exists. Table 1 shows the four phases of the case study in the Protect organization.

The *CBPE* model, with the aid of mobile technology, provides an opportunity for Protect to collaborate with the trades people nearest to the location of the work. The model generates revenue, as well as saving time for Protect.

The three case study studies have established the need of the *CBPE* model in the medium-sized and large organization. The proposed engineered processes for the individual organizations have demonstrated, using the BPMN diagrams, how the *CWBS* could enable collaboration across multiple organizations when these organizations are not necessarily known to each other.

*Table 1. The summary of the Protect case study*

| CBPE-BASED OUTCOME for PROTECT |
| --- |
| Arrange Fieldwork that is based on mobile devices and processes. Establish Billing Accounts that collaborate with various other internal services |
| Publishing the service required by Protect in order to enable electronic collaboration |
| Engineering additional process and re-engineering existing processes, the other external parties such as electricians, plumbers, meter checkers and readers can also find the required services offered by Protect. |

# RECOMMENDATION AND SUGGESTION
## Strategic Decision Making

The company needs strategic decision making for the future to continuously sustain the strength of the company in a collaborative environment. Good decision making can be attributed as one of the vital factors for collaboration that will help the business to achieve its core mission and objective. This alternative is helpful in a way that it can make the company more collaborative in the marketing environment.

## Implementation of Strategic Management

Strategic management is guiding the Protect to face the relative challenges and opportunities appearing in the collaborative environment. This collaborative environment is composed of those external parties that most directly affect organisational goal achievement and new goal development. Thus, organisation system design and management should complement strategic actions taken for productive subsystems, as well as those providing output delivery and other support functions for the collaborative nature of the organisation.

One of the potential benefits of strategic management is it make sure that the organisation only follows one direction or path and that is towards the achievement of its business mission, objectives and success. Through the use of strategic planning as part of the strategic management concept, the company will be able to determine the best approach to be used in order to efficiently attain the collaborative goals.

## Imposing Strategic Marketing

Marketing can be considered as one of the most important element for the success of any organization. Having a strategic marketing may enable the Protect to solve different issues and conflicts which have been one of the causes for the failure of the prior collaboration strategy.

## Channel Management

The Protect must enhance their collaborative channel in order to improve their collaborative efficiency and reduce support cost by giving channels with access to applications and information. This include the details about the products or services offers, the availability of such offerings, order status, literature, and training which facilitate and enhance the speed of the sales process.

The Protect should be able to utilize a unique collaborative channel management system which focuses in each of the divisions or services offered by the company. The company needs to use its branch, telephone and internet to ensure that they will be able to manage the collaborative business processes.

## Customer Relationship Management

Customer relationship management has emerged as a strategy used to learn more about customers' needs and behaviors. The understanding of customer's need and behavior allows the Protect to develop stronger relationships with their customers. In general, the company needs to value its customers and create a business strategy for managing and optimizing customer interactions.

Customer Relationship Management also helps the organization to respond in time and appropriately to their customer's requirements. More targeted and customized relationship strategies can result from better predictions of customer needs. Online CRM can enhance the importance of the relationship for both customers and the business.

Formation of customer management team could also help when it comes to implementation of CRM applications on the Web site, ensure customer acceptance of the change and also to educate the customer how to use and collaborate with the new system.

The team aims for enhancing the relationships with customers as well as providing better service quality by more understanding of customers' needs. This team aims to successfully manage the collaboration to achieve an effective integration with organization. The ability to integrate systems including both internal and external processes will prove pivotal, as each layer of the organization will need to be morphed into a complete e-business model.

## ACTION POINTS

1. Identify the collaborative business processes of your own organization and see where they match with the studied organization.
2. Consider the value that *CBPE* can bring in handling the energy situation on a global level – and see where it applies to your own organization.
3. Identify any further business processes that can be engineered in a collaborative manner that brings together various other organizations in the fold of energy services.
4. Evaluate the importance of the communication in your organization as seen here.
5. Consider the strategic decision making in your organization from the point of view of applying CBPE as undertaken in this large organization .
6. Identify how your organization will plan to enhance the collaborative channels.
7. Identify your organization's customer relationship management strategies.

# Appendices

## APPENDIX A: QUESTIONNAIRE

*The following is the survey that was used, in detail, to elicit data related to collaborative business, business processes and mobile technologies.*

### Study of the Issues of Mobility in Business – A Survey

**This Survey aims to study the effect of mobile technologies on large and medium sized business organizations as a partial fulfillment for a doctoral study. The responses are collected in order to understand and research into the use of mobile technologies and related issues when it is used as a tool in the business processes of a business organization. Your response would be collected and analyzed and classified using statistical methods to draw conclusions. Your help in filling up this questionnaire is greatly appreciated.**

The estimated time required to complete this survey is approximately 20 minutes; your kindness in completing this survey and returning it, in the envelope provided within a short duration is highly appreciated.

### 1.0 Your Organisation

1. **Which of the following best describe your organisation? (Please tick the most appropriate one)**
   - ☐ **Large:** Approximately employing 200 or more workers
   - ☐ **Medium:** Medium size operations employing more than 20 but less than 200 workers

2.  **Which of the following is the most appropriate industry category of your organisation? Please tick more than one category if required.**
    - ☐  Education & Training
    - ☐  Manufacturing and Processing
    - ☐  Building and Construction
    - ☐  Banking, Finance and Insurance
    - ☐  Professional services(legal, security, accounting)
    - ☐  Information Technology
    - ☐  Utility Services and equipment
    - ☐  Health and Community Services
    - ☐  Other (Specify)

3.  **Your position in the Organization**
    - ☐  Top Management
    - ☐  IT/MIS Manager, CIO
    - ☐  Marketing Manager
    - ☐  Customer care personnel
    - ☐  Sales and marketing
    - ☐  Executive Manager
    - ☐  Senior Manager/Officer
    - ☐  Systems Analyst/programmer
    - ☐  Technical support
    - ☐  Other (Specify

## 2.0 Mobile Technology Information

4.  **Is mobility/mobile gadgets very important to run the daily activities of your organisation? (Please tick the appropriate box)**
    - ☐  Yes (Please go to question 5)
    - ☐  Plan to use in the near future? (Please go to question 5)
    - ☐  Do not use and also no plans for the near future? (Please go to question 12)

5.  **Please tick off the utilised mobile devices in your organisation. (Please tick the appropriate box)**
    - ☐  Mobile Phones
    - ☐  Personal Digital Assistants
    - ☐  Laptops with mobile connectivity
    - ☐  Tablet PCs
    - ☐  Other- Please specify

6. **What are the current/perceived scenarios where mobile gadgets are/will be used in the organisation. (Please tick the appropriate box(es))**

☐ As a communication tool for day to day business activities, specifically as a cheaper method compared to over and above other communication methods

☐ As a technology used to contact employees any time any where in daily business activities

☐ As a special communication tool to contact employees under special circumstances (eg. In case of a fire etc.)

☐ As a special tool to reduce duplication of work and improve productivity (eg. Use of tablet PCs for signature for delivery of goods or use of lap tops to get data entry on customer site for sales people)

☐ As a tool providing flexibility to mobile employees (eg. top management, sales people, Managers)

☐ As a tool for enabling customers to contact at all times.

7. **Are there any new application/areas where mobile technologies could be included your daily business activities. Please tick the appropriate box for each point, out of six choices, in the table provided.**

P1) As a special technology to improve efficiencies in customer meetings
P2) As a special tool to advertise in a captured market
P3) As a tool to enable contacts with office for employees while on official travel
P4) As a method to track goods in transit
P5) Other (please specify)

**Legend**

| | |
|---|---|
| **VSA** – Very Strongly Agree | **SA** – Strongly Agree |
| **Ag** –Agree | **DA** – Disagree |
| **SD** – Strongly Disagree | **VSD** – Very Strongly Disagree |

| Point Number | VSA | SA | Ag | DA | SD | VSD |
|---|---|---|---|---|---|---|
| P1 | | | | | | |
| P2 | | | | | | |
| P3 | | | | | | |
| P4 | | | | | | |
| P5 | | | | | | |

8. **What do you consider to be the main advantages of using mobile devices in your organisation? Please tick the appropriate box for each point, out of six choices, in the table provided.**

P1)  Significant cost savings
P2)  Ability to connect employees anywhere and anytime
P3)  Improved Productivity due to better communications
P4)  Flexibility of employees thus improving morale of employees
P5)  Availability  for the customers to contact the organisation.

**Legend**

VSA – Very Strongly Agree      SA – Strongly Agree
Ag –Agree                      DA – Disagree
SD – Strongly Disagree         VSD – Very Strongly Disagree

| Point Number | VSA | SA | Ag | DA | SD | VSD |
|--------------|-----|----|----|----|----|-----|
| P1 | | | | | | |
| P2 | | | | | | |
| P3 | | | | | | |
| P4 | | | | | | |
| P5 | | | | | | |

9. **List the following factors which may be advantageous for the organisation? Please tick the appropriate box for each point, out of six choices, in the table provided.**

P1)  Demand for mobile technology is enhanced due to the interest by the employees in this technology
P2)  Demand for mobile technology enhanced by the interest of customers to use this technology
P3)  Demand for mobile technology is enhanced by the interest shown by the supply chain
P4)  Demand for mobile technology is enhanced due to socio-psychological factors(eg. New look for the organization)
P5)  Other (please specify)

**Legend**

| | | | |
|---|---|---|---|
| **VSA** – Very Strongly Agree | | **SA** – Strongly Agree | |
| **Ag** –Agree | | **DA** – Disagree | |
| **SD** – Strongly Disagree | | **VSD** – Very Strongly Disagree | |

| Point Number | VSA | SA | Ag | DA | SD | VSD |
|---|---|---|---|---|---|---|
| P1 | | | | | | |
| P2 | | | | | | |
| P3 | | | | | | |
| P4 | | | | | | |
| P5 | | | | | | |

10. **How could mobile technologies improve your daily work/activities? (Please tick the appropriate Box(es))**
    - ☐ Cost Savings
    - ☐ Time savings
    - ☐ Ability to contact any time, any where
    - ☐ More flexible approach towards work
    - ☐ Any other – Please specify

11. **What (problems/difficulties/complaints) are/(perceived to be) experienced by you in utilising existing mobile gadgets? (Please tick the appropriate Box(es))**
    - ☐ Not enough battery time available
    - ☐ Screen sizes are too small
    - ☐ The new mobile gadgets are too complicated to learn quickly
    - ☐ The lack of applications
    - ☐ Any other-Please specify

12. **What do you consider to be the main disadvantages of using mobile devices/applications? Please tick the appropriate box for each point, out of six choices, in the table provided.**

    P1) Cost of establishment of mobile technology and applications
    P2) Recurring cost to use mobile technology as a major tool
    P3) Technical drawbacks of current mobile systems such as coverage, call drop, network issues and low rate of data  transmission
    P4) Legal and privacy concerns in using mobile technology
    P5) Adoption and training related issues with regard to the use of mobile technology

P6) Other (please specify)

**Legend**

VSA – Very Strongly Agree     **SA** – Strongly Agree

**Ag** –Agree     **DA** – Disagree

**SD** – Strongly Disagree     **VSD** – Very Strongly Disagree

| Point Number | VSA | SA | Ag | DA | SD | VSD |
|---|---|---|---|---|---|---|
| P1 | | | | | | |
| P2 | | | | | | |
| P3 | | | | | | |
| P4 | | | | | | |
| P5 | | | | | | |
| P6 | | | | | | |

## 3.0 Mobile Technology Management

The Mobile Technology Management (MTM) Issues are further divided into two sub-classes. The following lists each sub-class and its corresponding MTM issues.

13. **Mobile network and infrastructure. The drawbacks of these areas are a concern for your organisation. Please tick the appropriate box for each point, out of six choices, in the table provided.**

P1) Lack of national mobile communication infrastructure

P2) Lack of mobile network systems for data transmission

P3) Lack of mobile network protocols

P4) Lack of planning and managing mobile communications and support by the providers

P5) Mobile transmission issues and coverage

P6) Other (please specify)

**Legend**

VSA – Very Strongly Agree     **SA** – Strongly Agree

**Ag** – Agree     **DA** – Disagree

**SD** – Strongly Disagree     **VSD** – Very Strongly Disagree

| Point Number | VSA | SA | Ag | DA | SD | VSD |
|:---:|:---:|:---:|:---:|:---:|:---:|:---:|
| P1 | | | | | | |
| P2 | | | | | | |
| P3 | | | | | | |
| P4 | | | | | | |
| P5 | | | | | | |
| P6 | | | | | | |

14. **Mobile - General issues. This deals with some general drawbacks. Please tick the appropriate box for each point, out of six choices, in the table provided.**

P1) Improving data integrity, reliability and quality assurance for mobile transmissions

P2) Integration of data processing, office Automation with mobile communications

P3) Effective rules and regulations to manage mobile communications

P4) Moving to open systems/standards for mobile applications

P5) Ease of navigation on mobile devices

P6) Other (please specify)

**Legend**

**VSA** – Very Strongly Agree      **SA** – Strongly Agree

**Ag** –Agree                      **DA** – Disagree

**SD** – Strongly Disagree         **VSD** – Very Strongly Disagree

| Point Number | VSA | SA | Ag | DA | SD | VSD |
|:---:|:---:|:---:|:---:|:---:|:---:|:---:|
| P1 | | | | | | |
| P2 | | | | | | |
| P3 | | | | | | |
| P4 | | | | | | |
| P5 | | | | | | |
| P6 | | | | | | |

15. **Please specify any other MTM issues that are important to your organisation but not included in the above questionnaire.**

1. _____

2. _____

3. _____

4. _____

5. _____

## 4.0 Mobile Technology and Process Issues

The Mobile Technology Process Issues are used to investigate any issues relating to how mobiles are used in the business processes by organisations when adopting mobile technology. Any process is a set of business activities happening in an organisation that leads to serving a customer.

16. **Which points would you consider as Mobile Technology advantages when used in organisational business processes? Please tick the appropriate box for each point, out of six choices, in the table provided.**

   P1)  Mobile technology's flexibility to integrate with business processes
   P2)  Mobile technology's any time any where contactability
   P3)  New mobile applications in the market providing a competitive advantage to business
   P4)  Mobile technology's individual to individual relationship
   P5)  Mobile technology's breakthroughs (eg. faster transmission, better screen sizes, etc.)
   P6)  Other (please specify)

**Legend**

| VSA – Very Strongly Agree | SA – Strongly Agree |
|---|---|
| Ag –Agree | DA – Disagree |
| SD – Strongly Disagree | VSD – Very Strongly Disagree |

| Point Number | VSA | SA | Ag | DA | SD | VSD |
|---|---|---|---|---|---|---|
| P1 | | | | | | |
| P2 | | | | | | |
| P3 | | | | | | |
| P4 | | | | | | |
| P5 | | | | | | |
| P6 | | | | | | |

17. **Mobile Technology Limitations. Please tick the appropriate box for each point, out of six choices, in the table provided.**

P1)  Limitations on the existing mobile network bandwidths
P2)  Limitations on available time due to battery limitations
P3)  Limitations of existing mobile applications
P4)  Limitations with the mobile devices such as small screen sizes
P5)  Other (please specify)

**Legend**

| VSA – Very Strongly Agree | SA – Strongly Agree |
|---|---|
| Ag –Agree | DA – Disagree |
| SD – Strongly Disagree | VSD – Very Strongly Disagree |

| Point Number | VSA | SA | Ag | DA | SD | VSD |
|---|---|---|---|---|---|---|
| P1 | | | | | | |
| P2 | | | | | | |
| P3 | | | | | | |
| P4 | | | | | | |
| P5 | | | | | | |

18. **Mobile Technology process considerations. Please indicate the areas that would be considered important to your organisation. Please tick the appropriate box for each point, out of six choices, in the table provided.**

  P1)  A method for systematic transformation of business processes into mobile processes

  P2)  Identifying any new processes needed with the introduction of mobile technology?

  P3)  Re-visiting organisational objectives in the context of mobile technology and applications

  P4)  Re-visiting the customer relationship with regard to mobile technology

  P5)  Changing the existing processes to allow mobile gadgets

  P6)  Other (please specify)

**Legend**

  **VSA** – Very Strongly Agree      **SA** – Strongly Agree
  **Ag** –Agree                      **DA** – Disagree
  **SD** – Strongly Disagree         **VSD** – Very Strongly Disagree

| Point Number | VSA | SA | Ag | DA | SD | VSD |
|:---:|:---:|:---:|:---:|:---:|:---:|:---:|
| P1 | | | | | | |
| P2 | | | | | | |
| P3 | | | | | | |
| P4 | | | | | | |
| P5 | | | | | | |
| P6 | | | | | | |

19. **Mobile Technology Methodology drawbacks. Please indicate the areas that would be a concern to your organisation. Please tick the appropriate box for each point, out of six choices, in the table provided.**

  P1)  Training of employees with the new processes and applications

  P2)  Shifting the focus of the organisation to adopt the new technology and work flow

  P3)  Eliminating any processes which are redundant when using mobile technology

  P4)  Other (please specify)

**Legend**

| | | |
|---|---|---|
| **VSA** – Very Strongly Agree | | **SA** – Strongly Agree |
| **Ag** –Agree | | **DA** – Disagree |
| **SD** – Strongly Disagree | | **VSD** – Very Strongly Disagree |

| Point Number | VSA | SA | Ag | DA | SD | VSD |
|---|---|---|---|---|---|---|
| P1 | | | | | | |
| P2 | | | | | | |
| P3 | | | | | | |
| P4 | | | | | | |

20. **Sociology Issues with regard to people when mobile technology is introduced. Please indicate the areas that would be considered important to your organisation. Please tick the appropriate box for each point, out of six choices, in the table provided.**

P1) The pressure from customers and employees to adopt new processes
P2) Adoption of new processes by the competitors
P3) Ethical considerations of some processes with regards to privacy issues (eg. Calling customers Outside their regular business hours)
P4) Legal issues in using mobile devices in certain situations such as when driving etc.
P5) Legal issues in handling mobile applications such as pushing advertisements in certain locations etc.
P6) Other (please specify)

**Legend**

| | | |
|---|---|---|
| **VSA** – Very Strongly Agree | | **SA** – Strongly Agree |
| **Ag** –Agree | | **DA** – Disagree |
| **SD** – Strongly Disagree | | **VSD** – Very Strongly Disagree |

| Point Number | VSA | SA | Ag | DA | SD | VSD |
|---|---|---|---|---|---|---|
| P1 | | | | | | |
| P2 | | | | | | |
| P3 | | | | | | |
| P4 | | | | | | |
| P5 | | | | | | |
| P6 | | | | | | |

## 5.0 Web Services

The Web Services are used in collaboration with the business processes of different organisations while adapting to new technology. The questions in this section refer to Web Services adaptation.

21.  **What do you consider as the major technological drawbacks in using Web Services. Please tick the appropriate box for each point, out of six choices, in the table provided.**

P1)  Issues with unfamiliarity with the concepts of the Web Services
P2)  Limitations on Web Services
P3)  New technology. How do we adapt and adopt it.
P4)  Limitations with handheld devices
P5)  How the collaboration process will take place

**Legend**

**VSA** – Very Strongly Agree    **SA** – Strongly Agree
**Ag** –Agree    **DA** – Disagree
**SD** – Strongly Disagree    **VSD** – Very Strongly Disagree

| Point Number | VSA | SA | Ag | DA | SD | VSD |
|---|---|---|---|---|---|---|
| P1 | | | | | | |
| P2 | | | | | | |
| P3 | | | | | | |
| P4 | | | | | | |
| P5 | | | | | | |

22.  **What do you consider as the major methodological drawbacks in using Web Services. Please tick the appropriate box for each point, out of six choices, in the table provided.**

P1)  How the existing processes will be affected when Web Services are introduced
P2)  Training of employees with the new processes and applications
P3)  If the concept of competition will change to collaboration
P4)  Shifting the focus of the organisation to adopt the new technology and work flow
P5)  Change Management issues with the introduction of Web Services.

**Legend**

| | |
|---|---|
| **VSA** – Very Strongly Agree | **SA** – Strongly Agree |
| **Ag** –Agree | **DA** – Disagree |
| **SD** – Strongly Disagree | **VSD** – Very Strongly Disagree |

| Point Number | VSA | SA | Ag | DA | SD | VSD |
|---|---|---|---|---|---|---|
| P1 | | | | | | |
| P2 | | | | | | |
| P3 | | | | | | |
| P4 | | | | | | |
| P5 | | | | | | |

23. **What would be the Social issues with respect to introduction of Web Services. Please tick the appropriate box for each point, out of six choices, in the table provided.**

P1)  The pressure from customers and employees to adopt new way of trade

P2)  How the competitors might react in such a scenario

P3)  How could competitors be trusted if Web Services are use to collaborate with them

P4)  What happens with the organisations we are already collaborating with (If they do not adapt Web Services)

P5)  Legality of sharing the customer information with other organisations

P6)  Other (please specify)

**Legend**

| | |
|---|---|
| **VSA** – Very Strongly Agree | **SA** – Strongly Agree |
| **Ag** –Agree | **DA** – Disagree |
| **SD** – Strongly Disagree | **VSD** – Very Strongly Disagree |

| Point Number | VSA | SA | Ag | DA | SD | VSD |
|---|---|---|---|---|---|---|
| P1 | | | | | | |
| P2 | | | | | | |
| P3 | | | | | | |
| P4 | | | | | | |
| P5 | | | | | | |
| P6 | | | | | | |

24. **Please specify any other process issues that are important to your organisation in regards to the Web Services but not included in the above questionnaire.**

1. _____

2. _____

3. _____

4. _____

5. _____

## END OF QUESTIONNAIRE

**The following *Optional* information may help in clarifications of the responses, if required by the research team.**

| | |
|---|---|
| Name of your organisation: | |
| Contact person | |
| Phone no.: | Fax no.: |
| Email address: | |
| Web : | |

## Thank you for your time.

## APPENDIX B: EVOLUTION OF THE INTERNET

*This historical perspective on the Internet will come in handy for early students of the Web. This list puts in perspective the increasingly complex utilization of the Web by the business.*

**August 1991**
Tim Berners Lee officially introduced the Internet. He said that the aim of this technology is to link the scientific column. However the linking was introduced in prior years he combined this linkage with the Internet.

**12 December 1991**
The first server outside the Europe was introduced. The American scientists visited the Cern labroatouary in Geneva. The Slac server was equipped with Mr. Berner's software.

**26 November 1992:**
The number of the servers for public use was increasing all around the world.

**22 April 1993:**
The *Mosaic* first browser for windows was launched. This program was giving the opportunity to ordinary people to browse the Internet.

**30 April 1993:**
It was announced that the using the Internet is free. Ordinary people would get the opportunity to use the facilities for free.

**May 1993:**
MIT published the first newspaper (The Tech) online.

**June 1993**
HTML was introduced.

**November 1993:**
The first Internet camera transmitted the first image on the internet. This camera was invented in Cambridge University.

**February 1994:**
The American students launched Yahoo.

**April 1994:**
BBC launched the first .net site for showing their TV programs.

**13 October 1994:**
Bill Clinton placed the white house site on the Internet.

**25 October 1994:**
The first advertisements were placed on the internet. These advertisements belonged to ATT Company and Zima soft drinks.

**February 1995:**
HK radio was the first 24 hours radio online.

**1 July 1995:**
Amazon.com started their operation on the Internet. The first internet book shop cadabra.com was already in operation. Today, they sell music instruments, electronic devices and even furniture.

**August 1995:**
18957 sites exist on the Internet.

**9 August 1995:**
The .com boom in New York financial markets.

**24 August 1995:**
Internet explorer was introduced in Win 95.

**September 1995:**
eBay the first auction online started their operation on the Internet. The first item was a laser targeting device sold for $1383.00. Today eBay is the biggest auction online.

**15 December 1995:**
Alta Vista as a first multi language search engine was introduced.

**4 July 1996:**
Hotmail launched the free email on American Independence Day.

**August 1996:**
342081 sites exist on the Internet.

**May 1997:**
The BBC used the Internet for their news in regards to 1997 election.

**June 1997:**
The Business.com domain was sold for $150000.00

**1 March 1998:**
Kozmo.com promised to deliver their sold item within an hour.

**September 1998:**
Google opened the first office in a house garage in California.

**19 October 1998:**
*Open diary* the first virtual community was introduced.

**May 1999:**
Shawn Fenning, a student in Boston developed Napster. Napster was the first program for file transfer (Data Communication). Right after, the music companies sued the Napster.

**19 August 1999:**
The first version of MySpace for file transferring was launched.

**November 1999:**
Boo.com started their operation for selling clothing items online.

**January 2000:**
The price on .com shares were in fact increasing.

**7 February 2000:**
8 important sites such as Yahoo!, CNN and Amazon were attacked by viruses.

**August 2000:**
More than 20 million sites exist on the Internet.

**11 January 2001:**
Jimmy Wales introduced wikipedia.

**4 September 2001:**
Google received an award for their web page order design.

**22 November 2001:**
Pop John Paul the second sent his first email from his laptop.

**11 December 2002:**
For the first time FBI placed the list of American most wanted online.

**27 January 2004:**
Amazon made profit for the first time.

**5 February 2004:**
The naked part of Janet Jackson breasts was placed on the Internet. Her name was placed on all search engines more than any other world.

**July 2004:**
Tim Berners Lee received the Sir title from the Queen of England.

**19 August 2004:**
Google shares were available for the public to purchase. Very soon the shares jumped from $85 to $400.

**9 November 2004:**
Mozilla Firefox was launched.

**October 2005:**
More than 17 millions sites were added to the list of existing websites.

**12 April 2006:**
Google is offering more services by introducing the GU and GE sites.

**2006:**
More than 92615362 websites on the Internet. 49 millions are belonging to American sites. Close to 80% are .com sites. 7 millions are .net. 3 millions are .info. Germany, Canada, England and China in order are coming after USA.

**2007:**
**Maturing** growth, at a rate of **25%** per year. Arrive at more than **131 millions websites by December 2007 used by 20% of the world population.**

## 2008:

The close of the first quarter saw a total base of more than 162 million domain names. This represents a 26 percent increase over the same quarter in 2007, and 6 percent growth over the fourth quarter of 2007. That pace of quarterly growth is about the same as the average quarterly growth rate from 2007. By June 2007, 21.9% of the world population had access to the Internet.

# APPENDIX C: ADDITIONAL USE CASES FOR DEVELOPMENT OF CWBS

*Following are some example use cases that were developed by Dr. Abbass Ghanbary during his action research studies. These use cases can be used as starting point for development of full requirements for collaborative business. Corresponding activity graphs also need to be developed.*

## PERPETUAL RESOURCES GROUP

## Use Cases

The Use case demonstrates that Perpetual Resources Group (PRG) can hire staff from the other security guard provider to finalise the required number of the staff for the specific venue when PRG is unable to supply staff.

| Use Case 1: | Requesting Staff (from other venues) |
| --- | --- |
| **Actors:** | PRG, Collaborative Web Based System CWBS, Directory level 1 and Directory level 2 |
| **Description:** | PRG submit a request form asking for staff from other venues. These venues might not be known to PRG. |
| **Pre-Condition:** | PRG is Using Web Services |
| **Post-Condition:** | PRG will receive a report that request is published ready to be consumed. |
| **Type:** | Very complex |
| **Normal Course of Events:** | 1. CWBS accept the request and identifies the member area (A1)<br>2. Directory level 1 checks Directory level 2 to identify the party capable of handling the requests<br>3. CWBS responds by eliminating the options that are not meeting the environmental boundaries (geographical, budget, financial issues, etc.)<br>4. PRG provides details of clients who have provided requests for security staff.<br>5. CWBS processes the PRG request and collaborates with selected available members regarding request.<br>6. CWBS flags the members involved in the process not to receive the next query.<br>7. Process request (A2)<br>8. CWBS prompts a message to PRG informing the outcome of the requested application<br>9. PRG roster the staff on Power force<br>10. Submit the roster to those members. |
| **Alternate Course of Events:** | A1: If the industry does not exist the CWBS prompt a message denying the request.<br>A2: If other industries should be involved in the request, the system will go through the process of locating them. |
| **References** | |

## Use Case: Requesting Staff from other Venues

The following Use case demonstrates the advertisement of Perpetual Resources Group for the provided services. Perpetual Resources Group publishes the performed services and people in need of these services consume them and can contact Perpetual Resources Group on the Web-based system.

| Use Case 2: | Advertise Performed Services |
|---|---|
| **Actors:** | PRG, Collaborative Web Based System CWBS, Directory level1 and Directory level 2 |
| **Description:** | PRG submit form advertising for the services performed by PRG. |
| **Pre-Condition:** | PRG is Using Web Services |
| **Post-Condition:** | PRG will receive a report that request is published ready to be consumed. |
| **Type:** | Very complex |
| **Normal Course of Events:** | 1. CWBS accept the request and identify the members in need of such services  (A1)<br>2. Directory level 1 checks Directory level 2 to identify the party capable in handling the requests<br>3. CWBS eliminates the options that are not meeting the environmental boundaries (geographical, budget, financial issues, etc.)<br>4. CWBS process the PRG request and collaborate with selected members in need of such a request.<br>5. CWBS prompts a message to PRG informing the outcome of the requested application. |
| **Alternate Course of Events:** | A1: If the industry does not exist the CWBS prompt a message denying the request.<br>A2: If other industries should be involved in the request, the system will go through the process of locating them. |
| **References** |  |

## Use Case: Advertised Performed Services by Perpetual Resources Group

The following Use case demonstrates the advertisement of Perpetual Resources Group as for recruitment on a monthly basis. The Operation Manager of Perpetual Resources Group place the guards with less worked roster on the inactive list at the end of the financial year based on the operational work such as disciplinary action, work availability and the guard's general performance.

| Use Case 3: | Job Advertisement and Recruitment |
|---|---|
| **Actors:** | PRG, Collaborative Web Based System CWBS, Directory level1 and Directory level 2 |
| **Description:** | PRG submit form informing that PRG recruit staff. |
| **Pre-Condition:** | PRG is Using Web Services |
| **Post-Condition:** | PRG will receive a report that request is published ready to be consumed. |
| **Type:** | Very complex |

| Normal Course of Events: | 1. CWBS accept the request and identify the members in need of such services (A1)<br>2. Directory level 1 checks Directory level 2 to identify the party capable in handling the requests<br>3. CWBS eliminates the options that are not meeting the environmental boundaries (geographical, budget, financial issues, etc.)<br>4. CWBS process the PRG request and collaborate with selected members in need of such a request.<br>5. CWBS accept the resume of the interested people.<br>6. CWBS submit the resume to PRG.<br>7. Operation Manager will read the resume.<br>8. Inform CWBS of the result. (A2)<br>9. CWBS prompts a message to PRG informing the outcome of the requested application. |
|---|---|
| Alternate Course of Events: | A1: If the industry does not exist the CWBS prompt a message denying the request.<br>A2: If the resume is accepted books an appointment.. |
| References | |

# Use Case: Job Advertisement and Recruitment Online

## PROTECT A

## Use Cases

The following Use case demonstrates registration of Protect A in the proposed portal. This Use case shows that by registering in the portal, Protect A can publish their products and services online.

| Use Case: | Registration of Prospective Member (Protect A) |
|---|---|
| Actors: | Member, Collaborative Web Based System ( CWBS), Prospective member |
| Description: | Prospective Member is getting registered in the CWBS<br>Please note that this is a generic use case. Different prospective members could come in to register. |
| Pre-Condition: | Prospective Member is using Web Services.<br>Prospective Member is willing to work through the CWBS |
| Post-Condition: | Prospective Member is upgraded to a Member |
| Type: | Complex |

| Normal Course of Events: | 1. Prospective Member connects to the CWBS and requests to register in the Directory level 1 <br> 2. CWBS prompts the appropriate member registration form to the member <br> 3. Prospective Member enters his details in the registration form (A1)(A2) <br> 4. CWBS prompts that the registration form is to be submitted. <br> 5. Prospective Member submits the registration form <br> 6. CWBS registers Prospective member sending a unique registration number <br> 7. Member logs out of the CWBS. |
|---|---|
| Alternate Course of Events: | A1: Information entered is insufficient or incorrect. Prospective Member is asked to input correct member ID. <br> A2: It is crucial for the Prospective member to fill all details specifically identifying the relevant industry |
| References | • A prospective member is Protect A <br> • After the registration process Protect A is a member. |

## Use Case: Registration in Proposed Collaborative Web Based System

The following Use case demonstrates how the *Collaborative Web Based System (CWBS)* register the Protect A in the protal and place the organisation within the right industry.

| Use Case: | Place the registration in the directory |
|---|---|
| Actors: | Collaborative Web Based System(CWBS), Directory level 1, Directory level 2 , Administrator |
| Description: | When the CWBS place the registered members in the right place in order to locate and consume them. |
| Pre-Condition: | Registration has taken place |
| Post-Condition: | Directories communicates with each other |
| Type: | Very complex |
| Normal Course of Events: | 1. CWBS identifies the relevant member area from the registration form (A1) <br> 2. Directory level 1 will receive an identification number from that specific member <br> 3. CWBS Register the member details of the member in Directory level 2. <br> 4. Member details are stored in the database. |
| Alternate Course of Events: | A1: If the industry does not exist in the Directory level 2 the CWBS will inform the administrator for further direction. |
| References | This is an automated use case. Only instance of human actor involvement will occur when the specified industry is not available in CWBS. |

# Use Case: Place the Registration in the Directory

The following Use case demonstrates how the *CWBS* publishes the products and services offered by Protect A. This publication enables other organisations to consume and contact Protect A if they need these services and products.

| Use Case: | Publish Product/Services |
|---|---|
| Actors: | Protect A, Collaborative Web Based System CWBS, Directory level1 and Directory level 2 |
| Description: | Protect A publishes the consumable applications |
| Pre-Condition: | Protect A is Using Web Services |
| Post-Condition: | Protect A will receive a report that request is published ready to be consumed. |
| Type: | Very complex |
| Normal Course of Events: | 1. CWBS accept the request and identify the members in need of such services (A1)<br>2. Directory level 1 checks Directory level 2 to identify the party capable in handling the requests<br>3. CWBS eliminates the options that are not meeting the environmental boundaries (geographical, budget, financial issues, etc.)<br>4. CWBS process the Protect A request and collaborate with selected members in need of such a request.<br>5. CWBS prompts a message to Protect A informing the outcome of the requested application. |
| Alternate Course of Events: | A1: If the industry does not exist the CWBS prompt a message denying the request.<br>A2: If other industries should be involved in the request, the system will go through the process of locating them. |
| References | |

# Use Case: Publish the Product/Services Offered By Protect A

# PROTECT B

# Use Cases

The following Use case demonstrates the registration of Protect B on the CWBS enabling the organisation to become part of the proposed collaborative environment.

| Use Case: | Registration of Prospective Member (Protect B) |
|---|---|
| Actors: | Member, Collaborative Web Based System ( CWBS), Prospective member |

| Description: | Prospective Member is getting registered in the CWBS<br>Please note that this is a generic use case. Different prospective members could come in to register. |
|---|---|
| Pre-Condition: | Prospective Member is using Web Services.<br>Prospective Member is willing to work through the CWBS |
| Post-Condition: | Prospective Member is upgraded to a Member |
| Type: | Complex |
| Normal Course of Events: | 1. Prospective Member connects to the CWBS and requests to register in the Directory level 1<br>2. CWBS prompts the appropriate member registration form to the member<br>3. Prospective Member enters his details in the registration form (A1) (A2)<br>4. CWBS prompts that the registration form is to be submitted.<br>5. Prospective Member submits the registration form<br>6. CWBS registers Prospective member sending a unique registration number<br>7. Member logs out of the CWBS. |
| Alternate Course of Events: | A1: Information entered is insufficient or incorrect. Prospective Member is asked to input correct member ID.<br>A2: It is crucial for the Prospective member to fill all details specifically identifying the relevant industry |
| References | • A prospective member is Protect B<br>• After the registration process Protect B is a member. |

## Use Case: Registration in Proposed Collaborative Web Based System

| Use Case: | Place the registration in the directory |
|---|---|
| Actors: | Collaborative Web Based System(CWBS), Directory level 1, Directory level 2 , Administrator |
| Description: | When the CWBS place the registered members in the right place in order to locate and consume them. |
| Pre-Condition: | Registration has taken place |
| Post-Condition: | Directories communicates with each other |
| Type: | Very complex |
| Normal Course of Events: | 1. CWBS identifies the relevant member area from the registration form (A1)<br>2. Directory level 1 will receive an identification number from that specific member<br>3. CWBS Register the member details of the member in Directory level 2.<br>4. Member details are stored in the database. |
| Alternate Course of Events: | A1: If the industry does not exist in the Directory level 2 the CWBS will inform the administrator for further direction. |

| References | This is an automated use case. Only instance of human actor involvement will occur when the specified industry is not available in CWBS. |
|---|---|

## Use Case: Place the Registration in the Directory

The following Use case demonstrates the publication of the request when the organisation (Protect B) is in need of specific trade's people within specific geographical boundary.

| Use Case: | Publish Request |
|---|---|
| Actors: | Protect B, Collaborative Web Based System CWBS, Directory level1 and Directory level 2 |
| Description: | Protect B publishes the consumable application |
| Pre-Condition: | Protect B is Using Web Services |
| Post-Condition: | Protect B will receive a report that request is published ready to be consumed. |
| Type: | Very complex |
| Normal Course of Events: | 1. CWBS accept the request and identify the members in need of such services (A1) <br> 2. Directory level 1 checks Directory level 2 to identify the party capable in handling the requests <br> 3. CWBS eliminates the options that are not meeting the environmental boundaries (geographical, budget, financial issues, etc.) <br> 4. CWBS process the Protect B request and collaborate with selected members in need of such a request. <br> 5. CWBS prompts a message to Protect B informing the outcome of the requested application. |
| Alternate Course of Events: | A1: If the industry does not exist the CWBS prompt a message denying the request. <br> A2: If other industries should be involved in the request, the system will go through the process of locating them. |
| References | |

## Use Case: Publish the Service Required by Protect B

# About the Authors

**Bhuvan Unhelkar** (BE, MDBA, MSc, PhD; FACS) has over 26 years of strategic as well as hands-on professional experience in information and communication technology. He earned his doctorate in the area of object orientation from the University of Technology, Sydney. He has authored/edited fourteen books including this one, and has extensively presented and published research papers and case studies. He is the founder of MethodScience.com and has notable consulting and training expertise in software engineering (modelling, processes and quality), enterprise globalisation, web services, enterprise architecture and mobile technologies. Wearing his academic hat, he teaches, amongst other units, object oriented analysis and design and IT project management, and leads the Mobile Internet Research and Applications Group (MIRAG).He is a sought-after orator, a Fellow of the Australian Computer Society, Life member of Computer Society of India, a Rotarian (Paul Harris Fellow) and a previous TiE Mentor.

**Abbass Ghanbary** (PhD) earned a full scholarship from University of Western Sydney (UWS) in Australia to complete his PhD. Abbass's thesis focused on the issues and challenges faced by businesses in incorporating Web services in businesses integration that resulted in the creation of a model for collaborative business process engineering. His investigation mainly concentrated on the improvements of the Web services applications across multiple organisations. Abbass is also a respected consultant in the industry in addition to his lecturing and tutoring in the university. He is a member of the Mobile Internet Research and Applications Group (MIRAG) within Advanced enterprise Information Management Systems (AeIMS) research group. Abbass is also a member of Australian Computer Society and is active in attending various forums, seminars and discussion; and a committee member that runs the of Quantitative Enterprise Software Performance (QESP).

**Houman Younessi**, PhD is professor of science, engineering and management at Rensselaer Polytechnic Institute–Hartford Graduate Campus where he also is in charge of all academic programs. Houman is an internationally renowned educator, practitioner, consultant and investigator. He is the inventor of the SBM (state behavior modeling) method and the co-inventor of the OPEN methodology and the new paradigm of recombinant programming. Dr. Younessi combines world class research based knowledge with recognized industry experience to bring forth innovations in research as well as in the classroom and to industry where his consultation is regularly sought by many leading organizations. A multi-disciplinarian, he has publications and expertise in many fields including software engineering, information systems, business and enterprise management and enterprise modeling and co-design, decision science, managerial economics and econometrics, and quantitative finance. Dr. Younessi is regularly invited to speak at many prestigious venues.

# Index